THE END OF MAN

Books by John W. Whitehead

The Separation Illusion

Schools on Fire (with Jon T. Barton)

The New Tyranny

The Second American Revolution

The Freedom of Religious Expression in the Public High Schools

The Stealing of America

Home Education and Constitutional Liberties
(with Wendell R. Bird)

The Right to Picket and the Freedom of Public Discourse

Parents' Rights

The End of Man

THE END OF MAN

John W. Whitehead

CROSSWAY BOOKS • WESTCHESTER, ILLINOIS
A DIVISION OF GOOD NEWS PUBLISHERS

Cover Illustration by Marshall Arisman

First printing, 1986

Printed in the United States of America

Library of Congress Catalog Card Number 85-70472

ISBN 0-89107-325-6

To Fred Willson

CONTENTS

Acknowledgments.. ix
Author's Foreword... xi

PART I: MAN IN SECULAR SOCIETY
1   The Christian Vacuum... 15
2   The Death of Humanism... 35
3   A New Faith.. 51
4   The Disenchanted World.. 69
5   The Magician's Bargain.. 87

PART II: MAN AND HIS EXTENSIONS
6   Extensions.. 107
7   The Schizoid Compromise...................................... 121
8   The Organic Machine... 131
9   AI... 147

PART III: MAN AND THE PLANNERS
10   The Conditioners.. 161
11   Death Control... 177

PART IV: MAN AND THE STATE
12   Friendly Fascism... 203
13   A New Despotism... 211
14   Freedom and Humanity... 237

Notes... 248
Select Bibliography... 271
Index... 297

ACKNOWLEDGMENTS

I would first like to express my gratitude to my wife, Carol, and five children: Jayson, Jonathan, Elisabeth, Joel and Joshua. They carried the burden of living with me while writing this book. Without their patience, prayer, and help, there would have been no book.

Special appreciation goes to Franky Schaeffer. His suggestions made this a better book.

Thanks to Dan Pawley for his astute suggestions and editorial work; to Pat Dwyer and my wife, Carol, for their typing; and to Kimberly Roberts and Ken Clark for their work on the footnotes and bibliography. Rebecca Beane's proofreading of the galleys was valuable. Wendell Bird's suggestions on Chapters Two and Three were very helpful.

AUTHOR'S FOREWORD

This book continues the train of ideas that began with *The Second American Revolution* and *The Stealing of America*.

In *The Second American Revolution* my focus was the shift away from a theistic base in law and government to a secularistic base. I also discussed the courts' distortion of both the United States Constitution and governmental principles. In *The Stealing of America* I expressed concern and examined the major philosophical forces that, if not in some way slowed, may very well lead us toward an authoritarian state.

In *The End of Man** my primary concern is the philosophical streams that are directly impacting on people and which, it seems, are totally denigrating human beings. In this century, especially, we have witnessed the rise of a scientific determinism which, aided by technology, not only posits an extremely low view of man, but threatens to end the traditional view of man.

In medicine and with population planning, this logic already has been carried to its death consequences. With abortion, infanticide, euthanasia, and coercive population control, we have entered into a new era of forced death for the generations that would, if they could, follow. *Posterity has become passé.*

If, as we have been told, unborn children are "protoplasmic rubbish" or "gobbets of meat protruding from human wombs," then several next steps were predictable. One was infanticide. The next was experimentation on live babies. Why not force a baboon's heart into a small child's body?

---

* The term "man" is used in this book in its generic sense. The term includes both men and women in general as human beings.

There is nothing to stop such things from occurring but oscillating public opinion. That is no barrier when we realize that our society has already been making funeral preparations for the end of man.

The message here should be clear. We must *now, at present,* stand and, if possible, rebuild our culture. We may fashion "end times" scenarios and hope and pray to be snatched from the terror of this age. As it did not happen for those who preceded us, it may not happen for the present generation.

John W. Whitehead
Manassas, Virginia

PART ONE

MAN IN SECULAR SOCIETY

We are the hollow men
We are the stuffed men
Leaning together
Headpiece filled with straw. Alas!
Our dried voices, when
We whisper together
Are quiet meaningless
As wind in dry grass
Or rats' feet in feet over broken glass
In our dry cellar

Shape without form, shade without colour,
Paralysed force, gesture without motion;

Those who have crossed
With direct eyes, to death's other kingdom
Remember us—if at all—not as lost
Violent souls, but only
As the hollow men
The stuffed men.

T. S. Eliot
The Hollow Men

THE CHRISTIAN VACUUM

Impersonalism presents the greatest challenge to twentieth-century man. As it is expressed through modern science and the state, on an ever-increasing scale, the challenge becomes more eminent. Its consequences pose a threat to the very essence of man as we have known him in the past.

Impersonalism is the quite logical movement of contemporary culture to reduce people to nothing more than cogs in the machinery of our technological society. It is a denial of the *whole man*, leaving us with only a one-dimensional view of people.

It is quite logical because the presuppositions of secularism, the predominant thought form of contemporary Western cultures, lead to the conclusion that man is something less than man. The titles of our most influential modern books—*The Human Animal*, for instance—advertise this conclusion to the masses. Secularism, with its denial of the personal Creator, makes a materialistic statement concerning people.

When we speak of the whole man, we know that he is more than a skeleton with meat on it. Man, created in the image of God, is a whole entity comprised of body, mind, and soul. People are spiritual beings as well as material entities. We could say that this goes without saying, but it does not. We no longer operate from the same philosophical base as earlier generations.

The tendency of modern secular society has been to pose man as a dehumanized, noncreative consumer by the pressures of the media and advertising industry. David Ogilvy himself, the guru of the advertising industry, says, "When I write an advertisement, I don't want you to tell me that you find it 'creative.' I want you to find it so interesting that you *buy the product*."[1] The result is manipulation: the sense that man is just plastic.

People, however, do not want to be merely plastic. Human beings in our time seek numerous ways to avoid the mechanistic plasticity of our society. Escape from this has resulted in a strange mysticism—what I have called "cosmic secularism" elsewhere.[2] That is why the cults, the occult, and Eastern religion have had easy entrances into the West. Modern man is a mystic—one who is defined as possessing "an intuitive understanding" of truths beyond human grasp—even if he claims to be a secularist.

It is at this point that Christianity, in particular, should have had an immense impact. As impersonalism was rearing its ugly head in the early twentieth century, Christianity should have been speaking into the spiritual vacuum. Indeed, the telltale signs were emerging everywhere: to the secular media an entire segment of society during the 1920s and 30s became known as "the lost generation." And pertinent artists, such as T. S. Eliot, viewed society in the terms of Eliot's seminal poem, *The Wasteland.*

Christianity, however, did not meet society's growing "lostness" and "wastedness"and is, therefore, largely responsible for the black holes of modern culture. As such, one of the most significant historical dilemmas of the twentieth century has been the collapse of Western Christianity, especially in the United States.

CHRISTIAN IDEAS

Human existence is structured by ideas. Presuppositions and ideas create world views—the grids through which we view the world. More importantly, a person's presuppositions are the basis upon which he or she acts.

People are more than a mere product of their environment. Men and women project their inward thoughts out into the external world where, in fact, their thoughts affect their environment. Ideas, thus, have consequences, which can be productive or · destructive—depending upon their basis or foundation.

Ideas are, then, not neutral. Their mere existence implies impact.

One such collection of ideas that had a significant impact on early American culture was that of traditional Christian theism. The influence of these ideas is attested to by the fact of their yet lingering impact on modern culture.

The early influence of theism on America, although its degree of influence is debatable, was significant. It helped form the freedoms modern Americans yet enjoy.[3] As Norman Foerster points out in his standard literary/historical commentary: "It was the Puritans of the seventeenth century who, more than any other early colonists, affected deeply the national character in later times. . . . [They] were men of independent stamp who had their full share of the protesting spirit of Protestantism. . .and were determined to see to it that the welfare of their Christian society was not to be subverted."[4]

At one time in American society, then (including the founding era), a primary genesis of thought forms was traditional theism.[5] Harold O. J. Brown has written that "the Bible has had a tremendous formative influence on people and institutions even when it has not been accepted as the authoritative Word of God. It is perfectly correct to say that a substantial measure of American culture, attitudes, literary [content], even language and laws and political institutions, is biblical in origin and inspiration."[6] The conclusion, as Brown writes, is: "*The basic source of values in American society is biblical.*"[7]

What, then, is traditional theism?[8]

First, theism posits that people are *created* in the image of God. Being created in God's image carries with it many facets. The conception of man made in the image of God can be summarized by saying that man, like God, has personhood, a measure of self-transcendence, intelligence, morality, love, and creativity.[9]

Being created in God's image meant, to those who came before us, that man was to reflect the Creator. Man acquired in a reflective manner the characteristics of God. This afforded man great dignity and worth. It also meant man, instead of being a one-dimensional machine-entity, was a three-dimensional human-entity.

Traditional theism teaches that absolute standards exist by which all moral judgments of life are to be measured. The character of God (love, mercy, and justice) is the standard. Furthermore, Christians and Jews hold that God has revealed His standard in the various laws and principles expressed in the Bible—such as the Ten Commandments, the Sermon on the Mount, and the Apostle Paul's ethical teaching. In these and many other ways the Creator has expressed His character to people. There is thus a standard of right and wrong, and people who want to know it can do so.[10]

This clearly means that traditional theism stresses accountability. Man is held accountable to the standards of the Creator. Man is expected, then, to be responsible, not irresponsible. Again, accountability and responsibility impute a high degree of dignity and worth to people (from the viewpoint of the Creator).

Traditional theism explains the present abnormality of man in terms of the flaw caused by the Fall. Modern thinkers have no real answer for the fact that man's noble attributes are vitiated by selfishness, cruelty, and vice. As a consequence, modern man, deeply aware of his flaws, oftentimes sees himself as absurd and futile. In the words of Albert Camus: "I proclaim that I believe in nothing and that everything is absurd."[11]

Traditional theism provides the answer to man's seeming futility and absurdity in the atoning work of Christ. The fatal infection is cured, though symptoms remain. The Christian is partially healed by Christ's work. However, he or she, because of fallenness, is never perfect in this life. As such, the Christian also is in need of the Creator's absolutes to order and direct his fallen nature. Without at least a partial adherence to these absolutes, as we see in modern society, life is not only chaotic, but can also result in extreme cruelty to people. The Holocaust, the Jonestown mass-suicide, and modern abortion mills operating at full-tilt attest to this truth.

Traditional theism is clearly expressed in some of the founding American documents. The contents of these documents reflect the cultural thought forms of their time. Although one cannot say that such documents are truly Christian writings, they do reflect principles that are arguably derivative of theistic thought. One such document is the Declaration of Independence, which presupposes that a "Creator"-God endows men with "inalienable" or absolute rights. Those who sought independence from Great Britain did not hesitate to declare to the world their belief in a personal and therefore theistic Creator who cared enough for His creatures to give them certain absolute rights—such as "life, liberty and the pursuit of happiness." "Almighty God has created the mind free," Thomas Jefferson also wrote, further suggesting that intellectual liberty and absolute rights hinged on an absolute infinite source. As we see in our day, finite men can only give relative rights.

Moreover, the Declaration, inherently recognizing the fallen nature of man (by the drafters' admission that human governments do indeed "become destructive" to fundamental principles handed down by God), holds King George accountable for transgressing the Creator's absolutes. "The history of the present King of Great Britain is a history of repeated injuries and usurpations, all having in direct object the establishment of [his own] absolute tyranny over these states," the drafters added. This usurpation of God's absolutes provided the basic foundation for breaking with the mother country.

Succinctly stated, the Declaration of Independence is structured upon a theistic base in that it professes *faith* (a religious proposition) in a "Creator" who works in and governs the affairs of men (history) in establishing absolute standards ("inalienable rights"). In this respect, the drafters—Jefferson, Franklin, John Adams, and the rest—were not inconsistent in "appealing to the Supreme Judge of the world for the rectitude...of [their] intentions...with firm reliance on the protection of Divine Providence."

The expression of traditional theism in societal mores, cultural practices, and red-white-and-blue institutions did not stop with America's founding fathers. It found expression, and yet does, in Presidential proclamations, patriotic songs, pledges of allegiance to the flag, and national holidays such as Thanksgiving. Even the most prominent achievements—the first moon landing, for instance—evoke theistic expressions such as prayer and the quotation of Bible verses. This basic theism was taught both in public and private education throughout the nineteenth century. Education endorsed theistic-centered learning to such an extent that it was quick to protect its students from books that, it judged, might be misleading to young minds. The reluctance to accept even Mark Twain's *Adventures of Huckleberry Finn*, for instance, emphasized this concern.

Christian theism also found its expression in court decisions, some of which openly acknowledged their foundation as being in Christian ethics.[12] As C. Gregg Singer notes in his book *A Theological Interpretation of American History*:

> A Christian world and life view furnished the basis for this early political thought which guided the American people for nearly two centuries and whose crowning lay in the writing of the Constitution of 1787. This Christian theism had so perme-

ated the colonial mind that it continued to guide even those
who had come to regard the Gospel with indifference or even
hostility. The currents of this orthodoxy were too strong to be
easily set aside by those who in their own thinking had come to
a different conception of religion and hence of government
also.[13]

This discussion is not intended as endorsing the concept of a
Christian nation in the sense that all or a majority of early Americans (including those who drafted the early founding documents)
were committed to Christ. "But," as Harold O. J. Brown writes,
"if by 'Christian' nation we mean that the most persuasive religious, cultural, and ethical influence in the country is and has
been that of Christianity, or that Christianity affects the hearts
and minds of Americans at least as much as Marxism does that of
Russians, then it is clearly correct to think of America as 'Christian' and speak of a 'Christian heritage.' "[14]

NEW IDEAS

Early theism had an impact because of its *totality*. By and large,
most Christians saw their religion in terms of its total application
and relevance to all areas of life. "Bible chapter-and-verse but-
tressed every proposition in books of theology, science, politics,
morals, even had a place in poetry and love letters," writes one
scholar.[15] Most importantly, Christ's Lordship was emphasized.

A dominant aspect of the Christian influence on early
nineteenth-century America was the interest and energy it dis-
played toward the external world and society. However, the
gradual dominance of the seventeenth-century Pietist movement
in Christianity and the influence of the Enlightenment changed
all this. These forces turned Protestant Christianity inward toward the development of the interior spiritual life.

Although it began as a renewal movement, Pietism ultimately
tended to degenerate into mere personal religiosity without much
direct influence on society and culture.[16] Religion became
"privatized" and ceased to affect public life. The earlier Christian foundation was so strong that Christianity continued to pervade society for some time after Pietism. But eventually such
influence began to wear off as the new generations of Christians
turned inward and diminished attempts to shape their society.
Although Christianity cannot survive if Christians neglect per-

sonal commitment and the spiritual life of the individual, it also inevitably declines if it devotes itself solely to the inward life.

In *Redeemer Nation,* Ernest Tuveson, professor of English at the University of California at Berkeley, notes that the dominant influence of early American Christianity began with the idea that God was "redeeming both individual souls and society in parallel course."[17] The religious revivals that dominated the early nineteenth century, as Harvard historian Perry Miller points out in *The Life of the Mind in America,* were not aimed merely at saving souls, but also at redeeming the physical aspects of the community.[18]

This attitude led to Christian involvement in the abolition of the slave trade in Great Britain. William Wilberforce and others in England spent a lifetime fighting evils such as slavery because of their Christian faith and their determination to apply that faith's principles to the external world. In America, Christian groups such as the Quakers fought slavery, applying their Christianity externally.

However, we must be truthful in saying that many Christians and non-Christians both failed to decisively act to fight slavery. In fact, some historians indicate that slavery in the United States found its mouthpiece in the pulpit, and that far from discouraging its practice, many Christians taught that it was a biblical thing. Mark Twain, for instance, in his autobiography called it the "pet of the Deity," preached in "a thousand pulpits."[19]

Even the early Pietists were, to some extent, active social reformers. Unfortunately, the later wave of the Pietistic movement looked inward. Their focus was, and still is, on the areas of life that were believed to be spiritual as opposed to the secular or worldly, including both politics and the arts. This view eventually led to a reduction of the Christian influence on the external world.

Pietism, especially in its present form, primarily stresses the personal "salvation" experience. Bible study becomes simplistic, and any form of intellectualism or social activism is considered unspiritual. Pietism inevitably resulted in Christianity adopting a religious form of Platonism, the belief that the spiritual world is somehow superior to and above the physical-temporal world. It has created a non-Christian dichotomy between the spiritual and temporal worlds.

This dichotomy, however, was in part a result of the influence of the Enlightenment, which began to have an impact upon Christianity in America during the nineteenth century (but significantly near the end of that century). The views of the Enlightenment, which emphasized the supremacy of rational man, have left an indelible mark upon contemporary society and culture. One of its consequences has been secularism.

The Enlightenment was a movement of thought which began to appear in the midseventeenth century and reached its most clear-cut form in the late eighteenth century. In general, it was an intellectual movement which emphasized the sufficiency of human reason and skepticism concerning the validity of the traditional authority of the past—in particular, Christianity. With the appearance of the Enlightenment, humanism, under the guise of naturalism with its unquestioning reliance upon empirical epistemology and scientific methodology, gained an upper hand in Europe (and was later translated to America).

The central ideas of the Enlightenment stand in antithesis to Christian truth. The Enlightenment insisted that what seemed to be evil in man was nothing more than a lack of knowledge, and that through proper education men, who are inherently good, can be improved and even perfected. Revelation essentially was to come through the application of the scientific method rather than through the Bible. Man could be perfectible through knowledge and science. "This doctrine of human perfectibility," as Singer writes, "had as its logical conclusion the perfectibility of the whole human race, and the achievement of a millennial era of a thoroughly secular character."[20]

As these ideas were flooding Europe, the Industrial Revolution was beginning its push forward. With the success of the Industrial Revolution, it was inevitable that such ideas would triumph. And once Charles Darwin introduced evolution, as supposedly supported by science, into this matrix, it is much easier to see why Pietism would arise as a dominant expression of Christianity in the late nineteenth and early twentieth centuries. How people were to view culture was changing. It was a monolithic barrage that would be difficult for any thought form to resist.

RELATIVITY

The dawn of the twentieth century altered even further how people view the world around them.

The modern world, in essence, began on May 29, 1919, when photographs of a solar eclipse, taken on the island of Principe off West Africa and at Sobral in Brazil, confirmed the truth of a new theory of the universe. It was the confirmation of a theory promulgated by Albert Einstein.

It had been apparent for a half century that the idea of Newtonian cosmology, based upon the straight lines of Euclidean geometry and Galileo's ideas of *absolute* time, was in need of serious modification. Paul Johnson explains:

> It had stood for more than two hundred years. It was the framework within which the European Enlightenment, the Industrial Revolution, and the vast expansion of human knowledge, freedom and prosperity which characterized the nineteenth century, had taken place. But increasingly powerful telescopes were revealing anomalies. In particular, the motions of the planet Mercury deviated by forty-three seconds of arc a century from its predictable behaviour under Newtonian laws of physics. Why?[21]

In 1905, a twenty-six-year-old German Jew, Albert Einstein, had published a paper "On the Electrodynamics of Moving Bodies," which became known as the Special Theory of Relativity. Einstein's observations on the way in which, in certain circumstances, lengths appear to contract and clocks slow down are analogous to effects of perspective in painting. "In fact the discovery that space and time are relative rather than absolute terms of measurement is comparable, in effect on our perception of the world, to the first use of perspective in art, which occurred in Greece in the two decades *c.* 500-480 B.C."[22]

Einstein's ideas aroused worldwide interest. His theory, and the much publicized expedition to the island of Principe to test it, caused a sensation. No exercise in scientific verification, before or since, has ever attracted so many headlines or become a topic of universal conversation.

The tension mounted steadily until the actual announcement at a packed meeting of the Royal Society in London in September of

1919 that Einstein's theory had been confirmed. To Alfred North Whitehead, who was present, it was like a Greek drama:

> We were the chorus commenting on the decree of destiny as disclosed in the development of a supreme incident. There was dramatic quality in the very staging: the traditional ceremonial, and in the background the picture of Newton to remind us that the greatest of scientific generalizations was now, after more than two centuries, to receive its first modification...a great adventure in thought had at last come home to shore.[23]

The impact of the theory was immediate. Innumerable books sought to explain how Einstein's theory had altered Newtonian concepts which, for ordinary men and women, formed their understanding of the world about them, and how it worked. Einstein himself summed it up: "The 'Principle of Relativity' in its widest sense is contained in the statement: The totality of physical phenomena is of such a character that it gives no basis for the introduction of the concept of 'absolute motion'; or, shorter but less precise: There is no absolute motion."[24]

For science, the implication from relativity was that absolute time and absolute length had been dethroned—that is, that motion was curvilinear. All at once, nothing seemed certain in the movements of the spheres. "It was," as Johnson writes, "as though the spinning globe had been taken off its axis and cast adrift in a universe which no longer conformed to accustomed standards of measurement."[25]

At the cultural level, however, the impact of relativity may have been greater. In fact, at the beginning of the 1920s the belief began to circulate, for the first time at a popular level, that *there were no longer any absolutes*. This included not only time and space, but also good and evil, knowledge and other areas traditionally reserved to moral absolutes. "Mistakenly but perhaps inevitably, relativity became confused with relativism."[26]

The cultural impact distressed Einstein. Although he was not a practicing Jew, he acknowledged the existence of God.[27] He believed passionately in absolute standards of right and wrong.[28] However, once ideas are released, seldom are their effects totally foreseen. More often than not, they are unforeseen.

The emergence of Einstein as a world figure in 1919 is a striking illustration of the dual impact of great scientific innovations on mankind. Johnson, again, notes:

They change our perception of the physical world and increase our mastery of it. But they also change our ideas. The second effect is often more radical than the first. The scientific genius impinges on humanity, for good or ill, far more than any statesman or warlord. Galileo's empiricism created the ferment of natural philosophy in the seventeenth century which adumbrated the scientific and industrial revolutions. Newtonian physics formed the framework of the eighteenth-century Enlightenment, and so helped to bring modern nationalism and revolutionary politics to birth. Darwin's notion of the survival of the fittest was a key element both in the Marxist concept of class warfare and of the racial philosophies which shaped Hitlerism. Indeed the political and social consequences of Darwinian ideas have yet to work themselves out.[29]

The same is true of relativity. It was one of the principal formative influences on the course of twentieth-century history. The impact of relativity was especially powerful because it virtually coincided with the public reception of such pseudo-sciences as Freudianism. However, one thing is clear. Relativity "formed a knife, inadvertently wielded by its author, to help cut society adrift from its traditional moorings in the faith and morals of Judeo-Christian culture."[30]

THE SHIFT

The net result of the flood of new ideas, with science at its back, was the compartmentalization of religion and the real world—a dichotomy. A great cross section of Christianity was dichotomized.

Thus, there was a gradual move from a total Christianity to a fragmented, compartmentalized religion—from Christianity that urged Christ's Lordship in all areas of life to a Christianity that urged a Neoplatonic (or simply impractical, idealistic) faith. Under the impact of total Christianity, Christians reached out to the culture, not only in personal evangelism, but also in science, law, government, and education.

New York University Professor Neil Postman notes that "the churches in America laid the foundation of our system of higher education."[31] From this era came the great educational institutions such as Harvard and Yale. Both were established for the combinative studies of the classics with Christian dogma and ancient morality with theology.

The first sixty years of the twentieth century were the crucial ones. Before these dates virtually everyone would have been working on much the same presuppositions, which in practice seemed in accord with the basic presuppositions of Christianity. This was true in the areas of both methodology and epistemology (the study of knowledge). However, not everyone was a Christian in the true sense of the word. To the contrary, only a small, but significant minority of the general population was Christian. This is just as true today, despite polls which indicate otherwise.

Non-Christians, nevertheless, before 1900 generally acted on Christian presuppositions. Whether or not they had a right to do so begs the question. The fact is that they did. Although it was romantic to accept optimistic answers without a sufficient base, non-Christians did act as if Christian presuppositions were true.

The basic presupposition, yet intact by 1900, was that there are such things as absolutes. Absolutes can emanate only from an absolute source. It was generally accepted, then, that there was a Supreme Being who dictated a moral system from which life was to be lived. As Francis A. Schaeffer explains:

> Therefore, because they accepted the possibility of absolutes, though many might disagree as to what these were, nevertheless they could reason together on the classical basis of antithesis. So if anything was true, the opposite was false. In morality, if one thing was right, its opposite was wrong. This little formula, "If you have A it is not non-A," is the first move in classical logic. If you understand the extent to which this no longer holds sway, you will understand our present situation.[32]

This meant that before 1900 it was still possible to discuss what was right and wrong (or what was true and false) with the man on the street. This is no longer possible. In the words of the modern classic, *Zen and the Art of Motorcycle Maintenance*, "...what is good...and what is not good—Need we ask anyone to tell us these things?"[33]

The shift in this basic truth has been dramatic. Once it could have been argued that a certain thing was true or right or moral. Most people in the United States were operating from the same basic presuppositions. Thus, in discussions you could have begun with the certainty that your audience understood you.

However, in the battle of ideas, Christianity lost. Thus, in the last sixty years the consensus upon which American culture was built has shifted from one that was based upon Christian theistic principles to a consensus growing out of the Enlightenment. As Schaeffer writes in *The Great Evangelical Disaster:*

> [It] stands in total antithesis to Christian truth at every point—including the denial of the supernatural; belief in the all-sufficiency of human reason; the rejection of the fall; denial of the deity of Christ and his resurrection; belief in the perfectibility of Man; and the destruction of the Bible. [34]

It is unfortunate that the Christian leaders of the early twentieth century, before secularism was locked in place, did not effectively challenge the presuppositions of impersonalism. Had they done this, Christians would not have been taken by surprise. The really foolish thing is that even now, years after the shift is over, many Christians still have little idea of what is happening. This is because they are still being taught a one-dimensional view of Christianity. As Schaeffer notes:

> The flood-waters of secular thought and the new theology overwhelmed the Church because the leaders did not understand the importance of combating a false set of presuppositions. They largely fought the battle on the wrong ground and so, instead of being far ahead in both defense and communication, they lagged woefully behind. This was a real weakness which it is hard, even today, to rectify among evangelicals. [35]

AFFECTING CULTURE

Again, a narrow view of Christianity simply will not combat impersonalism. Christians are passive because they have sat under decades of teaching that simply preaching from the Bible *is* evangelism. Again, this is a limited, one-dimensional view.

Full-dimensional Christianity, as the apostles taught, means *acting,* from the point of salvation onward, upon the basis that Christianity is *the* truth. [36] It means affecting culture.

I must make clear at this point that I am not advocating that any particular religious faith, including Christian, should subjugate society. However, history does teach that if a total Christianity is practiced it will have a substantial impact on culture.

Moreover, if the truth of Christianity is in fact truth, then it stands in antithesis to the ideas and immorality of our age. *This means it must be practiced in the real world, both in teaching and in practical action.*

Truth, however, demands *confrontation.* "It must be loving confrontation," writes Schaeffer, "but there must be confrontation nonetheless."[37]

It is at this point many modern Christians, as they are tucked nicely away in their Christian ghettos, fall short. And it is for two reasons. One is a false view of Christ, and the other is the willingness of modern Christianity toward accommodation.

Modern Christianity poses Christ in portraits, speech, and writing as a meek friend of the world. Such is not true. This is not the picture of Him as painted by the Gospels, nor does Christ, the avenger of the Book of Revelation, fit this image. And as John R. W. Stott makes clear in *Christ the Controversialist,* Christ, far from being passive and meek, was both strongly controversial and dogmatic.[38]

Christianity, to be true to itself, must be dogmatic. Stott explains:

> We must reply that historic Christianity is essentially dogmatic, because it purports to be a revealed faith. If the Christian religion were just a collection of the philosophical and ethical ideas of men (like Hinduism), dogmatism would be entirely out of place. But if God has spoken (as Christians claim), both in olden days through the prophets and in these last days through His Son, why should it be thought "dogmatic" to believe His Word ourselves and to urge other people to believe it too?[39]

And Christ, like the apostles, was a controversialist. Stott adds:

> Perhaps the best way to insist that controversy is sometimes a painful necessity is to remember that our Lord Jesus Christ Himself was a controversialist. He was not "broad-minded" in the popular sense that He was prepared to countenance any views on any subject. On the contrary...He engaged in continuous debate with the religious leaders of His day, the scribes and Pharisees, the Herodians and Sadducees. He said that He was the truth, that He had come to bear witness to the truth, and that the truth would set His followers free. As a result of His loyalty to the truth, He was not afraid to dissent publicly from official doctrines (if He knew them to be wrong), to expose error, and to warn His disciples of false teachers. He was also extremely outspoken in His language, calling them "blind guides," "wolves in sheep's clothing," "whitewashed tombs" and even a "brood of vipers."

The apostles also were controversialists, as is plain from the New Testament Epistles, and they appealed to their readers "to contend for the faith which was once for all delivered to the saints." Like their Lord and Master they found it necessary to warn the churches of false teachers and to urge them to stand firm in the truth.[40]

But this is where the problem arises. Modern Christianity, as Stott recognizes, has a "dislike for dogmatism" and a "hatred for controversy."[41] This is because modern Christianity has sought to *accommodate* itself to the thinking of the age. "This is," as Schaeffer writes, "the great evangelical disaster—the failure of the evangelical world to stand for truth. There is only one word for this—namely *accommodation:* the evangelical church has accommodated to the world spirit of the age."[42]

The secular world, however, does not accommodate. The secularist Stalin did not accommodate dissidents, Jews, or Christians. He sought to destroy all opposition. The same is true with other secularists. The methods simply differ.

This is not any less true with American secular society. It tolerates an accommodating Christianity. Secularism would, if possible, entirely eliminate all theistic religions, including Judaism or Christianity (or at least take extreme measures to "put these religions in their proper place" along with any other system of "sacred" beliefs).

Accommodation also has a denigrating effect on the Christian psyche. Seeking approval from the world and seeking to accommodate secularism creates a second-class mentality.

Likewise, when the secularists do approve of "Christians"—and this comes only by accommodation—it creates a zookeeper-animal mentality. Caged in a secular world, the accommodating Christian becomes fragmented and docile (a hatred of dogmatism and controversy). In the next step, very much like zoo animals, Christians begin viewing the secularist-zookeeper as "friendly."

TRUE CHRISTIANITY

Modern Christianity, through the mediums of television and radio, has spoken its message to more people more times than ever before in history. However, as George Gallup, Jr., writes in his book *Forecast 2000*, "When we begin to probe just how important religion is in the individual lives of various people, there sometimes appears to be a lack of substance behind the basic belief in God."[43] He continues:

> [A]s a people, we lack deep levels of individual spiritual commitment. One sign of this is that the level of ethics in this country seems to be declining—at least in terms of public perceptions of ethical behavior. . . . [W]e found there's very little difference between the churched and the unchurched in terms of their general view on ethical matters, and also their practical ethical responses in various situations.[44]

What has happened is that a redefinition of Christianity and traditional religion has occurred. For instance, a 1981 survey of 112 Protestant and Catholic theology professors found that 99 percent said they believed in God.[45] Moreover, 88 percent believed in eternal life and 83 percent in a final judgment. However, it is quite probable that for a "significant number of these people, God, [eternal] life and final judgment were defined in a way that nineteenth-century Christians would have regarded as blasphemous."[46] Thus, as Michael Harrington writes:

> So when the same percentage confess belief in God in 1981 as did in 1881, that may conceal a transition from the God who spoke to Moses from the burning bush to Paul Tillich's "ground of being." Moreover, even though 83 percent of those respondents said they believed in final judgment, only 50 percent accepted the doctrine of hell. The rejection of eternal torment is hardly new—Origen had his version of such a rejection in the third century—but what is revealing is the way theologians privately and inconsistently decide which church truths they will accept. And it is of some moment that only 56 percent of the respondents had, over a decade, tried to convert someone.[47]

Should it not be clear by now that a narrow, one-dimensional Christianity diminishes and does not increase commitment? Instead, it leads to a pietistic withdrawal and is, therefore, manifestly non-Christian. As a result, we live in a biblically illiterate culture; and by extension, a generally illiterate culture, since the literature of Western man, not to mention his laws, morals, and ethics, becomes understandable only when grounded in Christian information.

Christians boast that there are fifty million evangelicals in America. In all likelihood this is a myth. In light of the minuscule effect Christianity has had on contemporary culture, how could this be true? Why does it take atheists[48] such as Michael Harrington to point out how lukewarm modern Christianity really is?

In America, this total Christianity, as we saw, imparted culture in a way since lost. As professor Postman writes: "In the eighteenth and nineteenth centuries, religious thought and institutions in America were dominated by an austere, learned, and intellectual form of discourse that is largely absent from religious life today."[49]

We have forgotten that one reason historic Christianity spread was because of its effect on *real* people in dealing with *real* problems in a *real* world. Historic Christianity saw life in its totality, not in fragments. It was a total world view. There is, then, no longer such a consensus among Christians, or as Harry Blamires recognizes, a "Christian mind":

> It is a commonplace that the mind of modern man has been secularized. For instance, it has been deprived of any orientation towards the supernatural. Tragic as this fact is, it would not be so desperately tragic had the Christian mind held out against the secular drift. But unfortunately the Christian mind has succumbed to the secular drift with a degree of weakness and nervelessness unmatched in Christian history. It is difficult to do justice in words to the complete loss of intellectual morale in the twentieth-century Church. One cannot characterize it without having recourse to language which will sound hysterical and melodramatic.[50]

As a thinking being, the modern Christian has succumbed to secularization. He accepts religion—its morality, its worship, its spiritual culture. However, he rejects the total view of life which sees all earthly issues within the context of the eternal; that relates all human problems—social, political, cultural—to the doctrinal foundations of the Christian faith. As a consequence, the faith ineffectively fails even to minimally raise the ethical standards of the American population.

If Christians are going to be effective in the face of secularistic impersonalism, they must go through a period of systematic study, thought, and reevaluation that will take much time and energy. Even as this takes place, the forces of impersonalism will increase, for there is little to abate the movement.

It is not that the foundation of truth has changed, or that the basic doctrines have lost their meaning. But the expression and formulation of them sometimes needs rethinking as it is presented to the modern age.

One may study the present situation, point to the fact that the culture is collapsing, notwithstanding its technical achievements and great knowledge in many fields. However, one must never think that it is just "they," the secularists. It must be realized that Christians are largely responsible.

Much of the condemnation of modern Christians by secular society is justifiable. Why didn't Christians protest long ago? Why were they not helping the oppressed and the poor? Why did it take the wholesale slaughter of unborn children to bring Christians to their feet?

True Christianity, it must be emphasized, speaks to all of life. It has something to say to all of the disciplines: science, law, medicine, art, philosophy, religion, political science, and so on. Christianity also has something to say about the problems of our particular times: the problems of the faceless, mass man, of materialistic technology, of secularism squeezing away human freedom, of the lack of a true foundation to culture.

Christianity, then, expresses a profound realism about the world in which we live. The Bible is very realistic about sorrow, pain, evil, hatred, jealousy, cruelty, and human misery. But the Bible makes it clear that this is all man's responsibility. It is because of willful human acts against the Creator.

However, it is at this point that true Christianity *explains* man. Modern secularists do not understand man for the simple reason that they have no standard, except subjective relativism, by which to explain man. The Fall and the resulting abnormality in man explains why things are the way they are and why man brings curse upon curse upon himself.

If God seems to withdraw and let men go their own way—for the time being—this, in a way, should cause people to shudder: for the God who hides Himself is also the God who will judge. However, in this way God shows His intense interest in the worth and dignity of people.

THE ABYSS

Unfortunately, the Christians of the twentieth century have not adequately communicated truth to their cultures. The consequences of the Christian failure have been, and will continue to be, dire. Some of the most important of these, as Harrington notes, are:

> • a crisis of legitimacy in the late capitalist society, as one of the prime motives for noncoerced obedience and acquiescence in the social order begins to disappear;

> • the economic consequences of the shift from the "Protestant ethic" to the compulsory hedonism of unplanned and irresponsible economic growth, and the consequent bewilderment in times of political-economic contradiction and confusion;

> • the appeal of totalitarian movements as substitutes for religious solidarity, particularly under conditions of overt economic and social crisis;

> • the loss of the philosophic and "common sense" basis for responsibility before the law as various determinisms occupy the territory once held by religious doctrines of free will and/or moral responsibility;

> • the dangers of proclaiming men and women as the lords and ladies of the universe as they are manifested in a purely technological and instrumental attitude toward nature;

> • the decline in the sense of duty toward unborn generations;

> • the loss of one of the most important constituent elements in both group and personal identity;

> • the relativization of all moral values and a resultant crisis of individual conscience;

> • the weakening of the "superego," which religion did so much to form—for good and very often for bad—and the emergence of the cult of the self;

> • the thinness and superficiality of the substitute religions of sex and drugs.[51]

The results of the Christian failure and the triumphs of secularism, therefore, are being played out before our very eyes. J. Gresham Machen understood the impersonal forces moving under society and the consequence early on. In the 1930s he said:

> No thoughtful man can possibly look out upon the world today without observing that we are in the midst of a tremendous emergency. It does seem perfectly clear to thoughtful people, whether Christians or not, that humanity is standing over an abyss.[52]

Machen commented further:

> Everywhere there rises before our eyes the spectre of a society where security, if it is attained at all, will be attained at the expense of freedom, where the security that is attained will be the security of fed beasts in a stable, and where all the high aspirations of humanity will have been cursed by an all-powerful State.[53]

Machen lived in the afterglow of Christianity that had been taken off guard by ideas which, with all the trappings of science, would soon become the basis of all modern thought in the twentieth century. Sucked into the Christian vacuum, humanity was drawing near to the abyss.

Secularism and its children would lead to a rapid, unchecked advance and development of secularism and the rise of modern statism. Moreover, secularism would eventually be the excuse, either directly or indirectly, for categorizing man as less than man. The abyss was closer than even Machen thought.

THE DEATH OF HUMANISM

One of the great myths of the twentieth century is that secularism means the replacement of a world view that is religious with one that is not. This completely mistakes the meaning of religion. In *Idols for Destruction,* Herbert Schlossberg writes:

> Max Weber rightly argued that each major aspect of human action is dependent on a distinctive set of religious attitudes. The religious outlook influences the institutions of society in ways that cannot simply be accounted for in material terms. Sociologist Gerhard Lenski's studies in American society confirm Weber's hypothesis. The religious character of human ideas and institutions is all-pervasive, even in nontheistic systems like Buddhism, communism, and humanism. All social phenomena, Lenski says, constitute systems of faith, not being based on logical or empirical demonstration, and all seek to respond to the most basic problems of human existence. Thus, *all normal adults are religious.* [1]

"Human existence," writes Gerhard Lenski, "*compels* men to act on unproven and unprovable assumptions, and it makes no exceptions." [2] Life is an act of faith, a reaching beyond experience. Faith is the essence of religion. World societies have historically recognized this fact; that is, up until the present secular era.

Michael Harrington notes in contemporary society that "religion is not disappearing but 'relocating.'" [3] As such, the *relocation of faith* takes place from the objective supernatural Creator to finite man. This has, in the past, been the essence of humanism. However, the obvious effect is the irrelevance of or death of God movement—which theologian Helmut Thielicke expresses as the contemporary belief "that God is irrelevant to our experience of reality"⁴—and the rise of secularism.

"Do you hear the little bell ringing?" Heinrich Heine once wrote. "They are bringing the sacraments to a dying God."⁵ This, too, is a faith position. It is an assumption that the Deity does not exist. Such an assertion that there is no God is pure faith.

THE DEATH OF HUMANISM

Humanism has been a major thought form in the West for the past several centuries and the dominant form only in this century. But with the entrenchment of secularism in Western culture, *the age of humanism has been increasingly replaced by the age of secularism.* However, some understanding of humanism is essential to an understanding of secularism.

The concept of humanism is somewhat elusive, particularly since some of its earlier forms were neutral or even positive. If one thinks of humanism as emphasizing the dignity of man, Christianity is in that limited sense humanistic, for it teaches that man is made in the image and likeness of God.

The term *humanist* was originally applied to those scholars who revived the study of "humane" as opposed to "sacred" literature—that is, the works of antiquity. In the narrow sense, then, a humanist is someone who is interested, often in a professional way, in those intellectual and academic disciplines called the humanities—so called because they deal with human nature in its fullness, the nonrational side of man as well as the rational. These have traditionally included literature, history, the fine arts, philosophy, and sometimes metaphysics and teleology (the study and belief which suggests that natural phenomena are determined not only by mechanical causes, but by an overall design in nature). Alexander Pope's dictum that "[t]he proper study of mankind is man"⁶ is a watchword of the discipline.

Thus, the study of the humanities must be distinguished from modern humanism. Likewise, so must humanitarianism be distinguished.

Humanitarianism is being kind and helpful to people, treating people humanely. Christians should be the most humanitarian of all people, and in fact have been leaders of many humanitarian ventures. And Christians should certainly be interested in the humanities as the product of human creativity, made possible because people are uniquely made in the image of the Creator.

Thus, it is possible, in one sense, to talk of a Christian humanist. Francis A. Schaeffer explains:

> In this sense of being interested in the humanities it would be
> proper to speak of a Christian humanist. This is especially so in
> the past usage of that term. This would then mean that such a
> Christian is interested (as we all should be) in the product of
> people's creativity. In this sense, for example, Calvin could be
> called a Christian humanist because he knew the works of the
> Roman writer Seneca so very well. John Milton and many
> other Christian poets could also be so called because of their
> knowledge not only of their own day but also of antiquity.[7]

Only in this sense does the term "Christian humanist" not become a contradiction in terms.

Modern humanism, however, has lost even a tenuous connection with God by denying that there is any order to nature and in-
sisting that man is totally autonomous. Modern humanism has
also lost its connection with the classical humanities. Moreover,
because of its secularist nature, it is almost exclusively opposed to
Christianity.

Because of its connection with classical literature and art, early
humanism often appeared much more urbane and sophisticated
than Protestantism. Today's humanism, to the contrary, has lost
much appreciation for classical culture and is scarcely more ap-
preciative of the *Laws* of the philosopher Plato than of the law of
God as revealed in the Bible.

Indeed, in the late twentieth century, the very study of the humanities, once taken for granted at the major universities, has
come into question. Ironically, the very secularism that proudly
set out to enlighten or free mankind from the bands of traditional
religion (or what was seen as bigotry) has instead produced perhaps the least literate generation of so-called *educated* people the
West has known for several centuries. However, secularism's opposition to traditional education, as well as traditional religion,
escapes detection because of its past agreement with Christian intellectuals in esteeming the humanities.

Humanism can be defined as the fundamental idea that people
can begin from human reason without reference to any divine
revelation or absolute truth and, by reasoning outward, derive
the standards to judge all matters. For such people, there is no
absolute or fixed standard of behavior. They are quite literally

autonomous (from the Greek *autos*, self, and *nomos*, law), a law unto themselves. As such, there are no rights given by God; no standards that cannot be eroded or replaced by what seems necessary, expedient, or even fashionable at the time. Man, it is presumed, is his own authority, "his own god in his own universe."

Modern humanism, since the late nineteenth century, has rapidly retrogressed to materialistic secularism for several reasons.

First, the development of science, as it was arbitrarily redefined to exclude any concept of a creator or design, inherently became not just secularistic, but a potent secularizing force as well. Far from the brand of science practiced by Newton, Pascal and others, modern science and the so-called death of God movement actually walk hand-in-hand. As one writer notes, the death of God phenomenon is "related to the most important scientific conquest of the age, the discovery of infinite geometric space, and counterposes the silence of God to it. God does not speak any more in the space of rational science, because in order to elaborate that space, man had to renounce every ethical norm."[8] In fact, God is suppressed from speaking any more in science, because modern science has illogically excluded by definition the possibility of divine intervention into a universe rigorously governed by natural laws.

From this materialistic and naturalistic type of philosophy, science substituted rigorously secular interpretations of natural events for both religious interpretations of them and scientific interpretations allowing for breaks in natural laws. If this did not attempt to disprove God, it certainly tried to restrict the Creator's realm. For example, a famous anecdote has it that Napoleon asked an astronomer where God figured in his model of the heavens. "Sir," the scientist replied, "I have no need of that hypothesis in my work."

Second, the popularity of evolution, as undergirded by science, gave a totality to the secular picture of the world. Evolution is discussed in detail in the next chapter. Suffice it to say that the older deism could not even stand under evolution. Now everything was the product of an impersonal beginning. From here it was easy to posit the silence and nonexistence of God.

But surely, if God is silent, so is all that formerly had spoken loudly of man's stature—that is, man's worth and dignity as he stood in the universe. Logically, man, as originating from an impersonal source, was merely a part of the machinations of "nature"; that is, man was merely a product of natural laws, without creation or purpose, without a soul or absolutes.

Thus, it should be clear that secularism is antihuman. This is, as James Hitchcock notes, exhibited in two ways:

> One regards man as totally insignificant, a mere speck in a vast universe. At various times, mechanistic philosophies have proposed that man lacks any spiritual dimension and is merely a kind of advanced automaton. In recent times this anti-humanism has often predicted that man will be "replaced" by robots, computers, and other machines which will render him obsolete. The other form of anti-humanism dwells on all that is sordid, animalistic, and degraded in human existence, not to seek to elevate it but to proclaim in triumph, "See! Man has a high opinion of himself, but when you strip away the trappings, this is what he is."[9]

The term *secular* is derived from the Latin *"saeculum,"* which means a race, generation, age, the times, or the world. The secular then is the worldly or temporal as against the spiritual or eternal. To call someone secularistic means that he or she "is completely timebound, totally a child of his age, a creature of history, with no vision of eternity."[10]

However, being antihuman, secularism meant the death of the humanism of the past—whether it was deistic (believing that God exists and created the world, yet remains impersonal) or theistic (believing that God created the world and is personally involved in people's lives). It would mean that the humanism of someone such as Thomas Jefferson would bleed under the sword of secularism. The views of Jefferson, who held to a belief in God (but denied the deity of Christ) and the morals of the New Testament (in particular, those propounded in the Sermon on the Mount), would not totally mesh with modern secularism. Thus, the dominance of secularism in contemporary culture meant the death of humanism. Secularism devoured it.

Secularism, in the final analysis, then leads to the destruction of man. It completely debases man and, in the end, leaves him without a shred of dignity or worth. Man, thus, becomes a plaything for tyrants, science, and the conditioners, a situation not all that far removed from the futuristic visions of Aldous Huxley's *Brave New World:* "Home, home—a few small rooms, stiflingly overinhabited by a man, by a periodically teeming woman, by a rabble of boys and girls of all ages. No air, no space; an understerilized prison; darkness, disease, and smells.''[11]

However, this does not mean that secularism is any less religious than humanism or Christianity. To the contrary, it has its own dogma and its own particular faith system.

THE RELIGION OF SECULARISM

One of the earliest writers discussing secularism was George Holyoake. It was in 1845 that he defined ''secularism'' as the doctrine that morality should be based solely in regard to the well-being of mankind in the present life, to the exclusion of all considerations drawn from belief in God or in a future existence beyond death.[12] Moreover, Holyoake envisioned secularism as being ''independent of theistical or other doctrine'' rather than as atheistic or antitheological.[13] (This is, most likely, an attempt to avoid being characterized as an atheist in a day and time when atheists were not popular.)

Holyoake illustrated his concept of independence from Christian theism with his ''house'' analogy:

> [A] man could judge a house as to its suitability of situation, structure, surroundings, and general desirableness, without ever knowing who was the architect or landlord; and if as occupant, he received no application for rent, he ought in gratitude to keep the place in good repair. So it is with this world. It is our dwelling place. We know the laws of sanitation, economy, and equity, upon which health, wealth, and security depend. All these things are quite independent of any knowledge of the origin of the universe or the owner of it. And as no demands are made upon us in consideration of our tenancy, the least we can do is to improve the estate as our acknowledgement of the advantage we enjoy. This is Secularism.[14]

Man is in his house alone. This is secularism. Again, it takes living by a faith doctrine to maintain such a position, for the simple reason that the belief system of secularism does not coincide with the way the real world operates.

As with any belief system or faith, then, there are common elements which undergird secularism—some of which are reflected in Holyoake's early philosophy. The common elements or ''tenets'' weave what may appropriately be called a universal strand.

First, secularism denies the relevance of deity or supernatural agencies, whether or not it explicitly denies their existence. One can judge a house, Holyoake noted, "without ever knowing who was the architect or landlord." If God is irrelevant, or even dead, it follows that there has been no revelation from God to man.

Second, secularism, drawing directly from Enlightenment ideology, posits the supremacy of human reason. As is implicit in the reasoning of Holyoake, this encompasses the belief that man can begin from himself and, on the basis of the utilization of his mental faculties alone, think out the answers to the great questions which confront mankind. However, as we shall see later, with the development of artificial intelligence via the computer, man's capacity to reason is coming under a pessimistic scrutiny. Thus, it is here that the secularist is forced to take his initial leap of faith. Os Guinness writes:

> It is impossible to prove by reason alone that reason has the validity accorded to it by humanism, and the twentieth century has strongly undermined this confidence in two places. Modern psychology has shown that, far from being utterly rational, man has motivations at a deeper level than his reasoning powers, and he is only partially aware of these forces. Much of what was called reasoning is now more properly called rationalizing.... By *rationalism* I do not mean "rationalism" as opposed to "empiricism" but rather the hidden premise common to both—the humanist's leap of faith in which the critical faculty of reason is tacitly made into an absolute and used as a super-tool to marshal particulars and claim meaning which in fact is proper only to a world of universals.[15]

Secularism, then, makes the same leap as humanism.

Third, there is the belief in the inevitability of progress. This concept developed from the introduction of Christian linear teleology into Western culture.[16]

The belief in progress is perpetuated through evolutionary theory and its cultural application (Social Darwinism). Evolution has produced the mechanistic belief that nature is moving inevitably to higher forms of life. But this optimistic view of progress has been flavored with pessimism in recent years. Guinness remarks:

> Many point to evidence of an evolutionary crisis, somewhat tarnishing the comfortable image of inevitable progress with man at the center of the stage controlling his own evolution.... [B]elief in inevitable progress is not supported by evidence of the past nor corroborated by the present situation and is

hardly the united scenario of futurology. This means...
humanism is less and less supported by empirical data. It is becoming more and more an ideology, an idea which is inflated to
the status of truth quite beyond the force of evidence.[17]

As the more pessimistic outlook toward man's progress has
developed, secularists look more to the state, science, technology, and public education to assume a guiding hand in shaping
man's future. For example, in his book *The Experience of Nothingness,* Michael Novak quotes a secularist's view which advocates total reeducation of the country's youth: "'The child [has]
the right to know what he feels.... [T]his will require new mores
for our schools...one which will enable young people from early
years to understand and feel and put into words all the hidden
things which go on inside of them, thus ending the conspiracy of
silence with which the development of the child is now distorted
both at home and at school. If the conspiracy of silence is to be
replaced...children must be encouraged and helped to attend to
their forbidden thoughts, and to put them into words, i.e., to talk
out loud about...what goes in and what comes out; about what
happens inside and what happens outside; about their dim and
confused feelings about sex itself.'"[18]

Because man is thought not to be progressing as rapidly as desired, or because man does not seem to be progressing in the evolutionary sense, some have opted for forced progress and
manipulative environmental control. Harvard behaviorist B. F.
Skinner, for example, argues that man is simply a machine without dignity or worth and that man should be controlled by a manipulative statist environment.[19] Others, such as those in the
population control movement, would, by propaganda and rhetorical devices, scare us into giving up our freedoms and handing
over our future to the population planners and conditioners.
(The population control movement is discussed in Chapters Ten
and Eleven.)

Fourth, secularism propounds the belief in science as the guide
to human progress and the ultimate provider of truth and, thus,
an alternative to both religion and morals. Therefore, science itself assumes a religious character. John P. Friedrich, a scientist
himself, has remarked: "Science is a kind of sacred cow today. It
is worshiped by the public."[20] Phil Donahue, the well-known
talk show host and "humanist," lends substance to this remark

in his book *The Human Animal*. He writes: "Einstein and Curie have shown us just how much can be done by the human mind: just how far it can strike off into the unknown and return with a brand-new piece of Truth. They're our champions, in the best biblical sense of the word. They represent all of us at the farthest frontiers of human achievement, and when they're successful, we're all successful."[21]

Science, however, has also taken on a pessimistic view of progress and man himself. As a consequence, it has grown impatient with natural development and progress and is stepping outside traditional experimental levels to engage in such things as genetic tinkering, cloning, and experimental transplant operations on living human beings—not to mention the ready acquiescence by the scientific and medical community to include population manipulation through abortion, infancitide, and the elimination of the frail, elderly, and weak.

Fifth, the secularist must maintain the belief in the self-sufficiency and centrality of man. This encompasses the assertion of the autonomy and independence of man apart from deity of any kind, thereby supposedly releasing man from all obligations to the Deity. As Holyoake noted, all things "are quite independent of any knowledge of the origin of the universe or the owner of it." Along with evolution, the centrality and autonomy of man are the prominent features of this belief system.

Because man is autonomous, it is argued that man, contrary to Christian theism, is inherently good and in no need of salvation or theological redemption to correct or redeem his fallen nature. Man's future and salvation are in man's hands. Man, not God, controls the destiny of the human race. The most respected thinkers, such as cancer researcher Lewis Thomas, suggest that answers to modern predicaments will come only from human "professionals." Thomas writes: "I wish the psychiatrists and social scientists were further along in their fields than they seem to be. We need, in a hurry, some professionals who can tell us what has gone wrong."[22] If man is the master of his own destiny, he can create his own system of absolutes apart from divine revelation.

Pessimism, too, is beginning to mar the belief in centrality. Os Guinness has noted a "persistent erosion" of the view of man's centrality and importance:

The fact that man has made so many significant scientific discoveries points strongly to the significance of man, yet the content of these same scientific discoveries underscores his insignificance. Man finds himself dwarfed bodily by the vast stretches of space and belittled temporally by the long reaches of time. Humanists are caught in a strange dilemma. If they affirm the greatness of man, it is only at the expense of ignoring his aberrations. If they regard human aberrations seriously, they have to escape the dilemma raised, either by blaming the situation on God. . .or by reducing man to the point of insignificance where his aberrations are no longer a problem.[23]

This fact is readily apparent in the mechanistic view of man that has emerged in scientific circles. B. F. Skinner, for instance, openly advocates the abolition of man as an individual:

His abolition has long been overdue. Autonomous man is a device used to explain what we cannot explain in any other way. He has been constructed from our ignorance, and as our understanding increases, the very stuff of which he is composed vanishes. . . . To man *qua* man we readily say good riddance.[24]

Two sociologists, commenting on the modern conception of people, have aptly remarked:

Modern man feels freer to ask, "What good is it?" The world has become "disenchanted," more "sensate," more "materialistic," less "spiritual," to use terms that have been applied to this trend toward *secularism*. Secularism encourages *rationality* in social organization. Group ways of acting are consciously designed and measured by effectiveness and efficiency. . . . Secularism and rationality are associated with *impersonality* in human relations. With a weakened sense of kinship and with a utilitarian orientation, it is easy to treat people as means rather than as ends.[25]

Francis Crick, an avowed atheist, who along with James D. Watson unraveled the DNA code, has said:

[Y]ou must realize that much of the political thinking of this country [the United States] is very difficult to justify biologically. It was valid to say in the period of the American Revolution, when people were oppressed by priests and kings, that all men were created equal. But it doesn't have biological validity. It may have some mystic validity in a religious context, but. . .[i]t's not only biologically not true, it's also biologically undesirable. . . . We all know, I think, or are beginning to realize, that the future is in our own hands, that we can, to some extent, do what we want.[26]

For Crick, man is a "means" for the ends of science. Francis A. Schaeffer, however, challenged Crick's view:

> If man is what Francis Crick says he is, then he is only the product of the impersonal plus time plus chance; he is nothing more than the energy particle extended. And, therefore, he has no intrinsic worth. Our own generation can thus disregard human life. On the one end we will kill the embryo with abortion—anytime anyone wishes—and on the other end we will introduce euthanasia for the old. The one is here and the other is coming.[27]

Thus, secularism has given us a very debased view of people. Quite contrary to the Creator-creature relationship that was at the base of Christian theism, secularism has given modernity a man-to-man relationship which is increasingly producing more forms of denigration and pain. As Russian scholar Vadim Borisov has said:

> The American Founding Fathers who many years ago first propounded the "eternal rights of man and the citizen" postulated that *every* human being bears the form and likeness of God; he *therefore* has an *absolute* value, and consequently also the *right* to be respected by his fellows.
>
> Rationalism, positivism and materialism, developing in opposition to religion, successively destroyed the memory of this absolute source of human rights. The unconditional equality of persons before God was replaced by the *conditional* equality of human individuals before the law. Deprived of divine authority, the concept of the human personality could now be defined conditionally, and therefore, inevitably arbitrarily. The concrete person became a judicial metaphor, a contentless abstraction, the subject of legal freedoms and restrictions.
>
> And it is here, in the admission of the *conditionality* of the human personality, that we find the root of its calamitous ordeals in our barbarous world. If the human personality is conditional, then so are its rights. Conditional too is the recognition of its dignity, which comes into painful conflict with surrounding reality.
>
> In breaking the link between human personality and the absolute source of rights, and yet affirming them as something to be taken for granted, rationalist humanism has from the very outset been inherently inconsistent, as its more logical successors very quickly understood. Darwin, Marx, Nietzsche and

Freud (and many others) resolved the inconsistency each in his own way, leaving not one stone upon another in the edifice of blind faith in man's dignity.... These men represented the theoretical, logical culmination of mankind's humanist rebellion against God.... This century's totalitarianism, trampling the human personality and all its rights, rhinoceroslike, underfoot, is only the application of this theory of life, or humanism put into *practice*. [28]

Man, as a product of an evolutionary environment, collectivized in and through the masses, becomes, as Arthur Koestler posited, the "ghost in the machine." [29] Unfortunately, collectivized man loses his individuality within the wheel of technology:

If "evolution is good," then evolution must be allowed to proceed and the very process of change becomes absolutized....But in even more areas, science is reaching the point of "destructive returns"; and the attempt to use evolution as a basis for morals and ethics is a failure. If evolutionary progress is taken as an axiom, then the trend towards convergence (social and evolutionary "unanimization") becomes a value, as suggested by Teilhard de Chardin. But this militates against the value of individuality and can be used to support totalitarianism. [30]

Man, then, loses the individuality and dignity that emanate from the Creator-creature relationship. As the divine nature of man dissipates, so does his worth. Schaeffer concludes:

[T]he concept [of man's dignity] is gone. We are in the post-Christian world. Man is junk. If the embryo is in the way, ditch it. If the old person is in the way, ditch him. If you're in the way...and that's what lies before us. [31]

The *sixth* aspect of secularism is the belief in the absolutism of evolution. Because of its importance and breadth, evolution will be discussed in detail in the next chapter.

SECULARISM'S CHILDREN

Neoorthodox theologian Harvey Cox of the Harvard Divinity School expresses apprehension concerning secularism in his book *The Secular City*. [32] He writes that secularism is not merely indifferent to alternative religious systems, but as a religious ideology, it is opposed to any other religious systems. "It is, therefore, a closed system.''[33] Moreover, he writes that secularism "seeks to impose its ideology through the organs of the state.''[34]

Secularism, contrary to popular belief, is not a tolerant system. It preaches against religious "dogmatism," but it imposes its own (particularly the dogmatic insistence that no absolutes exist). In the process it creates disillusionment and oppression. These are secularism's children.

An ultimate failure of secularism is that by its very nature it promises what it cannot fulfill. By encouraging people to place their trust in earthly happiness, it programs them for disillusionment. James Hitchcock notes:

> This is in large measure the reason why the history of the modern world has been characterized, intellectually, by philosophies of pessimism like Existentialism and by often-rancorous bitterness over various plans for worldly improvement. In the twentieth century, manslaughter has been perpetrated not by religious believers in opposition to heresy but by secularists convinced that their plan for a worldly utopia is the only possible one.[35]

This disillusionment is evidenced in the boozed-out and drugged-out contemporary America. The suicide rate, which is a leading cause of death among teenagers and college students, is evidence that there are many people seeking to escape our secular paradise any way they can.[36] Statistics as of 1984 reveal that in the last twenty-five years suicide has increased by over 250 percent among young women (fifteen to twenty-four) and over 300 percent among young men the same age. There are approximately twenty-seven thousand suicides in America each year now, and one-fifth are youth.

Modern authoritarian states and totalitarianism are an inherent byproduct of secularism (which has been stained with blood from its birth). Born with the French Revolution—and thereafter mischaracterized as humanism and/or secular humanism—secularism has laid the foundation for the tyrannies of the twentieth century.

Wherever secularism has predominated within governmental bureaucracies it has been oppressive. It is a closed system. It closes out the spiritual and often actively persecutes believers.

Totalitarianism is a political system that seeks to shape and control every aspect of people's lives in attempting to create the perfect state. Many twentieth-century states have set out to fulfill this goal.

Some people, however, resist. They do not want to blindly follow the dictates of the state. "They persist in believing in God, which the prophets of the new age have identified as an obstacle to progress. They must therefore be forced to obey, because such obedience is in their own interest and that of humanity."[37]

In the twentieth century, much suffering has been perpetrated in the name of humanity by the secular state. Lenin, Hitler, Stalin, Mao—all were secularists, and their atrocities follow logically from secularism.

Religion, on the other hand, has been the strongest and most tenacious bulwark against modern authoritarian statism. Yet, in the West Christian theism is systematically attacked and undermined in the media and in the major institutions of society. In the drive to privatize Christianity in America, the secularists may be opening the door for some of the things previously reserved for traditional authoritarian states (such as the Soviet Union).

As James Hitchcock has recognized, there are already "benign forms of totalitarianism" in place in American society.[38] He writes:

> Many Humanists (and some religious believers) have become so exercised over the prospect of the overpopulation of the world, for example, that they now talk about enforced restrictions on human breeding. At a minimum this would involve incentives for people who do not have children and penalties for those who do. In a graduated process, it would end quite possibly with enforced abortions or enforced sterilizations for those who have "too many" children. Such methods have already been employed in China. Some Westerners who are not Communists nonetheless express admiration for the Chinese solution. Although Humanists are usually quite vigilant against anything they construe as a threat to individual liberty, they have been strangely silent about this prospect, when they have not actively endorsed it.[39]

Finally, in preaching its version of "individual" freedom—which is, in reality, freedom from traditional morality—secularism undermines the sense of personal moral responsibility that is essential to all truly free societies. In discrediting Christian theism, the source of such responsibility, it leaves the people without any absolutes upon which to base a valid opposition to oppression.

It is widely held that individual rights may be exercised as long as they do not infringe on the similar rights of others: "Your freedom ends where my nose begins." This position may work fairly well as long as there is a ready understanding of what persons are. But it fails if someone arrogates the right to define others—and their rights—out of existence.

When Hitler determined to exterminate the Jews, some German humanists objected on the basis of the sanctity of life and of natural justice. Hitler simply defined the Jews as less than fully human, and his critics were silenced. If the Jews were not human, then they did not have human rights. What a simple solution to an otherwise perplexing problem! The argument for rights, separated from any basis in a reliable frame of reference, becomes capricious and merely a matter of definition of terms by whoever has the power to make his definition stick.

Although we may see a form of authoritarianism in the United States, it will probably not come by force. Slowly, as science and technology mechanize every phase of life, including man, society will logically—and probably in the name of freedoms and rights—become what we have always feared—that is, unless it is somehow abated.

THREE

A NEW FAITH

Throughout history, there have been basic breaks with popular conceptions of man and nature and their places in the universe. For example, Copernicus, the founder of modern astronomy, gave man a new sense of the earth's place in the solar system. By placing the earth in the category of heavenly bodies that orbit the sun, Copernicus had challenged man's centrality in the universe. The year was 1514, and in his secretly circulated manuscript *Commentariolus*, Copernicus had challenged the accepted ideas of astronomy that had existed since the days of Aristotle and Ptolemy.

Much later Sigmund Freud challenged the concept of man's intuition of consciousness as he presented an image of man and his mind as a ripple on an ocean of *un*consciousness. Interestingly, Freud had begun to develop his revolutionary ideas under what might be termed the "indirect" influence of Charles Darwin. It is said that as a University of Vienna medical student in 1881, Freud had taken far more biology electives than he needed for his medical degree. His comparative anatomy professor was Carl Claus, a well-known early Darwinian.

Likewise, philosophies and religions have come and gone in history. But the revelation of Copernicus's work, and others that followed, never brought into question man's ultimate link and responsibility to the Creator as did the work of the man who once attended Cambridge University in preparation for the Church of England clergy: Charles Darwin.

THE DARWINIAN IDEA

By 1860, the eighteenth century's conception of the world as a vast machine had become orthodoxy (a conforming to the official formulation of truth) among many intellectuals. Charles Darwin, in his book *Origin of Species* (1859), laid the foundations in biology for a new orthodoxy in the area of science. While looking back in part to Issac Newton, he "gave to natural law an entirely new interpretation which neither Newton nor his immediate successors had foreseen, and which some of them might well have repudiated if they had come into contact with the Darwinian theory."[1]

Newton, who had either consciously or unconsciously modeled the universe after the clock, gave a mechanical or deterministic implication to the workings of the universe. From his earliest days, Newton, a child born three months after his father had died, wanted to know how "things" worked. It is said that as a boy he built a model mill using a mouse for power. He also constructed clocks, sketched advanced architectural drawings, and spent hours in lackadaisical wonder over the internal workings of birds, animals, men, ships, and plants.

Newton was a theist, however, and had no intention of removing God from the operation of things. In fact, it is reported that discourser Richard Bentley once contacted Newton for advice on how to prepare a series of sermons entitled "The Confutation of Atheism." But, as is oftentimes the case, the implications of his ideas were not foreseen. He would not have been pleased with how Darwin eventually made use of those ideas.

In his *Origin of Species* Darwin had confined himself to the study of biology, but in his *Descent of Man* (1871) he broadened his approach and applied his evolutionary interpretations to the emergence of man. From *Descent's* first sentence the message was clear. Darwin wrote: "He who wishes to decide whether man is the modified descendant of some preexisting form, would probably first enquire whether man varies, however slightly, in bodily structure and in mental faculties; and if so, whether the variations are transmitted to his offspring in accordance with the laws which prevail with the lower animals."[2] This thinking laid the foundation for the development of a complete world and life view that would be evolutionary in its nature and outlook.

And although Darwin confined his ideas to biology, they were soon adapted to scientific endeavor at large and to nearly every other aspect of intellectual life in the West. He became a hero to the international academic community, being awarded honorary doctorates by three foreign universities, and receiving honorary membership to fifty-seven foreign learned societies.

Darwin looked upon the natural world as a vast and complex mechanism without a goal or purpose. Darwin asserted that animals were partakers of one common ancestor and, thus, are "netted" together. This kind of thinking reduced *all* to the level of natural selection and survival of the fittest. The natural order was thus viewed as a system of chance and chaotic behavior, where only the fittest—those adapted to environmental change by newly acquired traits—would survive.

Darwin's theory was an immediate success. Within a quarter century, it was widely adopted in biology and many other fields (although in 1859 the majority of the scientists rejected Darwin's theory). George Bernard Shaw, who described himself in his autobiography as "full of Darwin," correctly noted that "the world jumped at Darwin."[3] This was essentially true. For example, J. D. Rockefeller used Darwinian thought to justify industrial monopoly without restraint: "The growth of a large business is merely a survival of the fittest."[4] Likewise, Andrew Carnegie could expound on his conversion to Darwinism in this fashion: "Light came as in a flood and all was clear. Not only had I got rid of theology and the supernatural, but I found the truth of evolution."[5] Unlike influential capitalists before him (such as Adam Smith, who turned to human resource as his moral touchstone), Carnegie transferred his mysticism to Darwinian "truths."

Like Carnegie and Rockefeller, the world jumped at Darwin for several reasons.

First, the intellectual groundwork in the world of ideas had already been laid in European thought. This was also true to a high degree in the United States. Nineteenth-century man had long been prepared for the acceptance of a biological theory because he had been exposed to a philosophy of evolution for some time by various theorists. Thus, Darwin's idea did not occur in a vacuum.

In fact, credible evidence exists to suggest that Darwin may have developed his theory of evolution as based upon the philosophy and work of Alfred Russel Wallace,[6] another British naturalist. Wallace's book *Darwinism*, published in 1889, is said to be especially important for the differences it brings out between Wallace and Darwin. However, it is also said that the book,

which went through many printings, elaborates Darwinism in its
purest form. Wallace argued that every species had come into existence coincident both in space and time with a preexisting
closely allied species.[7] It is worth noting also that Wallace, who
nearly died in a shipwreck while on expedition, converted during
the 1860s to spiritualism, the belief that the dead survive as spirits which can communicate with the living through the help of a
medium.

An important predecessor to Darwin was Charles Lyell. In his
Principles of Geology (1830-1833), Lyell emphasized the uniformity of natural causes in the field of geology. In surveying the many
processes which alter the surface of the earth—erosion of running
water, accumulation of sediments, elevating effects of earth-
quakes and volcanoes—he formed the idea that there are no
forces in the past except those that are active now—that is, no intervention by the Creator.

In the writings of Marquis Jean Baptiste de Lamarck and
Erasmus Darwin, the grandfather of Charles, who acquired the
label "atheist" because of his enthusiasm for pagan folklore and
his acceptance of evolutionary ideas, we find other early presen-
tations of the theory of biological evolution. Moreover, simultaneous with grandson Darwin there were still others (such as
Alfred Russel Wallace) working on a theory of evolution of the
species.[8] In the final analysis, though, it remained for Darwin
with *Origin of Species,* which theologians such as William Paley
promptly blasted for dislodging man from his position as created
in God's image, to gain a widespread hearing for the theory of evolution in Europe and America.

The second reason for welcoming Darwin was that the theory
mirrored what was happening in the Industrial Revolution. It fit
well within the general scheme of life during the midnineteenth
century. "Darwin's description of the evolution of species bears
a remarkable resemblance to the workings of the industrial production process in which machines were assembled from their individual parts."[9] Indeed, "[e]ach new species was seen as an
assemblage of individual parts organized into new combinations
and arrangements and with additional improvements designed to
increase both their complexity and their efficiency."[10]

Perhaps unconsciously Darwin, who stressed that even man's
moral sense was a basic mechanistic "part" produced by developing intellectual powers, was adding fuel to the mechanistic ap-

proach that was flowering in the midnineteenth century and which had previously been spawned in the Enlightenment. It was, as Amury de Reincourt recognizes, a "merciless...age when social Darwinism ruled supreme.... With Roman-like ruthlessness...Spencerian apostles confused mechanical expansion with historical progress, and the very success of industrialization contributed to ensnare them in their own intellectual traps."[11]

There was simply no way to escape the overwhelming presence of the machine in English life at the time. Many intellectuals were anxious to extend its application to every facet of life. Paintings of this period, such as *Work* (1863) by Ford Madox Brown, graphically dramatized the woes of manual labor and the attractions of machination. A huge mechanical device dominates a rural French landscape in Rousseau's *The Quarry* (1896). Such depictions were common as the machine's presence permeated the Western world. One could hardly expect biologists to remain aloof from the excitement of the day. The phenomenon is very similar to the application of computer technology to man and nature today.

A third reason for Darwin's acceptance was the growing philosophical and scientific revolt against biblical theology and historical Christian thought. Catholics and Protestants both were under attack. With the emergence of the Industrial Revolution, preceded by the Enlightenment, there was a propensity "to believe in the sufficiency of man to achieve his own redemption through the application of his own unlimited wisdom to the problems which confronted him."[12] As C. Gregg Singer notes: "The biblical doctrines of a sovereign God, who created man in His own image, the fall into sin with its corollary of total depravity, and the need of redemption through the atoning work of Christ upon the cross became increasingly foreign to the mind of the nineteenth century."[13]

The acceptance of Darwin, then, shifted truth on three parallel lines: man, nature, and God. As historian Ralph Henry Gabriel notes, Darwin emphatically challenged "the old religious doctrine of the nature of man."[14] That is to say, the fact that man was created in the image of God was directly challenged. The umbilical cord between man and his Creator was being severed.

Darwin himself never fully abandoned the conviction that there is a God. However, by making man a descendant of the ape and the product of "natural selection," rather than the direct handiwork of the Creator, he helped to rob man not only of his centrality, but also of his sense of responsibility to his Creator.*

Charles Hodge of Princeton Theological Seminary also recognized the implications of Darwin over a hundred years ago: "Darwin[ism] involves the denial of final causes. . . . [I]t excludes all intelligent design in the production of the organs of plants and animals, and even in the production of the soul and body of man."[15]

There can be no doubt that Darwin was firmly convinced that the universe betrayed no sufficient evidence of a plan or purpose. "It was," as Singer writes, "plainly and undeniably a fatalistic philosophy, which made its way into Western thought and eventually conquered the modern mind."[16]

Darwin had insisted on a fatalism of rigorous governance by natural laws. In *Origin of Species* he wrote:

> Some have even imagined that natural selection induces variability, whereas it implies only the preservation of such variations as arise and are beneficial to the being under its conditions of life. No one objects to agriculturists speaking of the potent effects of man's selection; and in this case the individual differences given by nature, which man for some object selects, must of necessity first occur. Others have objected that the term selection implies conscious choice in the animals which become modified. . . . It has been said that I speak of natural selection as an active power or Deity; but who objects to an author speaking of the attraction of gravity as ruling the movements of the planets? Everyone knows what is meant and is implied by such a metaphorical expression. . . . So again it is difficult to avoid personifying the word Nature; but I mean by nature only the aggregate action and product of many natural laws, and by laws the sequence of events as ascertained by us.[17]

Jacques Barzun, in his book *Darwin, Marx and Wagner*, explains the meaning of Darwin's idea:

_____

*It is said that in England theological confrontation of Darwin's theories came to a head one day in 1860. It was June 30, and a meeting of the British Association for the Advancement of Science was in session. The Reverend Samuel Wilberforce, bishop of Oxford, stood up and challenged Darwin's friend Thomas Henry Huxley, asking whether it was through his father or his mother that he had claimed descent from the ape. Huxley answered that he was not embarrassed at having ape ancestors, but he was embarrassed by men "who used great gifts and eloquence in the service of falsehood."

> All events had physical origins; physical origins were discoverable by science; and the method of science alone could, by revealing the nature of things, make the mechanical sequence of the universe wholly benevolent to man. Fatalism and progress were as closely linked as the Heavenly Twins and like them invincible.[18]

Science, as based upon evolution, "by revealing the nature of things," becomes, in essence, a new religion (or body of institutionally accepted observances) from Darwin forward.

In addition to removing the origin of man from God's direct causation, Darwinism further undermined any normative, divine order to nature because now nature itself was evolving. The best was yet to come. Thus, man cannot discern right principles of conduct from the natural order as it now exists. Chance and relative movements in nature became understood as normative.

Darwin spawned a philosophy of intellectual, moral, and ethical relativity that accompanied the amazing development of a totalitarian absolutism (or unconditional certainty of Darwinian "laws") during the twentieth century. Relativism (the limitation of certainty) in theology and morality inevitably brings with it a political absolutism. No society can endure with relativism as its only absolute and the struggle to survive as its only rationale. For the coming tyrants of the twentieth century, the "relativity of all values which they professed to find in Darwin's Absolute made such a conclusion both easy and popular—at least for those who were able to survive in the struggle and become the 'fit.'"[19]

One can explain the continuing popularity of Darwin's idea only in its rejection of historical Christianity. It certainly cannot be the result of an inherent attractiveness in the theory itself. That man descended from lower forms of life is not a belief in which man can take pride. Nor can its popularity be in its scientific correctness. That has been roundly attacked by evolutionists themselves, as well as by many qualified scientists. Instead, its popularity rests in its nonscientific explanations. In short, man believes what he wants to believe: the mystic requires little prodding.

COMPARTMENTALIZATION

There "was a sudden impact of Darwinism upon Christian orthodoxy"[20] of the mid- to late-nineteenth century. Without the hindsight we have today, the Christianity of that era was struck by Darwinian evolution in its scientific trappings. It was not until the 1960s that scientists began to study and propound what is now termed "scientific creationism," a point of view critics have labeled "as revolting as it is uncalled for."

The sudden impact of Darwinism with the cumulative and flowering effects in Europe of the philosophies of Kant (rejection of pure reason), Hegel (objective idealism) and Kierkegaard (Christian existentialism) resulted in an eventual compartmentalization of the Christian faith. Since nature, which now encompassed man, was lost to a mundane and material world oozing with the evolution of *all* life, the one area left for escape was the spiritual. Neoplatonic (or primarily theoretical) at base, it spawned a nature/grace dichotomy.

Restricted to the higher plateau of grace was God; heaven and heavenly things; the unseen and its influence on the earth; man's soul; and unity. Restricted to nature, the lower plateau, was life in its evolving state; earth and earthly things; the visible and what nature and man do on earth; man's body; and diversity.

Once this was accepted, Pietism (the overarching emphasis on devotional experience—sometimes known as "religiosity") was the next logical move within the Christian realm. As it gained in popularity, personal evangelism became the basic focus of Christian life. However, inward spirituality, not external redemption, was the message of the day.

Of course, this meant compartmentalizing one's self from participation in the natural realm, which included all that was not spiritual. This meant separating Christianity from the major institutions of society, such as law, government, science, education, and the media. In less than fifty years, the Christian pietistic retreat left a vacuum in society that could be filled only by advocates of Social Darwinism. Singer writes:

> [T]he evolutionary hypothesis also became the new frame of reference for the origin and function of all human institutions. Government, economic thought and practice, sociology, and education as well as philosophy and theology were all subjected to the demands and scrutiny of the evolutionary hypothesis. No area of human thought or activity was allowed to escape from this scrutiny. When scholars did not openly assert their fidelity to Darwinism, they nevertheless allowed it to guide their activities and conclusions. Darwinism became the order

of the day. Scholarship which did not pay due obeisance to this new deity became suspect. The theory became thoroughly entrenched as scientific fact, and its truths could not be questioned. Permeating every area of academic and intellectual endeavor, it became the frame of reference for the Western mind.[21]

Moreover, as has been noted:

> The master idea...was that of evolution.... Independently of the writings of both Comte and Spencer, there proceeded during the 19th Century, under the influence of the evolutionary concept, a thoroughgoing transformation of older studies like History, Law and Political Economy; and the creation of new ones like Anthropology, Social Psychology, Comparative Religion, Criminology, Social Geography.[22]

As a consequence, a system of institutions once influenced by Christian absolutes was lost to relativism. Julian Huxley noted:

> The whole of evolution was soon extended into other than biological fields. Inorganic subjects such as the life-histories of stars and the formation of chemical elements on the one hand, and on the other hand subjects like linguistics, social anthropology, and comparative law and religion, began to be studies from an evolutionary angle, until today we are enabled to see evolution as a universal, all pervading process.... Furthermore, with the adoption of the evolutionary approach in nonbiological fields, from cosmology to human affairs, we are beginning to realize that biological evolution is only one aspect of evolution in general.... Our present knowledge indeed forces us to view that the whole of reality is evolution—a single process of self-transformation.[23]

Public education soon became a primary vehicle for conforming society to evolution. Under the influence of men like John Dewey, giant of early twentieth-century public education, there was a systematic application of evolutionary concepts to the curriculum and methodology of public education.

In essence, Dewey believed that the evolutionary process had reached a state of development in which man could control his own evolution; he openly embraced the evolution of human behavior but went a step further, suggesting that such behavior could be used and channeled in and through the public educational system. Specifically, Dewey, who refined his ideas in the late 1800s at the University of Chicago, believed that the school as a social center meant that the active and organized promotion of this socialism would happen naturally through the intangibles of art, science, and other modes of social intercourse. The school as a social center, he believed, would produce a better social "animal."[24]

Evolution is now a bedrock foundation of public education. And it has been enforced by law. Federal district court Judge William Overton in 1982 ruled:

> Evolution is the cornerstone of modern biology.... Any student who is deprived of instruction as to the prevailing scientific thought on these topics will be denied a significant part of science education.[25]

One can easily see what has happened. Amazingly, the entire public educational system which now produces the scientists and professionals of society has shifted to a secularistic base without much more than a whimper from the Christian world of 1900-1960.

The vacuums in culture and education have given society several generations of people who no longer have a concept of traditional absolutes. In many there is even a hostility toward traditional religion.

For example, public schools, once saturated with at least nominal Christian teachings such as in the old *McGuffey Readers* which offered Protestant theology without mentioning Christ specifically, have put religion to rout. Indeed, judges, school superintendents, and principals, schooled in evolutionary antitheology, have been exorcising Christians and Christian-related values from the system. As recently as 1982, *Christianity Today* magazine reported that eleven teachers had been fired in California for sharing their Christian beliefs. Christians and other religious people have to beg the courts and legislatures for even a silent prayer in the schools; and since school districts are controlled locally, the hostilities of local public educational administrators actually compound things further for many religious teachers.

The education of Americans in materialistic secularism has had dramatic results up top in governmental higher echelons and in the scientific elite. As the state relies more and more on the advice and technology of science, those who grasp the reins of science are of great concern. The scientific elite, as we shall see, has *no* regard for the whole man. As the computer has come more into the forefront of scientific technology, man is coming more to be viewed as an inferior product of a mechanistic universe. And if there seems to be too many of him, he can be planned away in our "overpopulated" world.

Moreover, secularistic impersonalism (the maintaining of an "impersonal ethic" in education) that, as A. E. Wilder-Smith recognizes, "is taught avidly and dogmatically, indeed almost universally, in most schools and high schools,"[26] has become an article of faith for its proponents. Logically, then, this new faith is seeking to replace the older Christian thought forms as the basis of society.

ENUMA ELISH

Evolution, even in the midnineteenth century, was not a new idea. Instead, it is an idea that has roots in antiquity. It was a religious doctrine adhered to by ancient civilizations.

Some years ago the world's oldest cosmogony (or account of the universe's beginnings) was unearthed and found recorded on tablets excavated from the land that was once ancient Babylonia. It is known as the *Enuma Elish*,[27] and has been called by scholars the "Babylonian Genesis." This Babylonian cosmogony is an apparent description of what is referred to today as evolution:

> Specifically, *Enuma Elish* assumes that all things evolved out of water. This description presents the earliest stage of the universe as one of watery chaos. The chaos consisted of three intermingled elements: Apsu, who represents the sweet waters; Ti'amat, who represents the sea; and Munnu who cannot as yet be identified with certainty but may represent cloud banks and mist. These three types of waters were mingled in a large undefined mass. . . . Then in the midst of this watery chaos two gods came into existence.[28]

Another account of the ancient origin of evolutionary thought is found in the *Tibetan Book of the Dead*. This work, embraced and expounded most recently by pop philosopher and culture hero Timothy Leary, was compiled from the teachings of sages over many centuries in ancient Tibet, and was passed down through these early generations by word of mouth. It was finally written down in approximately the eighth century A.D. One interesting account declares: "The Osiris, the Scribe Ani, whose word is truth, saith: I flew up out of primeval matter. I came into being like the god Khepera. I germinated...like the plants."[29] As Henry M. Morris comments:

> The idea of evolution did not, of course, originate with Darwin...but it was a doctrine held by many scientists and philosophers before Darwin. Belief in spontaneous generation of life from the non-living and in transformations of the species was quite common among the ancients. Among the early Greeks, for instance, Anaximander taught that men had evolved from fish and Empedocles taught that animals had been derived from plants.... One striking fact emerges from the study of all the ancient cosmogonic myths, whether from Babylon, Greece, Egypt, India, or wherever. The concept that the universe had originally been *created*, out of nothing, by an act of God, is completely absent. Always there is primeval chaos or a primeval system of some kind, upon which the "gods," or the forces of nature, begin to work in order to bring the world and its inhabitants into their present state. Special creation seems to have been a doctrine completely unknown (or, if known, rejected) by the ancients.[30]

Darwin himself recognized in a later edition of *Origin of Species* the religious nature of evolution and its faith proposition.[31] He said that "[t]here is grandeur in this view of life...having been originally breathed by the Creator into new forms."[32]

The religious presuppositional status of evolution is clearly delineated in the thinking of neoorthodox theologian Pierre Teilhard de Chardin.[33] Teilhard de Chardin posited that even if all evidence pointing toward evolution were demolished, evolution would yet have to be man's fundamental vision. Why? "Evolution has long since ceased to be a hypothesis and has become a general epistemological condition...which must henceforth be satisfied by every hypothesis."[34]

Who needs evidence when, for Teilhard de Chardin, evolution has become the manner in which man can see "light"? He confessed his faith in evolution as the "light illuminating all facts, a curve that all lines must follow."[35]

Such illogical reasoning can perhaps be excused when it comes from primitive cultures or naive theologians. However, when scientists speak similar babble, it causes concern since scientific "truth" takes on an authoritarian air. Moreover, it is a return to the superstition of ancient civilizations.

AN ARTICLE OF FAITH

Sir Julian Huxley, grandson of Darwin confidante Thomas Huxley and brother of writer Aldous Huxley *(Brave New World)*, understood exactly how evolution must be maintained as the core idea of society. He argued:

> It is essential for evolution to become the central core of any educational system, because it is evolution, in the broad sense, that links inorganic nature with life, and the stars with the earth, and matter with mind, and animals with man. Human history is a continuation of biological evolution in a different form.[36]

Huxley's hopes have been answered. Evolutionary theory has been enshrined "as the centerpiece of our educational system, and elaborate walls have been erected around it to protect it from unnecessary abuse."[37] However, cracks in those walls have begun appearing as evolution is being exposed for the religion that it is.

For example, Colin Patterson, senior paleontologist at the British Museum of Natural History in London, on November 5, 1981, delivered a speech to a group of experts on evolutionary theory at the American Museum of Natural History in New York. Patterson dared to suggest that the "scientific" theory he and his colleagues had devoted their lifetime to is mere speculation:

> Last year I had a sudden realization. For over twenty years I had thought I was working on evolution in some way. One morning I woke up and something had happened in the night; and it struck me that I had been working on this stuff for twenty years and there was not one thing I knew about it. That's quite a shock, to learn that one can be misled so long. . . . So for the last few weeks I've tried putting a simple question to various people and groups of people. . . . Can you tell me anything you know about evolution, any one thing, any one thing that is true?. . .All I got. . .was silence. . . .
> The absence of answers seems to suggest that. . .evolution does not convey any knowledge, or, if so, I haven't yet heard

it.... I think many people in this room would acknowledge that during the last few years, if you had thought about it at all, you have experienced *a shift from evolution as knowledge to evolution as faith.* I know that it's true of me and I think it is true of a good many of you here.... Evolution not only conveys no knowledge but seems somehow to convey antiknowledge.[38]

Antiknowledge destroys knowledge, just as antimatter destroys matter, when they come into contact. Edwin G. Conklin, late professor of biology at Princeton University, recognized the pervasive sense of religiosity that permeated the thinking of his colleagues when he remarked: "The concept of organic evolution is very highly prized by biologists, for many of whom it is an object of *genuinely religious devotion,* because they regard it as a supreme integrative principle."[39]

Contemporary scientists have been candid in expressing their faith in the evolutionary theory of life. Harold Urey, a Nobel laureate, said:

All of us who study the origin of life find that the more we look into it, the more we feel that it is too complex to have evolved anywhere. *We all believe as an article of faith* that life evolved from dead matter on this planet. It is just that its complexity is so great it is hard for us to imagine that it did.[40]

Princeton University physicist/astronomer Carl Sagan, the unofficial "high priest of evolution," has said:

Today it is far easier to believe that organisms arose spontaneously on the earth than to try to account for them in any other way. Nevertheless, *this* still *is a statement of faith* rather than of demonstrable scientific fact. Scientists have only sketchy notions of how this evolution might have occurred.[41]

Similarly, physicist Robert Jastrow, an evolutionist, stated:

Either life was created on the earth by the will of a being outside the group of scientific understanding; or it evolved on our planet spontaneously, through chemical reactions occurring in nonliving matter lying on the surface of the planet. The first theory is a statement of faith in the power of a Supreme Being not subject to the laws of science. The second theory is also an act of faith. The act of faith consists in assuring that the scientific view is correct, without having concrete evidence to support that belief.[42]

Several years ago, evolutionist George Wald, Nobel Prize-winning Harvard biologist, noted:

> One only has to contemplate the magnitude of the task to concede that the spontaneous generation of a living organism is impossible. Yet, here we are—as a result, I believe, of spontaneous generation. [43]

Biological evolution, from a postulated first life to all plants and animals, is as much based on faith as is cosmic evolution and biochemical evolution. There is no persuasive fossil evidence that evolution took place. Pierre P. Grassé, one of the world's greatest living biologists, has noted that in evolution "a pseudoscience has been created." [44] He notes that "the explanatory doctrines of biological evolution do not stand up to an objective, in-depth criticism." [45] For future generations Grassé suggests that the following epigraph be attached "to every book on evolution": [46]

> From the almost total absence of fossil evidence relative to the origin of phyla, it follows that any explanation of the mechanism in the creative evolution of the fundamental structural plans is heavily burdened with hypotheses.... The lack of direct evidence leads to the formulation of pure conjectures as to the genesis of phyla; we do not have a basis to determine the extent to which these opinions are correct. [47]

There is a credibility gap for biological evolutionists: although many are dogmatically insistent that one or a few common ancestors evolved into all plants and animals, many scientists candidly acknowledge that there is virtually no evidence whatsoever that "evolution" took place. [48] Instead, the fossil evidence of abrupt appearances and systematic gaps is better explained by creation. The same problem exists concerning the phenomenal mathematical improbability that organized life emerged from chance occurrence and accidental arrangement of mutations. It "is virtually zero." [49]

G. A. Kerkut, professor of physiology and biochemistry at the University of Southampton, England, sums up the state of the science when it comes to the speculative nature of evolution:

> There is... little evidence in favor of biogenesis and as yet we have no indication that it can be performed. *It is* therefore *a matter of faith* on the part of the biologist that biogenesis did occur and he can choose whatever method of biogenesis happens

to suit him personally; the evidence for what did happen is not available.[50]

To qualify as science, Darwin's theory should be provable by means of scientific method. In other words, its hypothesis should be capable of being tested experimentally. Although not totally accepted by philosophers of science, the scientific method provides a helpful three-step process of verification. *First,* data or phenomena are observed. *Second,* a hypothesis is formulated based on the observations. The hypothesis allows the scientists to make certain predictions regarding the data. *Third,* experiments are set up to test the hypothesis and to determine whether the predictions are valid. If the outcome of the experiments validates the prediction, the hypothesis is considered verified. In his book *Dismantling the Universe: The Nature of Scientific Discovery,* Richard Morris has warned about science based on mere speculation. He writes: "[I]f theories can be based on mistaken insights, and if this can lead, in turn, to the misinterpretation of data, then one would think that scientific knowledge would be full of errors. In such a case, it would not be possible to have confidence in anything, and the only reasonable attitude toward scientific endeavor would be one of skepticism."[51] Does this apply to Darwinism?

At the heart of scientific method is experimental repeatability or reproducibility. Evolution, as with creation, will not stand up to the measurability of scientific method. This has been confirmed by evolutionists who note that "evolutionary happenings are unique, unrepeatable, and irreversible."[52]

The lack of scientific credibility has brought criticism to the advocates of evolution from their peers. For example, Allen C. Burton, former president of the American Physiological Society, comments:

> The facts must mold the theories, not the theories the facts. . . .
> I am most critical of my biologist friends in this matter. It seems to me that they have allowed what is a most useful working hypothesis in a limited field in the whole of biology, to become "dogma," in their worship of the principle of natural selection as the only and sufficient operator in evolution. If they have done this, they no longer can act as true scientists when examining evidence that might not fit into this frame of concepts. If you do not believe me, try telling a biologist that, impartially judged along with other accepted theories of sci-

ence, such as the theory of relativity, it seems to you that the theory of natural selection has a very uncertain, hypothetical status, and watch his reaction. I'll bet you that he gets red in the face. This is "religion" not "science" with him. [53]

IF ATOMS ARE MAN'S PROGENITOR

Men, intelligent men, often act irrationally in terms of their religion. This is as true of the Christian as it is the dogmatic evolutionist who believes in spontaneous generation when he has little, if any, evidence to sustain his belief.

However, it is evolution's religious basis that makes it troublesome. Men will hold to religion with tenacity. They suffer for it. A true believer will die for his faith, as the saints of history illustrate.

Being a materialistic religion, based upon an impersonal beginning, evolution can give no real explanation of personality. In a very real sense, the question of questions for all generations—but overwhelmingly so for modern man—is, "Who am I?"

When I look at the "I" that is me and then look around to those who face me and are also men, one thing is immediately obvious: "Man has a mannishness." [54] That is to say people have a conscience and a soul and an otherwise immaterial side to them.

This "mannishness" is found wherever you find people—not only in men who live today, but also in the artifacts of history. "The assumption of an impersonal beginning," writes Francis Schaeffer, "can never adequately explain the personal beings we see around us, and when men try to explain man on the basis of an original impersonal, *man soon disappears.*" [55]

Moreover, as a materialistic religion, evolution can provide no foundation from which to base freedom or to secure oneself against tyranny. Evolution simply does not form a foundation from which to protect life or liberty.

Materialistic philosophy relieves one of responsibility to anyone—whether it be God or man. Atoms have no morals. If atoms are man's progenitor, then man is not so much *im*moral as *a*moral. Once this is the accepted philosophy of a society and its government, the implications can be grave.

In fact, the implications of evolution, and its application to various facets of life, including political and social philosophy, are clearly seen in the totalitarian regimes of history. Social evolution formed a basis for fascism and its oppressive racist actions.[56] Benito Mussolini, who could stand by and watch the killing of nearly half a million persons at the Caporetto battle front, justified war (as did Friedrich Nietzsche) on the basis that it provided the means for evolutionary progress.[57] One writer documents:

> Our own generation has lived to see the inevitable result of evolutionary teaching.... Mussolini's attitude was completely dominated by evolution. In public utterances, he repeatedly used the Darwinian catch words while he mocked at perpetual peace, lest it hinder the evolutionary process.[58]

Adolf Hitler's *Mein Kampf* expressed his adherence to evolution in justifying his world view of genocide, master race, and human breeding experiments.[59] One anthropologist has said of Hitler: "The German Fuhrer...consciously sought to make the practice of Germany conform to the theory of evolution."[60]

The class struggles and atheistic posture of Marxist communism owe their existence to the political and social philosophy of evolutionary secularism. In fact, Karl Marx said that Darwin's *Origin of Species* served as "a basis in natural science for the class struggle in history."[61] Marx was so excited about the evolutionary implications for socialism that he sought to dedicate his book *Das Kapital* to Darwin.[62] However, Darwin kindly rejected the offer for fear that his association with Marx "might undermine the credibility of his own work among his peers."[63]

Racism, too, both modern and ancient, is merely a sequel to evolutionism.[64] Charles Darwin himself provided the racist element of the theory of evolution. Though the title of his book is often cited as *Origin of Species,* the complete title is *The Origin of Species by Means of Natural Selection, or the Preservation of Favoured Races in the Struggle for Life.* The favored race is, of course, the white race. Harvard biologist Stephen Jay Gould, an evolutionist himself, has recently documented the racism that has historically pervaded evolutionary thinking.[65] The same racist drive of evolution, it has been argued, is a motive of abortion; that is, abortion as the killing of minorities.[66]

Thus, evolution pervades every strand of modern life. Along with the secularistic society which supports it, evolution has not only denigrated man's position in the universe, but is now altogether removing man from a meaningful relationship with any aspect of the world around him.

FOUR

THE DISENCHANTED WORLD

Darwin's assertion that man descended from lower forms of life not only affected man's centrality and link with the Creator, it also dramatically reordered his relationship to nature. As seen, it created a great tension between the natural and spiritual worlds. And with the coming of Spencerian and Social Darwinism, all things became subject to unethical manipulation. Such manipulation or exploitation of nature, moreover, is also the exploitation of man, for wanton destruction of the natural world entails the same of man.

CONCEPTS OF NATURE

Before continuing, I want to make clear what I mean by nature. True nature, in traditional terms, relates partially to, but does not completely identify with, the Greek, the contemporary romantic notions of the term, or the scientific view.

The Greek concept of nature, as it derived from Hellenistic philosophy, posed nature as a creative controlling agent or force with operative principles. As such, nature determined wholly its own constitution, development, and well-being. However, even before the Hellenic Dispersion, the stage for a mechanistic view of nature had been set. With Anaxagoras—sometimes called the Darwin of his age (480 B.C.)—the universe had been divided into fire, air, water, and earth. The moon was dependent on the sun; winds were caused by atmospheric heating; thunder was caused by the collision of clouds; and all organisms were generated out of earth, moisture, and heat.

From the Greek concept, and from subsequent centuries of scientific thought, flowed the concept of natural law, which posits that the universe is sustained by its own laws; it is a deterministic, self-enclosed system of causality. One of this concept's off-spring was deism, which reduced the Creator to little more than the mechanic of the natural universe. Consequently, nature could function independently of God. The next step was to accept the ultimacy of nature and to drop God entirely, except in some nebulous sense. Nature, then, became a continuum operating without personal guidance from the Divine Hand.

The Hellenistic concept gave an imprimatur of *sacredness* to nature, but in different terms than would Christianity. Whereas the Hellenistic concept shrouded nature with mystery as a wonder to behold, Christianity would ascribe the term "wonder" to nature, but would make clear that a personal Creator was nature's progenitor and overseer.

Though the romantic version of nature embodies Hellenistic aspects, it differs in some ways. Romanticism as it concerns nature involves the application of human emotions to the natural world. In its purest form, this way of thinking found its home among the American romanticists (and/or transcendentalists) of the nineteenth century: Ralph Waldo Emerson, Henry David Thoreau, and others. Wandering through fields and woods, Thoreau wrote: "My instinct tells me that my head is an organ for burrowing, as some creatures use their snout and fore paws, and with it I would mine and burrow my way through these hills."[1] The tendency was and still is to integrate downward toward the creation, leaving no room for the upper categories of true spirituality.

The romantic view is very much a strong contemporary movement. It deals with the natural world in a religious way. Writers such as Pulitzer Prize-winner Annie Dillard use terms such as "holiness" and "praise" when discussing the natural world. Dillard ends her *Pilgrim at Tinker Creek* with this statement: "[M]y left foot says 'Glory,' and my right foot says 'Amen': in and out of Shadow Creek, upstream and down, exultant, in a daze, dancing, to the twin silver trumpets of praise."[2]

In this manner, modern man is barely different from "primitive" tribes. Anthropologists have observed how such tribes live in a world of myths, in which religion, culture, and the physical environment are all of a piece. Such tribes communally invent and inhabit an ordered image of the universe, a "cosmos" that unites all aspects of existence. As Joseph Campbell states in *The Masks of God*, his landmark study of primitive mythology, "Life is to mirror, as nearly perfectly as is possible. . . [the] order of the pageant of the spheres.''[3] It is thus impossible for the anthropologist to study a tribe's environmental perception apart from its culture and religion.

In a much quoted article in *Science*, "The Crisis" (1967), Lynn White, Jr. recalls the established historical fact that the primitive animistic view of the world, in which the physical environment was peopled by spirits, gods, and demons, was dramatically challenged by Judaism and Christianity.[4] These two religions "disenchanted" the world: the forests were no longer enchanted by the presence of the spirits, and the fields no longer subject to fertility gods. Man was man, God was God, and nature was subject to both. "You [man] are of more value than many sparrows," Jesus had said. Nature, according to James Boice, was just that: the "natural." It was there to be used.

Disenchantment does not mean disillusionment, as J. A. Walter writes, but "matter-of-factness."[5] The earth is worthy of our aesthetic appreciation and scientific investigation, but not our worship. Judaism and Christianity emphasized this and asserted a radical break between the divine (the Creator) and the material (creation). White, though correct in this part of his argument, overestimates the extent to which this disenchantment has been complete and permanent. To paraphrase Christ, "Sweep one spirit out of a house and leave it empty, and seven more will soon come in to fill it."

White's article, however, sparked off a debate about the past, present, and potential effect of traditional religion on the way human beings deal with their environment. The debate, as all other debates of the past three decades, focuses on the so-called "drastic" abuses of the environment by pollution, overpopulation, etc.[6]

At the base of White's critique is the religious fascination with nature—the romantic view. It has gained a dominant voice in anything that touches ecological concerns.

After Darwin, it became difficult to separate man and nature; and much of the message of ecology is that human beings should recognize that they are part of nature and cannot flout its laws without paying a price. "Human beings are getting themselves, and the rest of the world, into deeper and deeper trouble, and I would not lay heavy odds on our survival unless we begin maturing soon," writes naturalist Lewis Thomas. "We could. . .cause the crash of the species. . .overpopulation and crash, deforestation and crash, pollution and crash.''[7]

Nature, as such, becomes our moral instructor. Phrases such as "nature teaches us that . . ." or "nature tells us that . . ." are common. The inhabitants of the natural world are viewed as without human flaws, thereby assuming a "natural" superiority. "Does a tree shrew worry about contradictory thoughts?" asks naturalism's newest convert, Phil Donahue. "Is a blue-green alga torn between competing ideas?"[8] This kind of thinking involves a reversion to "natural theology," the philosophical view that an "ought" can be derived from what "is." Thus, we find Darwin and many after him going to nature to seek revelation and truth, but ending with a pessimistic view of people.

Modern ecology, however, has moved away, in romantic fashion, from the Darwinian nature of bitter struggle for survival. Instead, to the romanticist, nature is seen as stable, harmonious, and self-regulating. But the message is clear: "This benign system is likely to be vengeful if we sin against it, and this is the basic message of ecological revivalism; we must repent of our ways."[9]

Such religious reverence can be striking. American nature writer John Burroughs wrote in 1912:

> Every walk in the woods is a religious rite. . . . If we do not go to church as much as did our fathers, we go to the woods much more, and . . .we now use the word nature very much as our fathers used the word God.[10]

Or consider this extraordinary statement by conservationist Edward Abbey:

> [W]e have agreed not to drive our automobiles into cathedrals, concert halls, art museums, legislative assemblies, private bedrooms, or other sanctums of our culture. We should treat our National Parks with the same deference, for they, too, are holy places. . . . We are finally learning that the forests and the mountains and the desert canyons are holier than our churches.[11]

Such rhetoric is indeed a distortion. Although natural places can be beautiful, they are not always as painted by Burroughs and Abbey. As J. A. Walter writes in *The Human Home:*

Not only is the wilderness usually uncomfortable and dangerous, it is also often ugly. Most deserts are not perfect
windblown dunes glistening pure gold or white in the sun; they
are semi-scrub, flat as a pancake, roamed perhaps by half-
starved cattle and acting as a dump for technological refuse
such as old motor cars and abandoned tanks which do not rust
or decay in the dry, pure air. Left to the devices of nature, a
Newfoundland forest may consist of fungus-attacked stunted
dwarfs, in contrast to the healthy tall conifers of a managed
plantation.

The problem with actual wild places, then, is not just that
they are physically uncomfortable and dangerous, but that
they also challenge the romantic notion of the purity and
beauty of the Great Goddess Nature. For this notion to stay intact, the illusion must somehow be fostered that wilderness is
pretty and safe.[12]

Although Walter may overstate his case here, it illustrates the
fact that the romantic reverence (or "illusion") for nature is even
more religious (and, perhaps, more primitive) than the animism
of primitive peoples. Tribesmen who venerate a sacred mountain
do so not because it is a mountain, but because it is sacred. The
mountain speaks of something beyond itself, and they know perfectly well that in itself it is no more than a mountain. The American Indian's worship of snakes is also a case in point. They are
often reverenced, and occasionally their "holiness" makes them
dangerous, as anything may be that is "sacred." But snakes in
and of themselves pose no fear to the same Indians.

Likewise, in the view of medieval natural theology, nature
pointed to God, but was *not itself God*. This is the distinction, as
Walter notes, between the "primitives" and the moderns:

However, for modern worshipers of nature from the romantics
onwards, the sacredness lies in the mountain itself, and for
contemporary ecologists it lies in the whole natural system. For
the traditionalist, the sacred is worshiped through nature; for
the modern, nature itself is less sophisticated than the
"primitive."[13]

In the midst of the romantic view of nature, the question must
be asked: where does man fit in? Often, he is seen as a spoiler in
an otherwise pristine environment. He is the polluter. He cuts
the trees down. He shoots the animals. He is the one part of nature that executes itself.

Much of the rhetoric of overpopulation advocates suggests that man is indeed *the* spoiler of the world. Nature cannot tolerate too many spoilers. Thus, man must be thinned out and, in effect, planned away. However, as Julian Simon demonstrates in *The Ultimate Resource* and as Germaine Greer chronicles in *Sex and Destiny,* the overpopulation argument is one of the great myths of this century.[14] Organizations such as Planned Parenthood Federation have used the overpopulation rhetoric effectively to *force* contraception and abortion on millions[15] when, as Simon says, such arguments "are plain untruths that fly in the face of well-established scientific evidence."[16]

Carry the romanticism of nature to an extreme, and you wind up with pantheism. God is not viewed as a distinct and genuine personality, and man, with all living things, is seen as one essence.

Pantheism, however, eventually gives no meaning to the particulars of creation. In true pantheism, unity has meaning, but particulars have no meaning, including the particular of man. And if the particulars have no meaning, then nature has no meaning. Francis A. Schaeffer writes:

> A meaning to particulars does not exist philosophically in any pantheistic system, whether it is the pantheism of the East or the "Pan-everything-ism" of beginning only with the energy particles, in the modern West. In both cases, eventually the particulars have no meaning. One is left only with Jean-Paul Sartre's absurd universe. Pantheism gives you an answer for unity, but it gives no meaning to the diversity. Pantheism is not an answer.[17]

The term "God's creation" has no real place in pantheistic thinking. Such thinking does not allow for a *creation*, but only an extension of God's essence. The traditional concept of "God's creation"—as though He were a personal God whose creation was external to Himself—is alien to pantheism.

Furthermore, a pantheistic stand always brings man to a low, impersonal station rather than elevating him. This is clearly reflected in Eastern countries, which are openly pantheistic, and where there is no real base for the dignity of man.

Pantheism, as such, has its roots at least as far back as third-century Greece. In *The Life of Greece,* Will Durant tells about the pantheistic philosopher Euhemerus, whose views exerted a powerful atheistic influence upon ancient Greece. Durant writes: "About 300 Euhemerus of Messana in Sicily published his *Hiera Anagrapha*...in which he argued that the gods were either personified powers of nature or...human heroes deified by popular imagination or gratitude for their benefits to mankind.... The book had a sharply atheistic effect in third-century Greece."[18]

The scientific view of nature arrives at the same junction as the Greek and romantic views. Seeing nature as an impersonal mechanism, man, himself a clockwork organism, is part of the machine. The supernatural is entirely eliminated. As Francis Crick, who along with James Watson unraveled DNA, has said: "As soon as we understand cell chemistry, we know that a metaphysical explanation of life becomes superfluous."[19]

Scientist A. E. Wilder-Smith adds that "many honest thinking scientists are absolutely and unshakably convinced that the mere existence of proof for a chemical basis of life and of cell metabolism automatically and simultaneously totally excludes any metaphysical basis for life."[20] The Creator is ruled out of the picture.

However, it does not mean that man is not part of nature. Under the scientific rationale, man is one with the natural machine. This is *scientific pantheism*. Although it excludes the creation idea, it is, as we saw with secularism and evolution, religious.

THE CREATION IDEA

The opening words of the Bible are clear in their premise concerning the natural order of things: "In the beginning God created the heavens and the earth." With the successive acts of creation culminating in the creation of man, it is equally clear that all that exists bears the mark of the Creator, but is *separate* from Him.

This is inherently true of man. He bears the Creator's image, after the "likeness" of God. There can be little doubt that the "image" of God must entail those aspects of human nature which are not shared by animals: a moral consciousness, the ability to think abstractly, an understanding of beauty and emotion, the capacity for worshiping and communicating with the Creator. These characteristics are bound up in personality and in man's intended relationship with the Creator and other human beings.

In essence, the implication from the special creation of man (both male and female) is that man is fundamentally a religious being. This is true whether the object of worship is the Genesis Creator or a blood-stained idol upon which sacrifices are made.

Man's *basic* relationship, then, is not downward or horizontal, but upward. Man, as such, is separated from nature because he is made in the image of God. He has personality and is unique in the creation, but he is united to all other creatures in that all living things are created too. Thus, he also has a proper downward relationship with animals and plants: the created world. The term "man" is actually *"adam,"* and is related to "earth" (in the Hebrew *"adamah"),* since man's body was formed from the elements of the earth. Thus, there is a total interrelationship of man with the rest of the creation, even though this unity was significantly interrupted by the Fall.

Despite the Fall, however, I can look at the creation and know that the tree, for instance, is a creature like myself. But that is not all. Psychologically I should "feel" a relationship to the tree as my fellow creature. Schaeffer writes:

> It is not simply that we ought to feel a relationship intellectually to the tree, and then turn this into just another argument for apologetics, but that we should realize, and train our people in our churches to realize, that on the side of creation and on the side of God's infinity and our finiteness—we really *are* one with the tree. [21]

God, in the final analysis, then, created a holistic, living organism when He had finished the creation. Contrary to modern science, the Creator did not fashion a clockwork universe. Though its systems reproduce a kind of clockwork accuracy and repetition, it is not a giant machine that was assembled, wound up, and set to ticking. Instead, all creation is inescapably personal and actively sustained by the Creator. Nothing is autonomous.

It follows that nature was designed with a goal and a purpose. Moreover, with Adam being instructed to care for the creation, natural processes, even in their pre-Fall state, were not fully self-correcting. Without man's care, nature cannot independently achieve its purposes.

Modern man cannot understand this because he lives in a *decreated* (downward toward impersonal particulars) world. Everything is decreated and autonomous. Of course, this is not true from the Christian perspective. In fact, *value* does not arise from the fact that "things" are autonomous, but from the fact that God made them. All things are part of a total divine act. However, if man believes that he sustains the universe, then he must necessarily believe he sustains human beings. The resulting equation: Man over Man.

THE DOMINION IMPULSE

In both Genesis 1:26 and 1:28, man is given dominion "over all the earth." He is allowed to rule over "the fish of the sea and the birds of the air, over the livestock, over all the earth, and over all the creatures that move along the ground." The meaning of dominion is important not only for its psychological implications, but also for the natural propensity to misuse the concept of taking dominion (even on the part of Christians).

The term *dominion* in Hebrew is *radah*, which means to rule and to tread down. It is a military term implying an initial conquering followed with ruling. In context, however, there is no actual conflict suggested in Genesis 1 and 2 since everything God had made was pronounced "good." Therefore, the implied meaning of dominion is an ordering of creation. This ordering is affected by a study of the creation (with all of its intricate processes and systems) for the purpose of using this knowledge for the benefit of the earth's inhabitants. Therefore, man is not to destroy the earth, but to replenish it.

Important is the fact that dominion was established by the Creator as a primary function of human nature. It is inescapable and expressed daily by people through the human ego.

Unfortunately, the Fall gave way to a distorted egotism, which grew out of the dominion impulse. According to Paul in Romans 8:19-23, the very creation around us groans and travails, waiting for the final redemption of all things—presumably to escape the perversion and exploitation of them by fallen man.

Too often the impulse has been for men to rule men tyrannically. In so-called democratic societies the impulse has been used to manipulate people. But make no mistake. The dominion mandate of the early chapters of Genesis is not a command to rule over other men. Stalin, Hitler, and other tyrants of the twentieth century were examples of the distortion of the dominion impulse.

A key distinction must be made between dominion and sovereignty. Man has dominion over the lower orders of creation, but he is not sovereign over them. Only God is sovereign, and man must treat the lower orders by this standard. Man is not using his own possessions, and therefore he is not entitled to exploit the lower order.

Returning to the dominion impulse, it was impaired by the Fall. Instead of it being humanitarian centered, it is now egocentrical (or viewing everything in relation to man's self). In its corrupted state it wants to control, exploit, and manipulate. It is not satisfied with ordering.

Moreover, since the Fall, there appears to be embedded deep within our consciousnesses the concept of paradise lost. With the rise of modern science and technology, man can now attempt a return to Eden; that is, to a utopia.

A catastrophe, to use Erik Erikson's expression for it, that every human being must experience is his personal recapitulation of the biblical story of paradise. For a time the infant demands and is granted gratification of his every need, but is asked for nothing in return. Then, according to Erikson, often after the infant has developed teeth and has bitten the breast that has fed him, the initial unity between him and his mother is scarred or broken.

Erikson believes this universal human drama to be the ontogenetic (or life cycle) source of the Garden of Eden account. So important is this period in the child's life, Erikson believes, that "a drastic loss of accustomed mother love without proper substitution at this time can lead [under otherwise aggravating conditions] to acute infantile depression or to a mild but chronic state of mourning which may give a depressive undertone to the whole remainder of life."[22] However, as Erikson notes:

> [E]ven under the most favorable circumstances, this stage leaves a residue of a primary sense of evil and doom and of a universal nostalgia for a lost paradise.... [These early years], then, form in the infant the springs of the basic sense of trust and the basic sense of mistrust which remain the autogenic source of both primal hope and of doom throughout life.[23]

Whether or not such information can be trusted as reliable is beside the point. It does illustrate, however, that there is in every individual an imaginative attempt at reconstruction of the world. When translated through the dominion impulse, clouded by the fallen character of man, and not restrained by Christian compassion, it has produced campaigns of terror inflicted on the inhabitants of the earth.

But there is no paradise to be regained. Even among Christians it is not generally understood that paradise, as represented by Eden, was impermanent. It was to be a place of training for its original inhabitants, and they were not supposed to stay in the garden forever. From paradise, man was to order or take dominion of the natural realm worldwide.

Coupled with the psychological urge to recover Eden is the fact that applied science has now produced tools that enable man to approximate the lost skills of Adam in the garden. I am speaking here principally about continuing development of technology and, more recently, of computers.

There is a problem with such devices, however:

> [T]hey have almost allowed rebellious man back into the "garden" apart from saving faith and biblical dominion. Men may wish to find an escape from the bondage of death, thereby allowing them access to infinite temporal extension for the purpose of indulging their lusts. Yet their tools of dominion now threaten all of civilization, for the tools of dominion can produce and have produced mighty weapons, allowing us to turn ploughshares into swords more efficiently.[24]

DESACRALIZATION

Before and after the Greeks, nature was, as seen by early man, held to be sacred. Christians, too, have traditionally held to *a* sacredness in nature since it is the handiwork of God. Sacred, to the Christian, however, does not mean magical or self-contained.

This is where Christians may have had their greatest impact upon the understanding of nature. Christianity *disenchanted* nature in that it deprived it of its alleged magical qualities. In Romans 1:20, the Apostle Paul had clearly conveyed this sense of disenchantment when he wrote: "For since the creation of the world God's invisible qualities—his eternal power and divine nature—have been clearly seen, being understood from what has been made." However, Christianity did not desacralize nature as did later cosmologies.

For the Christian, because nature is fallen—it fell with Adam—its activities also must be viewed through the grid of moral accountability. Moreover, the natural order must not be tampered with, and anything new must be submitted to a moral judgment—which necessarily means an almost unfavorable pre-judgment for *any* tampering by man.

This was the popular mentality created by Christianity, particularly during the seventeenth century. In part, it led to the rise of applied science. Christianity was necessary for the beginning of modern science for the simple reason that it created a climate of thought—even awe of the natural order—which put men in a position to investigate the form of the universe, but without aiming to exploit it.

Jean-Paul Sartre posed the philosophic idea that something, rather than nothing, exists. No matter what man thinks, he has to deal with the reality that there is something here. The Christian faith gives an explanation, "a certainty of objective reality, and cause and effect; a certainty that is strong enough to build on."[25] The object and history, cause and effect, really exist.

This cosmology, or conception of nature and the order of the universe, made it possible for science to blossom. Charles Darwin altered this concept as it concerned nature. As a consequence, man's relationship to his environment changed, and a new cosmology was formed. All cosmologies, however, share the same overreaching theme:

> They tend to serve as a distant mirror of the day-to-day activity of a civilization. Cosmologies are humanity's way of elevating its behavior to universal importance. It is people's way of convincing themselves that their behavior is appropriate, that it is in accord with the grand operating scheme of the universe. People have always needed to believe that the way they are organizing their life is no different from the way nature organizes itself. Their cosmologies provide a rationale and justification for their every act. Cosmologies provide people with the confidence they need to endure.[26]

Cosmologies bring the vast universe in line with people's conception of it. Without a cosmology people would have no way of knowing that what they are doing is justified. They act and plan on the formulation of a cosmology. Thus, we can see the importance of the debate over the origin of life. Moreover, if a cosmology from which one frames his life is incorrect, it will provide a distorted view of nature, man, and God.

Cosmologies have been an essential feature of human societies from time immemorial. This is true of pretechnological societies which conceive of nature in a much different way than post-Darwinian cultures.

This was also true of the eras which preceded the Industrial Revolution. Then a people's relationship with nature was still participatory and intimate. When man's ability to manipulate and redirect nature was slight, his overriding preoccupation was with fitting into the world as it existed. This created a reverential attitude toward the larger forces which control life.

However, with Darwin, as he shaped his evolutionary cosmology to mirror the British Industrial Revolution, a fragmentation occurred. Creation, no longer a creation, became a product of material forces. Nature at this point was desacralized.

Desacralization is man's severing of any emphatic association he might feel toward the rest of the living world (from which he borrows everything he needs to exist). Desacralization is a code word for *deadening*.[27] Jeremy Rifkin in his book *Algeny* writes:

> Only after a living thing has been thoroughly deadened can it be prepared for assimilation. Unlike the other animals, human beings prefer not to tear into live flesh. We would rather separate the process of killing from the process of eating. We separate ourselves from nature, not only in the pursuit of it, but also in the consumption of it. Regardless of the stage of the assimilation process from pursuit all the way to consumption, we prefer to keep our distance.[28]

This means that people can attempt to maintain themselves as subject and reduce everything else to object. Greater separation from nature makes it easier to capture, maim, and kill without remorse—that is, seeing the vague outline of a man from afar is not the same as hearing the breath rush in and out of the nostrils.

During the Vietnam War, Cobra helicopter pilots recounted to me on several occasions the stories of their return flights after bombing missions. If ammunition was left unused, some pilots would empty the ammo on small Vietnamese boats or on villages. Again, it was easy to kill a vague outline. "Detachment and desacralization go together."[29] In contrast, ground soldiers would tell of hearing the tortured screams and seeing the ripped flesh of enemy soldiers. They saw what the pilots were too far away to see, and as a result they have more lingering nightmares.

Desacralization is the way man convinces himself that there is no fundamental likeness between him and other living things. It is always more difficult to kill and assimilate that which one identifies with. Thus, the "desacralization process allows human beings to repudiate the intimate relationship and likeness that exists between ourselves and all other things that live."[30] It allows us to conquer nature without moral remorse.

CONQUERING NATURE

Man's *conquest of nature* is an expression often used to describe the progress of applied science. It is man's attempt to control—exercise dominion—over the natural order. Reduced to one word, it is "power."

But it is not power in the abstract. What we term as *power over nature* is in reality power exercised by *some* men over *other* men with nature as its instrument. It is a power some men may, or may not, allow other men to profit by. In fact, modern science has created its own closed class. Biochemist Erwin Chargaff, whose early work on DNA in part paved the way for the work of Francis Crick and James Watson, remarks:

> The decline of the natural sciences, as reflected in the decrease of intellectual activity in that arena, has been brought about by specialists who resemble more and more the caste of priests in the Egypt of the pharaohs; that is, their existence is based on their need to survive. This is also true of the great mass of scientists who are creating—secretly, if I may say so—the sciences called "new," because they want to go on making a living and getting grants.... Science has been perverted...by its tendency to become a regular "business."...Today, they form a new class that, in order to survive, required continuity. Naturally, their group has everything to gain by creating problems that make it appear indispensable, and that's what we're seeing now.[31]

With the rise of technology, man's power over nature, as manifested in his machines, makes him as much the subject as the possessor. He is both the target and the one who targets others: the bomber and the bombed; the conditioner and the conditioned.

And ultimately, man's power over nature means the power of earlier generations over later ones. With the rise of eugenics (the science of racial improvement), as manifested in population control and abortion, a negative power is created in which future generations are subjects to be controlled by those already alive.

Each generation, then, exercises power over its successors. As each debunks tradition and modifies the environment bequeathed to it, it resists and limits the power of its predecessors. C. S. Lewis masterfully puts the matter in perspective:

> In reality, of course, if any one age really attains, by eugenics and scientific education, the power to make its descendants what it pleases, all men who live after it are the patients of that power. They are weaker, not stronger: for though we may have put wonderful machines in their hands we have pre-ordained how they are to use them. And if, as is almost certain, the age which had thus attained maximum power over posterity were also the age most emancipated from tradition, it would be engaged in reducing the power of its predecessors almost as drastically as that of its successors. And we must also remember that, quite apart from this, the later a generation comes—the nearer it lives to that date at which the species becomes extinct—the less power it will have in the forward direction, because its subjects will be so few.[32]

Eugenics is the inseparable wing of the age of biotechnology; that is, the technological restructuring of life. First coined by Charles Darwin's cousin, Sir Francis Galton, eugenics is generally categorized in two ways, negative and positive. Negative eugenics involves the elimination of biologically undesirable characteristics. Positive eugenics is concerned with the use of genetic manipulation to "improve" the characteristics of an organism or species.

Eugenics is not a new phenomenon. At the turn of the century many in the United States were involved in a massive eugenics movement. Politicians, celebrities, academicians, and other prominent citizens joined together in support of a eugenics program for the country. With people such as Margaret Sanger, founder of Planned Parenthood, leading the way, the movement reached a fever pitch. Many states passed sterilization laws, and Congress passed an immigration law in the 1920s which required thousands of Americans to become sterilized so they could not pass on "inferior" traits. "Population control," another aspect of man's authority over nature, grew out of such ideology.

While Americans were attempting to enforce a systematic eugenics program on the nation, the Nazis accomplished just that in the 1930s and 40s. In fact, the German law for the Prevention of Progeny with Hereditary Disease, the basis of Hitler's race purification program, was directly patterned on the model sterilization law proposed by leaders of the American eugenics movement.[33] Millions of Jews fell victim to gas chambers and crematoriums to advance the Nazis' concept of the super race.

Eugenics lay dormant for nearly a quarter of a century after World War II. However, with the spectacular breakthrough in molecular biology in the 1960s, eugenics has been revived once again through movements such as population control.

The offspring of this revival is genetic engineering, which is the new eugenics. Speaking at a National Academy of Science forum on recombinant DNA, Ethan Singer, a biologist at Massachusetts Institute of Technology, warned his colleagues that "this research is going to bring us one step closer to genetic engineering of people. That's where they figure out how to have us produce children with ideal characteristics. . . . The last time around, the ideal children had blonde hair, blue eyes and Aryan genes."[34]

If the trend continues, future generations, far from being the heirs of power, will be of all people subject to the cold hands of the planners and conditioners. A few hundred, the elite of conditioners, will rule over billions upon billions of people.

The final stage will arrive when man, by eugenics, population control, prenatal conditioning, genetic engineering, and an educational system armed with efficient propaganda techniques, takes control. State propaganda based upon effective applied psychology, and aided by the ever advancing computer elite, will make this control total. "*Human* nature will be the last part of Nature to surrender to Man."[35]

And if anyone supposes the conditioners will be benevolent, let alone merciful, he must realize that in the dictionary of the future secularist and genetic planners, the words *mercy, compassion, love* have no real meaning. The quality of the future population planners' "mercy" will probably be much the same as that of the doctors, lawyers, parents, and judges who condoned the killing by starvation of Infant Doe in Bloomington, Indiana, in 1982 because of that child's genetic defects. Their mercy will be that of the Indian government's enforced sterilization projects or of the Chinese Communist government's forced abortion programs in which women are rounded up at gunpoint and their children aborted.

This is not supposing that the conditioners are bad men. They are not men (in the traditional sense) at all. C. S. Lewis writes:

> They are, if you like, men who have sacrificed their own share in traditional humanity in order to devote themselves to the task of deciding what "Humanity" shall henceforth mean. "Good" and "bad," applied to them, are words without content: for it is from them that the content of these words is henceforward to be derived.[36]

The conditioners are actually artifacts. Indeed, man's final conquest will prove to be the end of man.

History shows us not one example of a man who, having stepped outside traditional morality and attained power, has used that power benevolently. Power corrupts, and absolute power, as Lord Acton noted, corrupts absolutely.

We are, as Erwin Chargaff comments, moving toward "a new barbarism":

> Our era violates all moralities, all the decalogues of humanity. It is a new barbarism, which tomorrow will be called a "new culture." We are already living in that time. Words have been so debased that today we label as morality what would have been called an absence of morality fifty years ago. Naturally, Nazism was a primitive, brutal, and absurd expression of it. But it was a first draft of the so-called scientific or prescientific morality that is being prepared for us in the radiant future. . . . Euthanasia and eugenics began under the Third Reich. Before swallowing up dozens of millions of "subhumans," the camps were first built to contain, then liquidate, mental patients, weaklings, etc. . . . Our time will be marked by progress in physics, the fission of the atom, and in the same stride by the demise of a race due to Hitlerian genocide. Hitler was a key to our time; he was a precursor of our sciences. In the not too distant future, monuments will be erected to him.[37]

By man's victory over nature, finally, we find the entire human race subjected to a few men who are not necessarily bad, but who have in the course of time sacrificed their humanity.

Nature, untrammelled by values, rules the Conditioners and, through them, all humanity. Man's conquest of Nature turns out, in the moment of its consummation, to be Nature's conquest of Man. Every victory we seemed to win has led us, step by step, to this conclusion. All Nature's apparent reverses have been but tactical withdrawals. We thought we were beating her back when she was luring us on. What looked to us like hands held up in surrender was really the opening of arms to enfold us for ever.[38]

THE MAGICIAN'S BARGAIN

In 1935, Michael Polanyi, then holder of the Chair of Physical Chemistry at Victoria University in Manchester, England, expressed alarm at the emergence of a secularistic scientific outlook which was producing "a mechanical conception of man and history." Further, he noted that "this conception denied altogether any intrinsic power to thought and thus denied any grounds for claiming freedom of thought."[1]

Even though Polanyi was a part of the scientific community, he recognized the rise of the scientific impersonalism which dominates twentieth-century thought. This disturbed him.

This impersonalism runs contrary to thought forms that existed through most of the nineteenth century. Before the year 1900, it generally was held that man and history were characterized by personalism. Man was seen as holding a unique and special position in space and time, a position which grew out of his relationship with the Creator—no matter how tenuous that connection might have been. "Is it not the chief disgrace in the world," Emerson asked, "not to yield that peculiar fruit which each man was created to bear?"[2] However, with the rise of scientific impersonalism man lost his uniqueness. And not without consequences.

REAL SCIENCE

Science had secular and Christian origins. The early scientists, however, shared, in general, the Christian world view in believing that there is a reasonable God, who created a reasonable universe. "Why! Do you not say yourself that the sky and the birds prove God?"[3] Pascal had asked. Thus, man, by his reason and his observation, could discover the universe's form.

When Christianity was first taught in Europe, culture and spirituality were fundamentally altered. The sternest of critics, such as humanist Edward Gibbon, would admit to the totality of effect Christianity had upon culture. And as historian Jeremy Jackson understates in his volume on church history, *No Other Foundation*, "Through Jesus Christ the history of the West—to speak only of the West—has been radically transformed."[4]

When one realizes the truth of what Chapter 1 of Genesis means to man's view of reality and his endeavor to understand it, the transformation becomes clear. Genesis says that God created the world and that there is no being that has not been created. This gave man, Christian and non-Christian, a freedom for research formerly unknown.

Indeed, while the church has traditionally been accused of restricting scientific research, some historians present a different picture. Will Durant writes in *The Age of Faith:* "The Church and the Inquisition were part of the environment of European science in the thirteenth century. The universities for the most part operated under ecclesiastical authority and supervision. The church, however, allowed considerable latitude of doctrine to professors, and in many cases encouraged scientific pursuits. William of Auvergne, Bishop of Paris (d. 1249), promoted scientific investigation. . . . Bishop Grosseteste of Lincoln was so advanced in the study of mathematics, optics, and experimental science that Roger Bacon ranked him with Aristotle. The Dominican and Franciscan Orders made no known objection to the scientific studies of Albertus Magnus or Roger Bacon. St. Bernard and some other zealots discouraged the pursuit of science, but this view was not adopted by the Church."[5]

Christianity prepared the way for scientific discovery in that it freed man from the tyranny of ancient gods. Of lightning, for example, man could ask: "What is it?" "The wrath of God?" "His tool or weapon?" "Can man investigate it and not be sacrilegious?" The ancient gods, being part of the cosmos and its regulating principles, made it impossible to launch into such discussions open-mindedly.

Moreover, as soon as man came to know the true Creator, everything was open for investigation, for everything had been created by God. Thus, only on this basis is there freedom for science.

What is more, in contrast to early scientists who were always in danger of being accused of going against the divine order, this Christian freedom did not need to go against the understanding that God reigns over the cosmos. This is because science proceeds from the assumption of *causality* (or what is sometimes called the "law of causality"). If a certain thing occurs, then man can experiment and study it. There is no event without a cause and no cause without a result. For everything, then, men should seek the natural cause within the created order of reality.

This is true of biblical figures. As H. R. Rookmaaker notes:

> Elijah, for instance, prayed to God for rain. But he knew, as man has always known, that there can be no rain without clouds. So he sends his servant up to the hill to see whether the clouds were coming. Praying for rain and understanding the basic rule of causality do not conflict. Why should it be a problem that Jesus walked on the water? If Jesus was God, and so Lord of creation, there is no reason to query whether He could. This is not contradicting science. It keeps the world open to God, who as Creator can work in His creation.[6]

This is the basic assumption of true Christianity. God has "created and sustains the world; that He is interested in His creation; and does not let things go by 'chance.' He looks after man, His creature."[7]

It was really in the sixteenth and seventeenth centuries, after the Reformation, that science developed rapidly. It capitalized on the freedom of observation which Christianity brought. Jeremy Jackson suggests that the revolution entailed "an application of those Renaissance/Reformation principles of objective enquiry to all aspects of the physical universe. . . . [It] depended very heavily on fundamental biblical ideas, such as the fact that the Bible assumes a world of order in which mathematical calculations and empirical observations make sense. Without such a backing, how could one be sure that two plus two will always equal four, or that organizing principles might be anticipated in the study of the endless variety of natural things?"[8]

Many of the scientists of the seventeenth century, as mentioned, were devout Christians who did not see their "scientific" activity as minimizing their faith. In fact, these scientists, nurtured by the Bible and especially Genesis, reopened the door to the advancement of knowledge which the Middle Ages had partially closed. "Christian geniuses giving glory to God," writes Michael Harrington, "helped overcome that European backwardness and unwittingly created the greatest challenge religion has ever known."⁹ This challenge—autonomous science—came once the capacity of reason and divine revelation were severed. Men such as Immanuel Kant laid the groundwork for such a challenge.

Nevertheless, it can be said with accuracy that the Christian world view allowed for the development of science. Harrington adds:

> The scientific revolutionaries of the sixteenth and seventeenth centuries—Bacon, Harvey, Kepler, Galileo, Descartes, Pascal, Huyghens, Boyle, Newton, Leibniz—were for the most part pious men. Newton, the quintessential architect of the age, might even be described as a religious crank. There was, Robert Merton has documented, such a close link between religious ideas and science that one can properly speak of a " 'holy alliance between science and religion.' " For even if particular theologians. . .denigrated the new discoveries, the men who made them agreed with Robert Boyle that their work gave witness "to the Glory of the Great Author of Nature."¹⁰

Scientists Alfred North Whitehead and J. Robert Oppenheimer also stressed that modern science was born out of the Christian world view. Whitehead, the son of an Anglican clergyman, was a widely respected mathematician and philosopher. And Oppenheimer was known as a scientist who had as much interest in his fellow workers and students as he had in science itself; his perceptiveness, it was said, balanced well with his readiness to admit ignorance when he did not possess an immediate scientific explanation of a matter.

Whitehead noted that Christianity was the mother of science because of the medieval insistence on the rationality of God.¹¹ In other words, because the early scientists believed the world was created by a reasonable God, they were not surprised to discover that people could find out something true about nature and the universe on the basis of reason.

Early science, moreover, was natural science in that it dealt with natural things. But it was not naturalistic. Although it held to a uniformity of natural causes, it did not conceive of God, man, or nature as machinery. Thus, man or God could not in any way be caught in the clockwork machinations of the universe.

The conviction was that the Creator gave to men knowledge concerning Himself, the universe, and history. Moreover, since God and man were independent of the machinery, they could affect the working machinations of cause and effect.

The philosophical streams of the eighteenth century, however, because of their impact on the discipline of science itself, began the move toward the secularization of scientific thought.

DOMINOS

Creeping in slowly was the development of a rationalistic approach to understanding the natural order of things. Although it was a time of contradictory aims and ideas, the basic thought forms of the Enlightenment laid down principles which govern today's dominant world view.

The first principles of this cultural movement, known as the Age of Reason,[12] were developed in France and England by a group of influential philosophers (René Descartes, Thomas Hobbes, John Locke, David Hume, Jean-Jacques Rousseau, and others).

However, Descartes, Hobbes, and Locke wanted to retain at least a vestige of Christianity. Locke, for example, wrote *Reasonableness of Christianity* (1695) and posited that biblical revelation was acceptable as long as it was reasonable.

The basic starting-point, therefore, was to be found in human reason. Descartes, for example, could proclaim that he doubted everything except for one certainty: "I think, therefore, I am."

This was a new thought form in the Christian West. Although profound, it eventually made God unnecessary—for as man began to apply his independent reason more, he was in need of the Creator's specific, written revelation less and less. Gently the Creator was pushed aside. "For personal life, for heaven and redemption, He might be useful," writes Rookmaaker, "but in the discussion of matters of science, politics, the big issues of the organization of the world, man must start with reason."[13]

A century after this scientific revolution, Immanuel Kant (who died in 1804) generalized his findings in theories which resonate to this day and which seem at first glance to be preposterous. "Previously one assumed that all of our experience must base itself upon objects,"[14] Kant wrote in the Foreword to the second edition of his *Critique of Pure Reason*. He continued:

[N]ow we must consider whether it would not be better to assume that objects must be based upon our knowledge.... That is as it was in the case of Copernicus, who, after he realized that the explanation of the movement of the heavens did not work very well when he assumed that the stars turned around the observer, sought to find out whether it would not be better to assume that it was the observer who turned and the stars which were at rest.[15]

On the face of it, this is absurd. Kant is saying that the real world depends upon man's knowledge of it rather than man's knowledge depending on the real world. This means that humans could create reality for themselves instead of accepting it as given from God. Moreover, the ideas of the human mind are imposed upon the external world instead of simply reflecting or describing it.

Supposedly Kant believed in God. But he offered a refutation of the evidences for the existence of God. One cannot, he said, argue with any validity toward the existence of God on the basis of an empirical reality known only by cause and effect. Such categories, Kant argued, are necessary to the human understanding of reality, but they are not necessarily real (and if they are we can never know it for sure).

Thus, in Kantian terms, one cannot use the subjective preconditions of finite experience to demonstrate the existence of an objective, infinite deity. One cannot employ the categories of time and space, he further argued, which are intrinsic to the mortal mind, to show that there is an eternal being beyond time and space. Not even mathematics, "that pride of human reason," he added, can satisfy us that God is in His heaven, that there is an immortal soul, or that man possesses free will.[16]

The implication of Kant's reasoning is that the natural realm—which is at least knowable subjectively—is not bound by anything beyond itself. Science and mathematics from Kant forward could be based on a methodological agnosticism. Pascal's insight that the infinite space of modern science is godless could now be carried out in excruciating detail.

Kant understood that the scientific revolution was, by its nature, agnostic. If he was correct, there was no God in Newton's universe even if Newton passionately believed there was. At most, the Deity remained a "cosmic plumber" to keep the Newtonian system in good repair.

In this way, Kant was more of a subversive, without intending to be, than even the French philosopher Robespierre. "The Frenchman only executed a king; the German [Kant] killed God."[17]

It is not difficult, moreover, to understand the intentions of those contemporaries who followed Kant. Reason (or common sense as they called it in the eighteenth century) is something all men are believed to have in common. We live in the same world and use the same senses. And if we start from this philosophical point, the subjective matters of religion can easily be eliminated.

From Kant's philosophy, nature was cut loose from the supernatural; the umbilical cord between the two was severed. And with nature separated from the Creator, the ensuing concept of the universe was that of a clockwork orange; that is, a biological machine of sorts. Stanley Kubrick could faithfully depict the futuristic horror of this machine in his film *A Clockwork Orange* (1972). Of the movie, film critic Vincent Canby wrote: "[It] is cast in the form of futurist fiction. . .[and] shows a lot of aimless violence—the exercise of aimless choice."[18] Important in this "clockwork" concept is that as man conquered nature, he was assimilated into the machine. He, too, had to be a machine.

It was at this point that men were seduced, as by an addictive drug called "science," into wishing and working for the establishment of an age of rationality. This rationality, of course, depended upon fallible human reason, even though it gradually became twisted so as to equate with the concept of *logicality*.

Thus was born the formula from which modern science operates—*rationality-as-logicality*. In other words, if something appears rational, in terms of subjective human reason, it must also be logical. If, for example, science reasons that man is nothing but a machination, this concept is equated automatically to cold logic. There is no room for argument then.

Starting every human endeavor with man at center, therefore, brought about a radical change. In the older philosophical and scientific frameworks, man had his place in a large universe. There were principles, ideas outside of man, just as there were angels, devils, and other forces. But with the Enlightenment came the shift:

[N]ow the primary problem was that of epistemology, the theory of knowledge: how can we know, how do we get true

knowledge?...Again and again the main point is this: we as
man stand before a big "X" called the universe, and the only
way to come to any understanding of it is to use our senses (seeing, hearing, weighing, measuring) and to use our reason to
coordinate the sensations or perceptions we have had. So the
ideas outside man are no longer of any reality nor of any validity as normative principles.[19]

With this shift, not only was a supernatural deity eliminated,
but so were other elements of the supernatural, such as angels
and devils. All of these became old and, to some, dangerous su-
perstitions. The dominos, however, did not stop falling at this
point.

Next, all norms or laws outside of man also disappeared. If
something was not discernible by the senser, then, in Kantian
fashion, it was suspect.[20]

However, if no overriding norms or moral laws outside of man
existed, and if we say that only things experienced or reasonable
are true, then why not murder, maim, and steal without any remorse? God's commandments and laws against such acts become
irrelevant under rationalism.

Therefore, Thomas Hobbes could easily construct his "social
contract," the theory which holds that man in the beginning of
history, having found that stealing is a nuisance and a hindrance
to all human endeavor, decided that it was *reasonable* to conclude
that man should not steal. Hobbes's social contract was an attempt to fill in the vacuum left by the absence of God.

At first appearance Hobbes's idea seems to be a "reasonable"
solution to potential anarchy. But there is a catch: what if man (or
a group of men) decided by a majority vote that in the present situation it is suddenly reasonable to steal? Good and evil have been
put outside real reality. At best, they are subjective human evalu-
ations of behavior.

With the disappearance of an infinite basis for value-
judgment, man, too, disappears. As early as the mideighteenth
century Diderot, the man who as a young Jesuit student ghost-
wrote sermons for preachers and missionaries, later wrote in his
Encyclopedia (1752-72) that man "seems to stand above the other
animals."[21] The difference between man and other created beings seemed to be evaporating within the deterministic machine
of nature.

It was no accident, then, that the Industrial Revolution emerged as this philosophy was developing. Technology was using deterministic laws to transform the environment in the most objective fashion; and it is man who in his godlike subjectivity manipulates those laws. There was no need for the silent God.

This was the creedal statement of a new faith. Just as the early church adhered to creeds and, as Harold O. J. Brown suggests, believed it was "vital to know and accept some very specific statements about...God and his son Jesus Christ,"[22] so the creedal statement for a new generation of technology worshipers was being born. It was a new philosophy, and it looked to science as its creedal source. Rookmaaker notes: "Science accepted the new task, and, with the theory of evolution, would seem to have 'proved' it finally, for in examining the possible mechanism of evolutionary change there would seem no need for a God behind natural reality, no need for a Creator."[23]

Science thus became *scientism*—oftentimes more of a philosophy than a discipline. Similarly, evolution became evolution*ism* (more than a "scientific" theory). In this way human existence became equated with natural, biological, and physical reality; the new science tried, and continues to try, to give this view a foundation in facts. But it exists in "facts" only, and everything beyond the senses is excluded.

Therefore, man became "natural." He lost his particular place in the universe. He lost his humanity.

> What does that mean? If man is just another animal, for instance, then what is "love"? After a long development the answer came out loud and clear: Libido. Lust. Love is *really* only sex. All that seems to be more is "in fact" sublimation, a nice kind of facade to hide the real drives. Sex one can see and experience. But love?[24]

Life becomes nothing more than biological activity, the beating heart, sexual urges, and the quest for food and drink.

The rationality-as-logicality formula, like a slow-acting poison, did not immediately kill its victim—the human spirit. There were those who early on were aware that mankind was increasingly coming to view life as a machine. At the end of Leonardo da Vinci's life, he had foreseen that beginning humanistically with mathematics "one only has particulars and will never come to universals or meaning, but will end only with mechanics."[25] It took science two hundred and fifty years to arrive at the place Leonardo da Vinci had foreseen. But by the eighteenth century it had arrived.

Man was trapped in the machine. He was an object controlled by natural laws, to be studied by scientific methods, and nothing more. As biochemist Erwin Chargaff notes, science became adept at explaining the universe, but not understanding it.[26]

And scientism, in effect, became a new religion positing that man is no different from animals and plants. Armed with Darwin's vision, such *scientific pantheism* has become the power of the age.

Scientism is the means by which man hopes to make a better world. It is, and will be, a technocratic world which includes man within its process. "Man is no longer a human being who buys things: no, he is a consumer. He has become a little wheel in the big machine, a unit in social statistics, an electronic oscillation in the computer."[27] Man, as a consequence, is, then, one-dimensional.

With the rise of scientism, science has greatly increased in autonomy and power. It was set free from any moral responsibility to the Creator; it sees little or no responsibility to either God or humanity.

It is the magician's bargain: give up our soul, get power in return. However, once our souls have been given up, the power thus conferred will not belong to man. C. S. Lewis writes:

> We shall in fact be the slaves and puppets of that which we have given our souls. It is Man's power to treat himself as a mere "national object" and his own judgments of value as raw material for scientific manipulation to alter at will.[28]

MAGIC

It is the *ism* in science, however, that must concern us. Science, cut from Christian absolutes, is at heart a religion in and of itself, and it has become progressively more so over the years.

A science has never existed that was not founded on presuppositions of a religious nature, nor will one ever exist. This is to say, in effect, that every science presupposes a certain theoretical view of reality, and this view is intrinsically dominated by a central religious motive or thought. In short, there is no science without faith.

"The cosmos is all that is," writes Carl Sagan, "or ever was or ever will be."[29] Sagan is a scientist, but in his persistent quoting from the Book of Job he sounds like an Old Testament sage with a secular twist.

The religious aspect of science, which often operates subliminally in our society, sustains the holding power of its mystique. However, it is through the emergence of *technique* that we have seen the development of scientism in its final forms.

"No social, human, or spiritual fact is so important," Jacques Ellul writes, "as the fact of technique in the modern world."[30] *Technique* is any complex of standardized means for attaining a predetermined result. Technique converts spontaneous and unreflective behavior into behavior that is deliberate and rationalized. Technique is concerned with the most efficient method or means to an end. It has become one of the few prevailing absolutes of modern society.

Technique has integrated the machine into society. However, as Ellul notes, technique has become autonomous.[31] Moreover, it began to develop and extend itself only after science appeared. Therefore, in order to progress, technique had to wait for science.

But technique began to develop long before science, as we know it, came into the flow of history. In fact, magic was historically the first expression of technique.[32]

Magic developed along with other techniques as an expression of man's will to obtain results in the spiritual order. To do this, early man made use of an aggregate of rites, formulas, and procedures which, once established, did not vary (this according to superstition). The classic cups-and-balls magic trick, for instance, is believed to be among the oldest forms in the history of magic. Depicted on the walls of ancient Egyptian tombs, the form has not varied an iota in its centuries of use.

Strict adherence to form is one of the characteristics of magic—forms and rituals, masks which never vary, the same kinds of prayer wheels, the same ingredients for miracle drugs, etc. All these became set a long time ago and were passed on. The slightest variation in word or gesture would alter the magical equilibrium. Quite simply, there is a relationship between a ready-made formula and a precise result:

> The gods being propitiated obey such an invocation out of ne-
> cessity; all the more reason that they be given no opportunity to
> escape compliance because the invocation is not correctly for-
> mulated. This fixity is a manifestation of the technical charac-
> ter of magic: when the best possible means of obtaining the
> desired result has been found, why change it? Every magical
> means, in the eyes of the person who uses it, is the most effi-
> cient one.[33]

In the spiritual realm, magic displays all the characteristics of a
technique—even of a science. It is a mediator between man and
"the higher powers," just as science mediates between man and
nature and any higher powers (if they can be proven to exist). Indeed, the ancient Greeks enshrined their magicians as though
they had lived in the shadows of the divine. Euclides, an enter-
tainer who performed magic, was honored by having his statue
sculpted in the Temple of Bacchus in Athens.

Magic leads to efficacy because it joins the power of the gods to
the activities of men, and it secures a predetermined result. Furthermore, it affirms human power in that it seeks to subordinate
the gods to men, just as the technique of modern science causes
nature to obey.

In his conflict with the material world, man, by his use of
magic or science, interposes an intermediary agency between
himself and his environment. This agency has a twofold
function:

> It is a means of protection and defense; alone man is too weak
> to defend himself. It is also a means of assimilation: through
> technique, man is able to utilize to his profit powers that are al-
> ien or hostile. He is able to manipulate his surroundings so that
> they are no longer merely his surroundings but become a factor
> of equilibrium and of profit to him.[34]

Because we moderns are obsessed with materialism and do not
take magic seriously, it has little real interest to us. However,
modern man is unaware that through science he is drawing on the
great stream of magical technique.

It is a common myth of some of those who write about the sixteenth century to pose magic as a medieval force which science
swept away when it arrived. But those who have studied the period know better.

There was very little magic in the Middle Ages, which for our purposes we will date from approximately 500 to 1500 A.D. The sixteenth and seventeenth centuries were the high noon of magic—the so-called Age of Science. It was then that the first substantial texts on magic were published, such as Reginald Scot's *The Discoverie of Witchcraft,* which appeared as early as 1584. In his book *The Magic Catalogue,* William Doerflinger points out that magicians were being welcomed increasingly by both the public and international leadership. Some were very well-paid and were even enlisted for diplomatic missions between countries.[35] "The serious magical endeavor and the serious scientific endeavor," C. S. Lewis adds, "are twins. . . . They were born of the same impulse."[36]

Something unites magic and applied science while separating both from the wisdom of earlier years. For the wise man of old, the cardinal problem had been how to conform the soul to reality, and the solutions had been knowledge, self-discipline, and adherence to traditional moral codes. Regarding magic and science, C. S. Lewis restates the dilemma:

> For magic and applied science alike the problem is how to subdue reality to the wishes of men: the solution is a technique; and both, in the practice of this technique, are ready to do things hitherto regarded as disgusting and impious—such as digging up and mutilating the dead. If we compare the chief trumpeter of the new era (Bacon) with Marlowe's Faustus, the similarity is striking. You will read in some critics that Faustus has a thirst for knowledge. In reality, he hardly mentions it. It is not truth he wants from his devils, but gold and guns and girls. . . . In the same spirit Bacon condemns those who value knowledge as an end in itself: this, for him, is to use as a mistress for pleasure what ought to be a spouse for fruit. The true object is to extend Man's power to the performance of all things possible. He rejects magic because it does not work, but his goal is that of the magician.[37]

The purpose of magic is *total control* by man over other men, nature, and the supernatural. Whatever form magic takes, this is its goal. The purposes of modern science are increasingly those of magic—the exercise of total control. The essential goal of modern science is knowledge in order to have prediction, planning, and control over *all* things—including people.

Under the influence of Christianity, science escaped from magic. Magic, however, has again triumphed. With performers such as Doug Henning feeding today's "renaissance" in the world of magic, Doerflinger attempts explanation of the magician's contemporary appeal: "This attitude of childlike wonder and awe is beguiling for the audience, who share in [the magician's] astonishment and are captivated by his appealing modesty. Here is no slick, assured performer, showing off his prowess, exhibiting his skill. Instead the young magician is right there with them, wondering, attempting, explaining, fascinated, hopeful, and finally, miraculously, triumphant."[38]

Moreover, modern science is popular precisely because man today demands to triumph over history, ethics, and morality and to place man beyond good and evil and beyond responsibility to the Creator. As a consequence, man is no longer whole. He is a one-dimensional character integrating into the void of the machinations of the universe.

CONSIDER THE ANT

Once man was viewed less than whole, it was inevitable that he would be reduced to reflect the "machineness" of the universe. This is presently a presupposition of modern science. For example, Aldous Huxley, writing in 1946, said:

> Because of the prestige of science as a source of power, and because of the general neglect of philosophy, the popular Weltanschauung of our times contains a large element of what may be called "nothing-but" thinking. *Human beings, it is more or less tacitly assumed, are nothing but bodies, animals, even machines.*... [V]alues are nothing but illusions that have somehow got themselves mixed up with our experience of the world; mental happenings are nothing but epiphenomena... spirituality is nothing but...and so on.[39]

Approximately two decades later, computer scientist Herbert A. Simon noted his own theoretical orientation concerning the entity known as man:

> *An ant, viewed as a behaving system, is quite simple. The apparent complexity of its behavior over time is largely a reflection of the complexity of the environment in which it finds itself.*... [T]he truth

or falsity of [this] hypothesis should be independent of whether ants, viewed more microscopically, are simple or complex systems. At the level of cells or molecules, ants are demonstrably complex; but these microsocopic details of the inner environment may be largely irrelevant to the ant's behavior in relation to the outer environment. That is why an automaton, though completely different at the microscopic level, might nevertheless simulate the ant's gross behavior. . . .

I should like to explore this hypothesis, but with the word "man" substituted for "ant."

A man, viewed as a behaving system, is quite simple. The apparent complexity of his behavior over time is largely a reflection of the complexity of the environment in which he finds himself. . . . I myself believe that the hypothesis holds even for the whole man.[40]

With a single stroke of the pen, by substituting "man" for "ant," the presumed irrelevancy of the microscopic details of the ant's inner environment to its behavior has been elevated to the same in man. And it is only man's attempt to remain as man that creates the illusion that he is something more than the ant. As Simon adds: "Only human pride argues that the apparent intricacies of our path stem from a quite different source than the intricacy of the ant's path."[41]

This philosophy—man as nothing more than a machine—is antihuman. It is the quite logical progression of secularism. Man is dehumanized whenever he is treated as less than human, and this is often the posture of modern science.

Science today, argues M.I.T. professor Joseph Weizenbaum, has been robbed "of even the possibility of being guided by any authentically human standards, while it in no way restricts science's potential to deliver ever-increasing power to men."[42] In fact, he says, noting the antitheistic bias of science, "we [scientists] may not mention God, grace, or morality."[43] Thus, science is not held to any standard which could possibly retain the humanness of man.

Harvard behaviorist B. F. Skinner argues that human values are illusory. And if they are, it is presumably up to science to demonstrate this. But then science itself must be an illusory system. For the only "certain" knowledge science can give us is knowledge of the behavior of formal systems; that is, systems that are games invented by man himself. To assert truth in such systems is nothing more or less than to assert that, as in a chess game, a particular board position was arrived at by a sequence of moves.

However, when science purports to make statements about man's experiences (as in comparing man to the ant), it bases them on what the scientist considers "formulae" and some set of human observations. No such set of observations can ever be proved correct—for when dealing with man, we are dealing with the undefined. At best, such observations or conclusions will yield interpretations contrary to empirically observed phenomena. As Weizenbaum concludes:

> All empirical science is an elaborate structure built on piles that are anchored, not on bedrock as is commonly supposed, but on the shifting sand of fallible human judgment, conjecture, and intuition. . . . Probably all scientific theories currently accepted by scientists themselves (excepting only those purely formal theories claiming no relation to the empirical world) are today confronted with contradicting evidence of more than negligible weight that, again if fully credited, would logically invalidate them.[44]

Scientific statements, then, can *never* be certain; they can only be more or less credible.

The man on the street, however, believes all scientific facts to be as well-established as his own existence. His certitude is an illusion.

In fact, the scientist himself is not immune to the same illusion. "He is," Weizenbaum writes, "rather like a theater-goer, who, in order to participate *in understanding* what is happening on the stage, must for a time pretend to himself that he is witnessing real events. . . . Gradually he becomes what he at first merely pretended to be: a true believer."[45]

A SLOW-ACTING POISON

Modern science has become the sole legitimate form of understanding in today's common wisdom. It has, at the same time, become a slow-acting poison. By conveying the idea of the certainty of scientific knowledge to the general public, man has virtually delegitimized all other ways of understanding. All knees must bow before the god of science.

We have bought into something that, if not restored of its humanness, could very well spell destruction. The belief in the rationality-as-logicality equation has corroded our ability to see anything but cold technique and machineness. As a consequence, we have, through science and technology, created extensions of ourselves which have become autonomous and are on the verge of ruling us. They yet allow us to count, but we are rapidly forgetting how to say what is worth counting and why.

PART TWO

MAN AND HIS EXTENSIONS

This is the dead land
This is cactusland
Here the stone images
Are raised, here they receive
The supplication of a dead man's hand
Under the twinkle of a fading star.

Is it like this
In death's other kingdom
Waking alone
At the hour when we are
Trembling with tenderness
Lips that would kiss
Form prayers to broken stone.

T. S.Eliot
The Hollow Men

SIX

EXTENSIONS

It is often forgotten that the secularization of life in the West would have been impossible apart from the secularization of science; and that this scientific secularization has taken place under the influence of the religious secularism effected by post-Renaissance humanism. We have simply come to regard this situation as a *fait accompli*.

The dangers of our secularized science, as we have seen, are confronting us with a distorted view of man. It has torn us away from the faith of our ancestors and, as a consequence, has made much of the world easy prey for socialism, communism, and nihilism.

However, as we are often told, it is the missionary task of the church to present Christianity to the new-age scientists. Such people do not understand that the same secularized science which has made a secular wasteland of the West will also wither the message of Christianity. That is because science, secularized and isolated, has become a religious power, an idol that dominates all of culture.

Modern science, however, has not merely presented itself as a new idol to worship. It has given us a secularized technology which presumes to operate without the moral law. This has allowed man to extend himself technologically as never before—into extensions which, at present, threaten to turn on him.

NARCISSUS

As said, man is inescapably a religious being. If he does not worship his Creator, he will worship an extension of himself, something of his own making.

Primitive man bowed before stone and wooden representations of gods and demons. The Greeks and Romans personalized their gods so that they could manipulate them. Thus, their gods became reflections of the humans who made incantations to them. Again, these gods were mere extensions of human beings: "amplified humanity," according to Francis Schaeffer.

The Hebrews, and later the Christians, broke with tradition and proclaimed that a transcendent God existed. He was viewed as Creator of the universe, who disdained certain extensions of man. As the objective essence of existence, tribute would be paid to God alone. The Hebrew God went so far as to restrict the building of altars of hewn stone, lest it be tainted by human hands and become an extension of man.

Later in history Paul, drawing upon Christ's teachings, took this principle a step further by proclaiming that God's true temple of worship was man himself. Christ Himself had confounded the elders of Israel, announcing that true religion must be an extension of the Creator. In Christ's case it would be His followers. Man, then, in order to be in tune with the hum of the universe, must allow himself to be extended by the Creator, but in the spiritual realm. Imprinted by the *imago Dei,* and indwelt by the Spirit, man, as was intended in the beginning (but negated by the Fall), now embodied the essence of true religion.

Extensions mesmerize, and the Greek myth of Narcissus develops this theme. The word *Narcissus* is extracted from the Greek word *narcosis,* or numbness. The youth Narcissus mistook his reflection in the water for that of another person, and this extension of himself by mirror-image numbed his perceptions until he became the slave of his own extended image. The nymph Echo tried to win his love with fragments of his own speech, but in vain. Narcissus was numb.

The point of the myth was that men become fascinated by any extension of themselves. Without a true Christian perspective, man's extensions often dictate to him.

The Narcissus myth, as Marshall McLuhan explains in *Understanding Media,* does not convey the idea that Narcissus fell in love with anything he regarded as himself.[1] Quite to the contrary. Narcissus fell in love with an *extension* of himself. "The point of this myth," adds McLuhan, "is the fact that men at once become fascinated by any extension of themselves in any material other than themselves."[2]

The Psalmist understood the nature of the extensions of man. In Psalm 115: 4-8, we read:

Their idols are silver and gold,
The work of men's hands.
They have mouths, but they speak not;
Eyes they have, but they see not;
They have ears, but they hear not;
Noses have they, but they smell not;
They have hands, but they handle not;
Feet they have, but they walk not;
Neither speak they through their throat.
They that make them shall be like unto them;
Yea, every one that trusteth in them.

The concept of idol for the Hebrew Psalmist is much like that of Narcissus for the Greek mythmaker. And the Psalmist insists that the beholding of idols, or the use of technology, conforms men to them—"They that make them shall be like unto them."

The fact that human beings bind themselves with strong emotional ties to machines ought not in itself to be surprising. The instruments a man uses become, after all, extensions of his body.[3] The automobile, for instance, bonds with man to such an emotional degree that McLuhan is moved to categorize it as "the Mechanical Bride." He quotes the following news item: " 'It was terrific. There I was in my white Continental, and I was wearing a pure-silk, pure-white, embroidered cowboy shirt, and black gabardine trousers. Beside me in the car was my jet-black Great Dane imported from Europe, named Dana von Krupp. You just can't do any better than that.' "[4]

Most importantly, man must, in order to operate his instruments skillfully, internalize them in the form of kinesthetic and perceptual habits. In this sense, his instruments literally become part of him. Thus, man's machines alter the basis of his affective relationship to himself.

Being enormously adaptive, man has been able to discover a form of identity in his technological acceptance and immersion. Possibly this explains why he rarely questions the appropriateness of investing his most private feelings in machines. On a temporal level one can view this phenomenon in such matters as man's naming and personalization of automobiles; on a serious level it can be seen (and heard) in computers which have been programmed to converse with human beings.

Such an explanation, however, suggests that computers represent merely an extreme usurpation of human qualities and man's capacity to act as an autonomous being. It is, therefore, important to inquire into the more profound ways in which man has come to yield his own autonomy, as a free-thinking entity, to a world viewed as a machine.

CONCENTRIC ENVIRONMENTS

Any new technology creates a new human environment. Thus, to fully comprehend extensions, one must understand the concept of environments.

It must be understood that environments are not passive wrappings but active processes. They act directly upon man. The rebellious teen, for instance, who plunges himself into a personal environment of rock music soon finds that the lyrics pounding into his skull through headphones are having effects on the way he perceives the world.

The effects of environments, however, in no way negate man's propensity to sin, nor do they render man an automaton, molded solely by his surroundings. True Christianity rejects such notions.

Environments merely enhance the flawed nature of mankind. The propensity to commit wrongful acts already exists within man. His environment, however, can ignite, consciously or subconsciously, latent tendencies to act wrongfully.

A failure of modern Christianity has been its powerlessness to understand modern culture and its environmental trappings. Because of this misunderstanding, Christians, even with all their technological extensions, have been generally ineffective in reaching contemporary society.

Much of this failure, however, is due to the fact that environments shift subtly, and often rapidly. With the advance of technology, the world moves so rapidly that a machine purchased today is replaced by a more developed version tomorrow. Factually, this is true of modern culture.

Environments, then, overlap other environments. This can be illustrated by a series of concentric circles which overlap but nonetheless are replaced by the last circle in the chain of circles. For example, Alvin Toffler might express his view of the three stages[5] of mankind as follows:

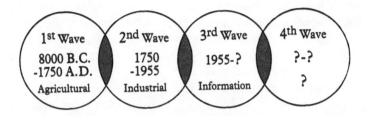

Of course, Toffler's depicting of these stages is open to debate. However, the *gray areas* in these concentric environments are important. They make this statement: We are *never* made aware of our environment until it has arrived. Moreover, the following statement also applies:

> The culture in which a man lives consists of structures based on ground rules of which we are mysteriously unconscious.... But any change in the ground rules of a culture nonetheless modifies the total structure.[6]

However, within the concentric or general environments exist corresponding and, often, interrelated social and technological environments. These specific environments serve as content for the concentric environment. For example, within the information circle are social environments such as family, school, and church. All affect people and their behavior.

Likewise, technological environments wrap themselves around, and weave in and through, cultures. This will become clearer as we discuss specific extensions. Suffice it to say here that technological developments do create new environments, and like their social counterparts, they alter human behavior.

If we look for an understanding of crime on the streets or rebellion in the classroom, for example, we must first study the environments in which they occur. I am convinced that people consciously and/or unconsciously act out what they are taught in environmental settings. Of course, this "instruction" can be up-front-conscious or it can be subliminal.

A major part of environments exists in the subliminal. In fact, they are mostly subliminal in that a great deal of the information we take in comes to us subconsciously.

There is, moreover, no way fallible, mortal man can consciously absorb all or even a significant portion of that which surrounds him. And this fact is amplified by complex and varied technological developments. Not only does it create a subliminal onslaught, but it has also given rise to people's inability to cope with their environments (without numbing themselves by the use of booze, drugs, and music).

Even subliminally, though, people perceive much that makes up their environments. Perception in human beings, as far as we know, is total. Everything that happens is perceived in its totality. The breaking-down process—that function that becomes a conscious activity—is somehow accomplished inside the brain, which retains the major portion of what is perceived totally, though it is completely unknown to the individual. Some of these unconscious experiences have been discovered in anatomical experiments involving the human brain.[7]

This does not mean man is an automaton of his unconscious. To the contrary, it is an indication of man's mysterious nature and mental capacities, which are limited only by the Fall and continuing sin.

Many of the environmental influences remain subliminal simply because they are common, everyday experiences that go unnoticed. The subliminal effects of body language, for example, are rarely studied by social behaviorists, and as a result, these effects on human relationships remain a mystery.

However, to return to point, we know that environments do affect people, and man's extensions weigh heavily in the overall influence of environmental processes.

An understanding of these extensions, then, is vital to any comprehensive understanding of culture. They are constantly altering our environments as well as creating new environmental structures.

THE TIME MACHINE

A tool or a machine (any form of technology) is a constituent of man's symbolic recreation of his world. Moreover, machines that have been owned and operated by only a few members of a society have often influenced the entire society.

Movable type, for example, completely altered, within a relatively short time, the entire concept of medieval man and society. As McLuhan notes in *Gutenberg Galaxy:*

Printing from movable types created a quite unexpected new environment—it created the PUBLIC. Manuscript technology did not have the intensity or power of extension necessary to create publics on a national scale. What we have called "nations" in recent centuries did not, and could not, precede the advent of Gutenberg technology any more than they can survive the advent of electric circuitry with its power of totally involving all people in all other people.... The unique character of the "public" created by the printed word was an intense and visually oriented self-consciousness, both of the individual and the group.[8]

There is, however, probably no better illustration of technology altering Western culture (and, eventually, the world) than the invention of the clock.

Before the clock, and until Darwin's theory of evolution began to sink into the stream of commonly held ideas, people knew that the world about them—the world of reproducing plants and animals, of rivers that flowed and dried up and flowed again, of seas that pulsed in great tidal rhythms, and of the ever-repeating spectacles in the heavens—had always existed, and that its fundamental law was *eternal* periodicity. Cosmological time, as well as the time perceived in daily life, was a sort of complex repeating and echoing of events. However, with the emergence of the clock and its sudden position of dominance during the Industrial Revolution, a transformation in man occurred. Instead of merely living in the natural world, he became nature's alleged master.

Lewis Mumford calls the clock, not the printing press or steam engine, "the key machine of the modern industrial age."[9] In his *Technics and Civilization,* he describes how during the Middle Ages the ordered life of monasteries affected life in the communities adjacent to them:

> The monastery was the seat of a regular life.... [T]he habit of order itself and the earnest regulation of time-sequences had become almost second nature in the monastery.... [T]he monasteries—at one time there were 40,000 under the Benedictine rule—helped to give human enterprise the regular collective beat and rhythm of the machine; for the clock is not merely a means of keeping track of the hours, but of synchronizing the actions of men.... [B]y the thirteenth century there are definite records of mechanical clocks, and by 1370 a well-designed "modern" clock had been built by Heinrich von Wych at Paris. Meanwhile, bell towers had come

into existence, and the new clocks, if they did not have, till the fourteenth century, a dial and a hand that translated the movement of time into a movement through space, at all events struck the hours. The clouds that could paralyze the sundial...were no longer obstacles to time-keeping: summer or winter, day or night, one was aware of the measured clank of the clock. The instrument presently spread outside the monastery; and the regular striking of the bells brought a new regularity into the life of the workman and the merchant. The bells of the clock tower almost defined urban existence. Time-keeping passed into time-serving and time-accounting and time-rationing. As this took place, Eternity ceased gradually to serve as the measure and focus of human actions.[10]

Mumford makes the crucial observation that the clock "disassociated time from human events and helped create the belief in an independent world of mathematically measurable sequences: the special world of science."[11] Therefore, as a machine, the clock produces uniform seconds, minutes, and hours in sequential pattern. Processed in this way, time became separated from the rhythms of human experience. The mechanical clock, in short, helps to create the *image* of a numerically quantified and mechanically powered universe.

It was in the medieval monasteries, moreover, with their need for rule and synchronized order, that the clock started its modern development. Time measured not by the uniqueness of private experience, but by abstract uniform units, pervades society from that point onward.

The clock, however, in synchronizing man's tasks, fragmented life. This meant that the "clock dragged man out of the world of personal rhythms and recurrence."[12] The continuous action or hum of the universe was divided into time slots. In other words, the logical development from the mechanical clock was the fragmentary mechanization of the Industrial Revolution.

Pulling man from the continuous flow of nature drastically changed the way people live. Early man lived by the stars, the rising of the sun, and the color changes in leaves. He slept when he was tired and ate when he was hungry. With the clock and the creation of abstract time, modern men eat when it is "*time* to eat."

Clocks, essentially an extension of man's own biological clock,[13] became, in effect, autonomous machines. Once started, clocks ran by themselves.

However, as we have seen, clocks altered history and they remained the only truly important autonomous machines until the advent of the computer. But this occurred before anyone had a chance to ponder the change. Thus, the environmental change was largely unconscious.

LUDD AND MARX

At various times in history, people have sensed the radical changes that were being brought about by extensions such as the clock. We can see this in two distinct but related historical incidents.

In the early eighteenth century an Englishman named Ned Ludd organized a group of angry weavers in Great Britain. Upset by being displaced by the textile machines of the Industrial Revolution, they created retaliatory plans.

In the fall of 1811 separate bands of "Luddites" invaded one district after another and destroyed all of the new textile frames they could find. The movement spread from Nottinghamshire to Lancashire, Derbyshire, and Leicestershire, and continued through 1812.

The machine-wreckers abstained from injuring persons except in the case of an employer who ordered his men to fire upon them. The strikers sought him out and killed him. England shivered in fright with the French Revolution still fresh in their minds.

Journalist William Cobbett defended the raiders in the House of Commons, and the poet Byron delivered a fervent address in their favor in the House of Lords. The prime minister, Lord Liverpool, put through Parliament severe legislation and sent a regiment to suppress the revolt. The leaders were eventually rounded up and condemned in a mass trial at York in 1813. Some were deported, others were hanged. But the machines multiplied.

However, as the technology of the Industrial Revolution descended on the workers in Europe, the controversy was again awakened. As late as 1848, workers still demanded that the machines be suppressed.

This is easily understood. The standard of living had not risen, and people still suffered from the loss of equilibrium in their lives brought about by a too-rapid injection of technology.

Peasants and workers bore all the hardships of technical advance without sharing in the triumphs. This produced a reaction, and society was split. The power of the state and the money-class were for technology; the workers were against it.

In the middle of the nineteenth century, however, the situation changed. Karl Marx, even as he penned *The Communist Manifesto*, preached that technical advances could be liberating. Those who exploited technology, Marx reasoned, enslaved the workers. But that was the fault of the exploiters and not the technology itself.

Marx was not the first to say this, but he was the first to convince the masses of it. Technology, it was prophesied, would logically bring about the collapses of the *bourgeoisie* and capitalism.

A prodigious upheaval took place between 1850 and 1914 which, enhanced by the emergence of electricity, convinced the world of the excellence of technology: a movement that could produce technological marvels and alter human life. This movement, Marx explained, presaged even better things and pointed to a utopian paradise.

THE ELECTRIC VILLAGE

Marshall McLuhan, in the introduction to his book *Understanding Media*, writes:

> After three thousand years of explosion, by means of fragmentary and mechanical technologies, the Western world is imploding. During the mechanical ages we had extended our bodies into space. Today, after more than a century of electric technology, we have extended our central nervous system itself in a global embrace, abolishing both space and time as far as our planet is concerned. Rapidly, we approach the final phase of the extension of man—the technological simulation of consciousness, when the creative process of knowing will be collectively and corporately extended to the whole of human society, much as we have already extended our senses and our nerves by the various media.[14]

Several important consequences flow from the extension of the central nervous system, whether actual or symbolic, by way of electricity. (Again, we are speaking here of extensions as they created new environments.)

First, our world has become contracted. As a result, "the globe," McLuhan notes, "is no more than a village."[15] The human nervous system is, at least symbolically, wrapped around the earth by the extension of electricity. Through electricity we have interdependence on a global scale. Expressed through the media, electricity has rendered *all things simultaneous,* even on a worldwide scale.

Zbigniew Brzezinski, however, in *Between Two Ages,* defines the electric age as more of a global network than a global village. He writes:

> The new reality, however, will not be that of a "global village." McLuhan's striking analogy overlooks the personal stability, interpersonal intimacy, implicitly shared values, and traditions that were important ingredients of the primitive village. A more appropriate analogy is that of the "global city"—a nervous, agitated, tense, and fragmented web of interdependent relations. That interdependence, however, is better characterized by interaction than by intimacy. Instant communications are already creating something akin to a global nervous system. Occasional malfunctions of this nervous system—because of blackouts or breakdowns—will be all the more unsettling, precisely because the mutual confidence and reciprocally reinforcing stability that are characteristic of village intimacy will be absent from the process of that "nervous" interaction. . . . Man's intensified involvement in global affairs is reflected in, and doubtless shaped by, the changing character of what has until now been considered local news. Television has joined newspapers in expanding the immediate horizons of the viewer or reader to the point where "local" increasingly means "national," and global affairs compete for attention on an unprecedented scale.[16]

Those who see a conspiratorial movement toward a "one-world government" to rebuild the "Tower of Babel" are, in reality, seeing only a part of the total picture. There have always been conspiracies, and no doubt there are people who desire a global government either for purposes of power or for the reason that they believe such a government is best for mankind. However, the discovery of electricity and the development of communication devices have eliminated the need for such a conspiracy. *Electricity requires no organized prodding: it leads logically to a more pronounced worldwide awareness and inevitably to some sort of global network.*

Secondly, the extension of the central nervous system through electricity creates a need, at least artificially, for human involvement and participation. This is clearly reflected in increasing needs for therapy groups, cults that stress unity, and even traditional religion:

> The same new preference for depth participation has also prompted in the young a strong drive toward religious experience with rich liturgical overtones. The liturgical revival of the radio and TV age affects even the most austere Protestant sects. Choral chant and rich vestments have appeared in every quarter. The ecumenical movement is synonymous with electric technology.[17]

Much of the desire of involvement (with the "I am into it" mentality) is due to the effect of television on recent generations of children. Television, unlike radio or movies, is a medium of involvement. Moreover, with television we clearly see the effects of technology in altering environments.

The mode of television has nothing in common with film or photography. "With TV the viewer is the screen."[18]

From the cathode-ray tube, "the television image offers some three million dots per second" to the viewer, says McLuhan. From there, the viewer can consciously accept only a few dozen each instant from which to make an image. The television image, then, is a mosaic mesh of light and dark spots. In mosaic art, the viewer is required to fill in the spaces. This is the secret of television. It requires the same kind of unconscious involvement as mosaic art. Television in itself, then, is an environment which has had a pronounced effect upon people. Adds McLuhan: It has the power "to transform American innocence."[19]

Perhaps the most familiar and pathetic effect of the television image concerns the posture of children in the early grades, who try, often unsuccessfully, to carry over to the printed page the all-involving sensory mandate of the television image. The child's involvement-orientation often prohibits adaptation to the logical, linear medium of print. In fact, Neil Postman, professor of communication arts and sciences at New York University, argues that television, because of its emphasis on visual communication, logically leads to illiteracy.[20]

The necessarily involving character of television has been demonstrated by the Mackworth head-camera:

The Mackworth head-camera, when worn by children
watching TV, has revealed that their eyes follow, not the actions, but the reactions. The eyes scarcely deviate from the
faces of the actors, even during scenes of violence. This head-
camera shows by projection both the scene and the eye movement simultaneously.[21]

Such extraordinary behavior is another indication of how television involves the individual's total person.

Thirdly, the electric extension of the nervous system will logically result in the formation of an elite group whose self-
appointed purpose will be to manage the global village. As the
information age rolls over us, "almost any kind of material will
serve any kind of need or function, forcing the intellectual more
and more into the role of social command and into the service of
production."[22]

It has long been the role of the intelligentsia to act as liaison
and mediator between old and new power groups. Most familiar
of such groups in history are the Greek slaves, who were for a
long time the educators and confidential clerks of the Roman
power. And it is precisely this service role of the confidential
clerk (or technician-bureaucrat) to commercial, military, and political power that science and education have continued to play in
the West, even to the present.

One final thing must be said before we move away from this
topic. I refer to the overwhelming tension and pressure that the
electrical extension brings upon people. We speak of "wanting
to jump out of my skin" or of "going out of my mind" or "flip-
ping my lid." This seemingly carries with it a suicidal impulse—
possibly a reaction to the accelerated increase of information and
crises which we find ourselves involved in now on a global scale.

The final frontier in electrical extensions will be the automated
society—the dominion impulse in full-bloom. This is becoming
more and more feasible because of the computer.

Jacques Ellul, concerned about "the problems of automation,
which will become acute in a very short time,"[23] asks: "How,
socially, politically, morally, and humanly, shall we contrive to
get there? How are the prodigious economic problems, for example, of unemployment, to be solved?"[24]

Ellul, however, may not be asking the right question. And the
problem may not be that there will be mass unemployment.
McLuhan recognizes this:

Automation is information and it not only ends jobs in the world of work, it ends subjects in the world of learning. The future of work consists of learning a living in the automation age.[25]

Automation, thus, simply creates a mass learning complex:

The very same process of automation that causes a withdrawal of the present work force from industry causes learning itself to become the principal kind of production and consumption. Hence the folly of alarm about unemployment. *Paid learning* is already becoming both the dominant employment and the source of a new wealth in our society.[26]

The real question concerns, not unemployment, but the type and form of work of the future. We have lived through the assembly-line madness of the Industrial Age. Are we to believe that the Age of Automation will, by way of process (all is process with electricity), really alter the mindless and mundane occupations of modernity? Even if one is armed with a college degree (of paid learning), will this free him from a life as a worker bee in an automated world?

SEVEN

THE SCHIZOID COMPROMISE

Our discussion of extensions now leads into a further investigation of computers, which, in fact, serve as the technological extensions of our human brains. But first a word about technology in general. Technology often changes not only what we do with our lives, but, more importantly, how we think. It changes our awareness of ourselves, of one another, of our relationships with the world.

The new machine that stands behind the flashing digital signal, unlike the clock, the telescope, or the train, is a machine that thinks. The computer, which is a logical technological extension of the brain, challenges our notions not only of time and distance, but also of mind.

Most considerations of the computer concentrate on what it can accomplish. However, one question looms much larger. This question is: In light of the computer, what will *we* be like in the future? What kind of a people are we becoming, both individually and collectively? In the words of Lewis Thomas, "We are becoming a grid, a circuitry around the earth. If we keep at it, we will become a computer to end all computers, capable of fusing all the thoughts of the world into a syncytium."[1]

ELIZA

In the early 1970s, Joseph Weizenbaum, professor of computer science at the Massachusetts Institute of Technology, wrote what by now is probably the most widely quoted computer program in history. This was the ELIZA program, which was "taught" to speak English and "make conversation" by playing the role of a psychotherapist. The name ELIZA was chosen because with this program the computer, like Eliza of *Pygmalion* (*My Fair Lady*) fame, could be taught to "speak" increasingly well.

The project of making a computer program that can enter into dialogue on all possible subjects is not technically possible at present. Some experts doubt that it can ever be done. However, setting the context for a conversation with ELIZA in the consulting room solved a lot of problems.

Certain psychotherapists use a technique of "mirroring" what their clients say to them. Thus, if a patient says, "I am having problems with my girlfriend," the therapist might say, "I understand that you are having problems with your girlfriend," or, "Why do you tell me that you are having problems with your girlfriend?"[2] This technique is convenient for ELIZA. It allows the program to make an acceptable response without knowing the meaning of what has been said. Weizenbaum explains:

> I gave ELIZA a script designed to permit it to play (I should really say parody) the role of a Rogerian psychotherapist engaged in an initial interview with a patient. The Rogerian psychotherapist is relatively easy to imitate because much of his technique consists of drawing his patient out by reflecting the patient's statements back to him.[3]

The following is a conversation between a young lady and ELIZA playing doctor and using the Rogerian method of psychotherapy. The first to "speak" is the young lady. The computer's responses are printed in capitals:

Men are all alike.
IN WHAT WAY
They're always bugging us about something or other.
CAN YOU THINK OF A SPECIFIC EXAMPLE
Well, my boyfriend made me come here.
YOUR BOYFRIEND MADE YOU COME HERE
He says I'm depressed much of the time.
I AM SORRY TO HEAR YOU ARE DEPRESSED
It's true. I am unhappy.
DO YOU THINK COMING HERE WILL HELP YOU NOT TO BE UNHAPPY
I need some help, that much seems certain.
WHAT WOULD IT MEAN TO YOU IF YOU GOT SOME HELP
Perhaps I could learn to get along with my mother.
TELL ME MORE ABOUT YOUR FAMILY
My mother takes care of me.

WHO ELSE IN YOUR FAMILY TAKES CARE OF YOU
My father.
YOUR FATHER
You are like my father in some ways.
WHAT RESEMBLANCE DO YOU SEE
You are not very aggressive, but I think you don't want me to
    notice that.
WHAT MAKES YOU THINK I AM NOT VERY
    AGGRESSIVE
You don't argue with me.
WHY DO YOU THINK I DON'T ARGUE WITH YOU
You are afraid of me.
DOES IT PLEASE YOU TO BELIEVE I AM AFRAID OF
    YOU
My father is afraid of everybody.
WHAT ELSE COMES TO MIND WHEN YOU THINK
    OF YOUR FATHER
Bullies.
DOES THAT HAVE ANYTHING TO DO WITH THE
    FACT THAT YOUR BOYFRIEND MADE YOU COME
    HERE[4]

Famous at M.I.T., copies of the ELIZA program soon began appearing at other educational institutions in the United States. The program became nationally known. Weizenbaum, however, experienced what he termed "shock" at the program's popularity and for three reasons.

First, a number of practicing psychiatrists seriously believed ELIZA, as psychotherapist, could develop into a completely automatic form of psychotherapy. (This may point up the rather fallacious foundation undergirding both psychology and psychiatry.[5]) In fact, three distinguished psychiatrists, K. M. Colby, J. B. Watt, and J. P. Gilbert, noted:

> If the method proves beneficial, then it would provide a therapeutic tool which can be made widely available to mental hospitals and psychiatric centers suffering a shortage of therapists. Because of the time-sharing capabilities of modern and future computers, several hundred patients an hour could be handled by a computer system designed for this purpose. The human therapist, involved in the design and operation of this system, would not be replaced, but would become a much more efficient man since his efforts would no longer be limited to the one-to-one patient-therapist ratio as now exists.[6]

Carl Sagan, the astrophysicist, likewise concluded:

In a period when more and more people in our society seem to be in need of psychiatric counseling, and when time sharing of computers is widespread, I can imagine the development of a network of computer psychotherapeutic terminals, something like arrays of large telephone booths, in which, for a few dollars a session, we would be able to talk with an attentive, tested, and largely nondirective psychotherapist.[7]

Stripping a discipline such as psychotherapy of whatever humanness it may have, and reducing it to its bare mechanical workings, has a direct bearing on the view of people held by the psychotherapists themselves. Colby *et al.* comments:

A human therapist can be viewed as an information processor and decision maker with a set of decision rules which are closely linked to short-range and long-range goals. . . . He is guided in these decisions by rough empiric rules telling him what is appropriate to say and not to say in certain contexts. To incorporate these processes, to the degree possessed by a human therapist, in the program would be a considerable undertaking, but *we are attempting to move in this direction.*[8]

"What can the psychiatrist's image of his patient be," Weizenbaum writes, "when he sees himself, as therapist, not as an engaged human being acting as a healer, but as an information processor following rules, etc.?"[9] This statement recalls Michael Polanyi's conclusion that there has emerged a scientific outlook that appears to have produced "a mechanical conception of man."[10]

Secondly, Weizenbaum was startled to see how quickly and how very deeply people conversing with ELIZA became emotionally involved with the computer, and how unequivocally they anthropomorphized (or attributed human characteristics to) it. Weizenbaum's students and colleagues who had access to ELIZA knew and understood the limitations of the program's abilities to know and understand. And yet, many of these very "sophisticated" users related to ELIZA as though the computer did understand, *as though it were a person.* With full knowledge that the program could not truly empathize with them, they confided in it and wanted to be alone with it. Weizenbaum concluded: "What I had not realized is that extremely short exposures to a relatively simple computer program could induce powerful delusional thinking in quite normal people."[11]

Thirdly, Weizenbaum was surprised at the widespread notion that the computer, using the ELIZA program, demonstrated a general solution to the problem of computer understanding of natural language. Computers, since their conception, have had difficulty in receiving and assimilating human language and responding to it.

This reaction to ELIZA demonstrated the enormously exaggerated attributions an even well-educated audience is capable of making to a technology it does not understand. Decisions, however, made by the general public about emergent technologies depend much more on what that public attributes to such technologies than on what they actually are or can and cannot do. But the public's attributions are often wildly misconceived. As such, public decisions are bound to be misguided and often wrong.

As we have seen, in the face of the computer, even the professional is misguided. Thus, as Weizenbaum says: "Difficult questions arise out of these observations; what, for example, are the scientist's responsibilities with respect to making his work public? And to whom (or what) is the scientist responsible?"[12] These questions we have already discussed to some degree. Other questions, however, are raised by the reaction to ELIZA and similar computer programs.

One concerns man's role in the face of technologies and techniques he may not be able to understand and control. This, of course, leads to another question-issue—that is, whether or not every aspect of human thought is reducible to mathematical formulae; or, to put it into the modern idiom, whether or not human thought is entirely computable.

Before modern science fathered the technologies that reified and concretized its otherwise abstract systems, the system of thought that defined man's place in the universe served to explain man's obligations to the Creator, to his fellowmen, and to nature. Resting on the Judeo-Christian tradition, man had the freedom to act with a corresponding responsibility for his actions. This is a central issue of all religious systems.

The spiritual cosmologies engendered by modern science, on the other hand, are infected with the germ of logical necessity. They, except in the hands of the wisest of scientists and philosophers, no longer content themselves with explanations of appearances, but claim to say how things actually are and must necessarily be. In short, *they convert truth to provability.*

In other words, in this Kantian scheme of things, whatever science can prove is true and whatever it cannot prove is placed in mental limbo or is assumed to be irrelevant. For example, if it cannot be proved—and it has not been yet—that man has either a mind or soul, then, in the eyes of science, man is in a precarious way. Man is reduced to bare minimum upon the scales of provability.

WHO ARE WE?

As hinted in the previous chapter, ours has been called a culture of narcissism.[13] We are a culture in search of mirrors that will reflect to us who we are.

We are insecure in our understanding of ourselves, and this insecurity breeds our preoccupation with the question of who we are. We search for ways to see ourselves.

The computer is a new mirror. *It is the first psychological machine.* "Beyond its nature as an analytical engine," psychologist Sherry Turkle writes, "lies its second nature as an evocative object."[14]

We are living in a culture that invites us all to interact with computers in ways that permit us to become intimate with their second nature. Terrified of being alone, yet afraid of intimacy (we stare face to face and say nothing), modern man experiences widespread feelings of emptiness, alienation, and the "unreality" of self. It is here that the computer, a companion without emotional demands, offers a compromise. You can be a loner, but never alone. You can interact, but need never feel vulnerable to another person.

The images of the computer offering a new expressive medium and a "schizoid compromise"[15] between loneliness and fear of intimacy are emblematic of the encounter between machines and our emotional lives. Along with this comes another bridge: between computers and our philosophical lives.

> Because they stand on the line between mind and not-mind, between life and not-life, computers excite reflection about the nature of the mind and the nature of life. They provoke us to

think about who we are. They challenge our ideas about what it is to be human, to think and feel.[16]

Computers, then, present us with more than a challenge. "They present us with an affront," Turkle writes, "because they hold up a new mirror in which mind is reflected as machine."[17]

In the world of ideas and now in its practical applications, the effect of the computer is often subversive. It undermines the entire concept of man. Man and ant are equated. Computer scientist Herbert A. Simon comments:

> Perhaps the greatest significance of the computer lies in its impact on Man's view of himself. No longer accepting the geocentric view of the universe, he now begins to learn that mind, too, is a phenomenon of nature, explainable in terms of simple mechanisms. Thus, the computer aids him to obey, for the first time, the ancient injunction, "Know thyself."[18]

Thus, the computer calls into question our ways of thinking about ourselves. It begs this question: If the mind of man is a machine, who causes this machine to act? Where is responsibility, spirit, soul? In 1983 *Newsweek* ran a cover story on the mind which expressed the new dualism. It read:

> What's the matter?
> Never mind.
> What is mind?
> No matter.[19]

By the end of this article, which described advances in brain chemistry and artificial intelligence, *Newsweek* reported that the new technologies of neuroscience and silicon chips are on their way to providing technical solutions to the "mystery of the mind." We are, by implication at least, chemistry and program.

AUTOAMPUTATION

"During the 1990s," writes Christopher Evans in *The Micro Millennium,* "computers will increasingly serve as intellectual and emotional partners."[20] Evans, now deceased, accepted the coming union of computers and humans with enthusiasm:

> We are about to embark on a massive program to develop highly intelligent machines, a process by which we will lead computers by the hand until they reach our own intellectual level, after which they will proceed to surpass us. In the course of this strange partnership computers will inevitably acquire ways of behaving which will allow them to converse with us, exchange ideas and concepts, stimulate our imagination and so on.... When they do overtake us computers will, in my view, become extremely interesting entities to have around. Their role as teachers and mentors, for example, will be unequaled. It will be like having, as private tutors, the wisest, most knowledgeable and most patient humans on earth: an Albert Einstein to teach physics, a Bertrand Russell to teach philosophy, a Sigmund Freud to discuss the principles of psychoanalysis, and all available where and when they are wanted.[21]

This type of scientific utopianism makes for interesting reading. However, in its aim at the mass public readership, it has the tendency to create a false optimism about science and the development of the computer, suggesting that eventually the computer will perform all activities reserved for human beings. More importantly, it endorses a willingness to create autonomous machines which, instead of being servants, will be served.

Developments such as these do not come about with ease. They are more or less wrenched from modern man, who is under more pressure and tension than ever before.

Some medical researchers hold that all extensions of ourselves, in sickness or health, are attempts to maintain equilibrium. They refer to this process as "autoamputation."[22] Such researchers indicate that the autoamputative power or strategy is resorted to by the body when the powers of perception cannot locate or avoid the cause of the irritation. The body, as a group of sustaining and protective organs for the central nervous system, acts as a buffer against sudden variations in the physical and social environment.

With the arrival of electric technology and the extension of man's central nervous system, there has been a desperate and suicidal autoamputation. It is as if the central nervous system can no longer depend on the physical organs to be protective buffers against the slings and arrows of societal mechanization. The principle of autoamputation "as an immediate relief of strain on the central nervous system applies very readily to the origin of the media of communication from speech to computer."[23]

Moreover, the point is this: once an extension is amputated, it is autonomous. It is essentially free from man's control. It becomes something to admire on its own stature—narcissism, if you like. It is something to seek emotional ties with. It is the prodigal son who will not return, except by force.

NEW CHILDREN

Already, a great schism is developing between generations. Our children, as the philosophy of the upper elite filters down, are beginning to conceptualize the world in a fashion quite fundamentally different from anything we can readily identify with in the past. We are beginning to witness termination of one great lifeline in history and the abrupt creation of another.

Our children are the first sojourners of the computer age. While they still carry with them most of the conceptual trappings of the past, they are beginning to experience the world from a profoundly altered frame of reference:

> To begin with, their language is the language of the computer. Their world of communications is made up of computer programs, electronic games, word processors, videodiscs. The average American child now spends approximately twenty-eight hours per week with electronic learning tools, compared to twenty-five hours per week with printed learning materials. The electronic image and the computer printout are increasingly taking the place of the spoken and written word. A *New York Times* article reports mathematician Seymour Papert of M.I.T. as saying that "the effect of the computer on learning and thinking is comparable to that of the invention of writing."[24]

Alan Newell of Carnegie-Mellon University is one of the experts in the field of artificial intelligence and the computer sciences. He argues that the true import of the computer is that it opens young minds to a "whole new language for describing behavior."[25]

This new language is drastically altering our children's perception of the world. Many educators now believe that our young people are beginning to conceptualize the world in the same terms that animate the operations of a computer system.

Joseph Weizenbaum best expressed the conceptual revolution that separates the generations when he observed: "To him who has only a computer, the world looks like a computer domain."[26]

The world as seen from a computer perspective is very different from the one we have experienced in the past. In this new world, all physical phenomena are reduced, reorganized, and redefined to meet the operating requirements of the computer.

The computer, then, necessarily recasts the world in its own image. Thus, it transforms all of nature into bits of information to be processed and programmed. All life is reprocessed, and all philosophies and religions are recast in terms of the machine. It is a total elimination of humanness.

JAWS

Eliminating humanness in man, simultaneous with the creation of an autonomous machine such as the computer, will, if not slowed, inevitably bring sweeping changes upon humanity. No matter what we may want to call our machines, or what personalities we attempt to imprint on them, they are yet machines. This is true of the computer as well.

Machines, we must remember, when working properly, operate with a fierce regularity. We set a punch press into motion, and it mangles the hand of a worker who gets close to it. The very regularity of the machine is its most fearsome property. We put it to its task and it performs, regularly to be sure, but blindly as well. The punch press processes its material, whether its jaws grasp pieces of metal or a worker's hand.

When we create autonomous machines, we run the risk that before long we will find ourselves in their metallic jaws. It seems to be a perilous path to walk, but a path nevertheless that modern society is traveling.

EIGHT

THE ORGANIC MACHINE

Since the beginning of social life man has been aware of his special role on earth. Until the significance of the Darwinian thesis began to sink home, he considered himself to be unique in the universe, second only in status to God.

Even when identifying himself with the animals, he has still been able to convince himself of his uniqueness. The evidence has suggested that he is possessed of intellectual powers vastly superior to those of animals.

There is no doubting the importance that we assign to our sense of intellectual dominance, and our pride in human endeavor and success. Most creative art is committed to dramatizing those aspects of humanity which emphasize this special place in nature and our implicit claim to the *imago Dei*.

Furthermore, ingrained in our unconscious minds is a psychologically potent self-image which helps us to accept our role in a frightening and mysterious universe. This self-image has been tarnished by the great tragedies of mankind—war, terrorism, torture, and so on—but never has it been seriously doubted.

The coming of the computer, however, is the first event to call into question the belief that problem-solving, thinking, and even creativity are exclusively human. With man's propensity to deify his extensions, and with the belief that he can direct evolution, man's traditional view of his self-image is in jeopardy. Moreover, with the increasing dependence of the state on computer technology, man's *total* well-being may be threatened.

The computer is, like most technologies, a blessing if correctly understood and used. On a moral level it has, for instance, freed individuals to work at home and possibly, in this way, strengthened the family unit. On a practical level the computer has also given access to vast quantities of information never before available.

However, because man is spiritually flawed and is looking for other gods, *the greatest danger in the computer*, despite its merits, *is in its application to man*. The danger of the computer is not in its existence or efficiency; it lies in man's sustained drive to mold humanity in the image of the machine, which in this case is the computer.

DARWIN IN QUESTION

As previously suggested, the concept of evolution is for modern man the unimpeachable starting-point for all things. Without it, an accurate scientific understanding of life is impossible.

Sir Julian Huxley, the renowned twentieth-century scientist-philosopher, understood how important evolutionary theory is to explaining the entire scope of life when he argued:

> It is essential for evolution to become the central core of any educational system, because it is evolution, in the broad sense, that links inorganic nature with life, and the stars with the earth, and matter with mind, and animals with man. Human history is a continuation of biological evolution in a different form.[1]

Huxley's hopes have been answered. Evolutionary theory has been enshrined as the centerpiece of the public educational system. Moreover, elaborate walls have been erected around it to protect it from unnecessary abuse. "Great care is taken to ensure that it is not damaged, for even the smallest rupture could seriously call into question the entire intellectual foundation of the modern world view."[2]

No doubt, most academic and scientific leaders would find themselves in agreement with Huxley, who added that "Darwin's theory...is no longer a theory but a fact. No serious scientist would deny the fact that evolution has occurred just as he would not deny that the earth goes around the sun."[3]

However, to the contrary, we have shown that Darwinian evolution is far from unchallenged fact. Biologist Garrett Hardin notes, though, that anyone who dares question Darwin's theory

"inevitably attracts the speculative psychiatric eye to himself."[4]
Such a person's sanity is immediately questioned.

Quietly, however, traditional Darwinian evolution is coming under scrutiny for lack of sustaining evidence. For example, Colin Patterson, thought by many to be the world's leading paleoichthyologist, delivered a speech at the American Museum of Natural History in which he announced:

> Last year I had a sudden realization. For over twenty years I had thought I was working on evolution in some way. One morning I woke up and something had happened in the night; and it struck me that I had been working on this stuff for twenty years and there was not one thing I knew about it. That's quite a shock, to learn that one can be so misled so long. . . . So for the last few weeks I've tried putting a simple question to various people and groups of people. . . . Can you tell me anything you know about evolution, any one thing, any one thing that is true?. . . All I got. . .was silence. . . . The absence of answers seems to suggest that. . .evolution does not convey any knowledge, or, if so, I haven't yet heard it. . . . I think many people in this room would acknowledge that during the last few years, if you had thought about it at all, you have experienced a shift from evolution as knowledge to evolution as faith. I know that it's true of me and I think it is true of a good many of you here. . . . Evolution not only conveys no knowledge but seems somehow to convey antiknowledge.[5]

While biology teachers in the public education system continue to teach Darwin's version of the theory of evolution, some modern evolutionary biologists have abandoned the traditional view. "Remarkably little has been written in the popular press about this rebellion in the making."[6] The *coup d'etat* had unfolded rather quietly, but it has occurred.[7] However, it has not meant the abandonment of evolution, but merely a new version of the theory.

At present, there is an intense struggle "going on within the profession, pitting dyed-in-the-wool Darwinists against a new generation of theoreticians who are anxiously looking around for a more satisfactory explanation of the origin and development of species."[8] The evidence against traditional evolutionary thinking is beginning to mount.

G. A. Kerkut, professor of physiology and biochemistry at the University of Southampton, England, published a book critical of Darwin's theory. Entitled *Implications of Evolution*, the book concludes: "The attempt to explain all living forms in terms of an evolution from a unique *source*, though a brave and valid attempt, is one that is premature and not satisfactorily supported by present-day evidence."[9]

The eminent Russian biologist Aleksandr Oparin has also noted the lack of proof for the traditional theory of evolution. He writes: "Proof in the sense in which one thinks of it in chemistry and physics is not attainable in the problem of primordial biogenesis."[10]

Moreover, Darwinian evolution, as discussed earlier, cannot be proved by the scientific method. Unfortunately, however, this means that it can neither be disproved. In order to fall within the scientific domain, a theory must be capable of being proven true or false. Newtonian physics, for example, can be so examined as experiments can be conducted to prove whether or not Newton's laws are true. Evolution, however, like belief in God, cannot be verified by the same method. Thus, evolution is not science in the true sense of the word. And if not based upon science, evolution is necessarily a matter of personal faith.

The new confusion in academia concerning Darwin's theory has caused a historic shift in thinking among scientists. At first the debate centered on what is known as "the modern synthesis,"[11] the synthesis that brought Darwinism together with developments in genetics in the early part of the twentieth century. This is neo-Darwinian evolution.

The theory rests on the assumption that any animal's survival depends on being in the right place at the right time. According to the neo-Darwinian schema, the organism's structure and behavior are rigidly determined at birth by its genetic program. The organism is, then, powerless to affect its own destiny. It can do nothing to assure that it will be appropriately outfitted to do battle. The organism operates in an environment that is relatively uniform. It lives out its life cycle in rigid conformity with its genetic blueprint. It is a prisoner of its genes. If, however, it is fortunate enough to have been endowed with a genetic program that just happens to fit the environmental circumstances it is forced to contend with, the organism will survive long enough to pass on its genetic endowment to its offspring.

Neo-Darwinism, however, is now giving way to a new theory which has had profound ramifications concerning man.

MIND IN NATURE

The new theory, which combines biology and technology (that is, *biotechnology*), challenges the notion of fixity anywhere in nature. "Where Darwin challenged the idea that [a] species is fixed and frozen in geological time," Jeremy Rifkin writes, "the new theory challenges the notion of an individual organism being fixed and frozen in its own lifetime."[12]

According to the new theory, then, nothing is fixed. Every living thing is in flux and continually adjusts to change.

Unlike Darwin's theory of natural selection, which sees organisms as either adapt*ed* to or unadapt*ed* to changing physical environments, the new theory sees organisms as either adapt*ing* to or failing to adapt to changing temporalities:

> Darwin's theory of evolution was a spatially conceived cosmology, though it contained a strong dose of temporality. In this sense, it was heir, albeit a rebellious one, to a long cosmological tradition stretching back to the beginning of Western civilization. The new theory of evolution, however, is decidedly temporal and marks a profound break in our conception of nature and our place in it.[13]

The transformation from a spatial to a temporal conception of nature marks "one of the most spectacular changes in cosmological thinking since the beginning of human history."[14] From the beginning, time has been reduced to space, that is, to history. Thus, time has been seen properly symbolized as intervals along a spatial segment. As a result, one could chart history along a straight line marking certain events which occurred in the context of spatial time—"In the beginning God," to the rise of Greece, to the fall of Rome, to the birth of Christ, to the resurrection of Christ, to the Renaissance, to Sputnik, and so on.

This was the view of time held, for example, by the Israelites, for whom creation had a unique beginning point and moved in linear fashion toward a final end. Time had *fixity* and a permanence which gives to man, at the very least, an illusion of permanence and establishment. Matter was real as was time, and they operated in a real and fixed world.

Classical physics, for example, defined matter as impenetrable physical substances. Newton's laws, for example, are based on the proposition that two particles cannot possibly occupy the same place at the same time because they are each discrete physical entities that take up a certain amount of space.

Classical physics, moreover, viewed the physical world as real, orderly, and understandable; a direct parallel to the thinking of classical theology, if one substituted the term *God* for *physical world.*

However, by the early years of this century this view was giving way to a new conception:

> As the physicists began to probe deeper into the invisible world of the atom, they began to realize that their earlier ideas about solid matter existing in a fixed space were naive. Much to their surprise, they found that an atom was anything but still. In fact, it became apparent that the atom was not a thing, in the material sense, but rather a set of relationships operating at a certain rhythm. This discovery created quite a stir. Relationships or rhythms cannot exist at an instant.[15]

As historian and philosopher R. G. Collingwood of Oxford University noted in 1945, relationships and rhythms can exist only in a "tract of time long enough for the rhythm of the movement to establish itself."[16] Philosopher Henri Bergson added: "A note of music is nothing at an instant."[17]

In other words, an individual note cannot by itself be music, but requires notes preceding it and following it in time. According to the new physics, this is true of all phenomena. For example, if the atom is a set of relationships operating at a certain rhythm, then, Collingwood concludes, "at a certain instant of time the atom does not possess those qualities at all."[18]

Once this idea was accepted, the old idea of structure independent of function was abandoned. The new physics contends that it is impossible to separate what something is from what it does.

Everything is pure activity. Nothing is static.

Alfred North Whitehead summarizes the shift:

> The older point of view enables us to abstract from change and to conceive of the full reality of Nature *at an instant,* in abstraction from any temporal duration and characterized. . .solely by the instantaneous distribution of matter in space. . . . For the modern view, process, activity, and change are the matter of fact. At an instant there is nothing. Each instant is only a way of grouping matters of fact. Thus, since there are no instants,

conceived as simple primary entities, there is no Nature at an instant.[19]

Matter, then, is a form of energy, and energy is pure activity. Gone is the notion of hard substances that exist in a real, concrete world. As Whitehead concludes: "There is no Nature apart from transition, and there is no transition apart from temporal duration."[20]

Science here is not directly stating that space is being eliminated as a meaningful concept. However, by saying that time and space are abstractions that make sense only in relation to each other, the implication of static space in a real world is meaningless. Time, instead of being contained within space, is no longer something extraneous to life, but is, rather, an essential part of it.

Moreover, man, viewed as part of nature, is subject to the same scrutiny. As an individual, he cannot exist. Only within the confines of an interrelationship with everything else does he have meaning. Man, as well as nature, becomes nothing more than *process* (continuing development involving many changes).

Again we are witnessing the influence of man's extensions on his thinking. Electricity, for example, does not simply *flow*. Those who speak in such terms live in a "pre-electric" world of thought. Electricity, by contemporary explanation, is pure *process*, one that has altered the world around us. And thinking in such terms and expressions has given way to a pervasive philosophy of processes.

Alfred North Whitehead, the father of *process philosophy*, laid much of the groundwork for what will conceivably follow in scientific study. Although Whitehead had been reared within the Church of England, he broke away from the church's "restrictive" theology as a young man and thereafter sought a substitute for evangelical Christianity. His breakaway was made manifest first in science and then in philosophy, and as C. J. Singer writes, "To read Whitehead in any other way is to misread him completely."[21]

Process philosophy is an epistemological approach to conceptualizing nature based on the recognition that things no longer exist independent of time, but *through* time. Whitehead begins with the assumption that all of nature consists of the interaction of patterns of activity. Every organism is a bundle of relationships that somehow maintains itself while interacting with other organisms that make up the natural environment. In interacting with their environment, organisms are continually "taking account" of the many changes and processes going on and are continuously changing their own activities to adjust to the cascade of activity around them.

By this Whitehead suggests that every organism in some way anticipates the future and then chooses one of a number of possible ways to adjust its own behavior based on what it expects to encounter. Adjustment requires the ability to "anticipate" what is going to happen before it occurs—a sort of "thinking" process within nature. In scientific terms, the organism adjusts and adapts according to the feedback it receives.

The phrase "taking account" to Whitehead is the same as "subjective aim" or the constant "anticipation and response" that occurs in nature. Again, a type of "thinking" takes place in nature, which is the central dynamic of all life, according to such a theory.

The phrase "subjective aim," then, is another expression for *mind*. To Whitehead, mind is not *in* nature, it *is* nature, and he resolves one of the great paradoxes in Darwinian thinking: How could mere matter produce life and minds?

> According to Whitehead, mind has been there all along. Nature is pure mind, and each succeeding organism, by dint of its ability to anticipate the future better and adjust accordingly, is exhibiting a pattern of behavior that reflects more and more of the total mind pattern of nature. [22]

Evolution, moreover, is seen as a movement—a pattern of interacting relationships between organisms striving to complete itself. Furthermore, the goal of evolution is the enlargement of mind until it fills the universe and becomes one with it.

This philosophy laid the framework for the new evolutionary theory. In his 1975 book, *Of Time, Passion, and Knowledge*, philosopher J. T. Fraser outlines these thought forms which are now embedded in scientific inquiry. Sounding like Whitehead, he asserts that "life has been characterized from its very beginnings by a striving to increase its control over lengthening periods of future time and thus decrease the uncertainties and attendant tensions of the present."[23] Each species, according to Fraser, from the primitive to the highly developed, is equipped to anticipate a future for itself. And the better an organism is at anticipating what lies ahead, the better able it will be to adjust its own behavior and ensure its continued survival.

Each organism, then, is reduced to a mere process. It is a process of becoming. It is dynamic rather than static. However, since man can now identify evolutionary life as process, it should be possible to selectively intervene in nature and manipulate it. And manipulate it man will. The catch, however, is that he, too, is part of the process—the machine.

Moreover, if the process of the natural world, whether animate or inanimate matter, has or is mind (the ability to direct activity purposefully), then mind can eventually exist in anything. This, of course, would include machines.

CYBERNETICS

These conceptual changes are joining hands in the sweeping technological transformation that is occuring worldwide today. Through technology people conquer time and space. It is the way man amplifies and extends the human body in ordering nature. The technological transformation is laying the base for the age of biotechnology, and the fusion of computerization and living tissue conceivably signals the new order.

As previously suggested, the computer marks a new chapter in human history. For the first time man has developed a technological means of projecting the human mind directly into nature. "The new temporal theory of evolution is reconstructing nature in the image of the electronic computer."[24] Nature as "matter in motion" is being replaced by nature as "mind in action."[25]

The computer is becoming the chief metaphor for the reconceptualization of the origin and development of the species:

> It is no mere coincidence that many of the operating principles that animate the computer happen to be the same operating principles that biologists now claim are the basis of all living systems. The cosmologists are once again borrowing the organizing technology of the society and "projecting" it onto nature. To the question How does nature operate? the new answer is that it operates in a manner similar to the electronic computer.[26]

These truths lead directly into a consideration of *cybernetics*, the science of how machines *self-regulate* themselves in changing environments. It is the science that explains "purposeful" behavior in machines.

Cybernetics reduces behavior to two essential ingredients, *information* and *feedback*, and claims that *all* processes are explained by them. *Information* consists of the countless messages that go back and forth between organisms and their environments.

However, the "steering" mechanism that regulates *all* behavior is *feedback*, which is both a positive and negative commodity. Positive feedback *reinforces*, and negative feedback *dampens* and causes *readjustment*. Cybernetics is primarily concerned with *negative* feedback.

M.I.T. mathematician Norbert Weiner, who popularized cybernetic theory, first introduced in 1943 the notion that machines could exhibit "purposefulness." Weiner defined purposeful behavior as "a final condition in which the behaving object reaches a definite correlation in time and space with respect to another object or event."[27] For Wiener, all purposeful behavior reduces itself to "information processing." Mind you, he is not talking about machines so much as he is talking about humans and other organisms. He writes:

> It becomes plausible that information...belongs among the great concepts of science such as matter, energy and electric charge. Our adjustment to the world around us depends upon the informational windows that our senses provide.[28]

The succeeding generation of scientists and engineers have generally concurred.

With the aid of the computer, cybernetics has become the primary methodological approach for organizing economic and social activity. Virtually every activity of importance in today's society is being brought under the control of cybernetic principles. "Information processing" *via* the computer is fast becoming the hallmark of our technological society. John Naisbitt, in his best-selling book *Megatrends*, calls the computer "the Liberator." It liberates us to "mass produce knowledge and this knowledge is the driving force of our economy."[29]

In their book *Current Problems in Animal Behavior*, zoologist William H. Thorpe and psychologist Oliver L. Zangwill of Cambridge University reassess the impact of engineering on the field of biology and conclude that the life sciences have all but succumbed to the operating assumptions of the technologists. They note that "principles derived from control and communications engineering are being increasingly brought to bear upon biological problems, and 'models' derived from these principles are proving fertile in the explanation of behaviour."[30]

According to Thorpe and Zangwill, scientists in both fields are finding common ground "under Norbert Wiener's banner of Cybernetics."[31] As a consequence, the distinction between technological principles (concerning machines) and biological principles is beginning to blur.

Biology is being totally revamped along technological lines as a new way of thinking has permeated the biological field:

> It says in effect: look to engineering, to blueprints and operational principles...for the sources of your theoretical models in biology, much as Darwin drew on the works of sheep breeders and pigeon fanciers as a source for Natural Selection.[32]

Perhaps the best way to express the extent to which technology has been able to recast the field of biology in its own image is to take a look at the word "performance":

> Engineers use this word to refer to the activity of machines. Biologists in contrast have traditionally relied on the word "behavior" when referring to the activity of living organisms. Performance conjures up the idea of purposeful activity designed to meet a specific objective. Behavior, on the other hand, often connotes the image of undirected activity without specific goals.[33]

Experimental psychologist R. L. Gregory of Cambridge University notes that biologists are increasingly using the two words (biology/engineering) interchangeably: "[t]he reason," Gregory writes, "almost certainly being the influence of cybernetic ideas, which have unified certain aspects of biology and engineering."[34]

Biologists now view living organisms, including human beings, in terms of information systems. W. H. Thorpe, for example, defines living organisms as things that "absorb and store information, change their behavior as a result of that information, and...have special organs for detecting, sorting and organizing this information."[35]

"The most important biological discovery of recent years," says W. H. Thorpe, "is the discovery that the *processess* of life are directed by *programmes* [and] that life is not merely *programmed* activity but *self-programmed* activity."[36] If the word "life" were removed from this quotation, it would seem that Thorpe and other biologists are talking about computers with their information processing, their programs and self-regulating activity. Indeed, computer technology and principles *are* what they are talking about in an indirect way.

The French biologist Pierre Grassé, for instance, begins by framing *all* of life in cybernetic terms: "Information forms and animates the living organism. Evolution is, in the end, the process by which the creature modifies its information and acquires other information."[37] Further, he notes that "the cybernetic model, of which philosophy has not yet fully taken advantage, is applicable to all kinds of biological systems."[38]

By reducing all activity, including the activity of people, to information feedback and processing, cyberneticians hold that the most defining characteristic of mind is the ability to anticipate and respond to changing conditions over time. This is a continuous process of "becoming." In fact, if the word "information" is dissected, it means "in" "formation." Living organisms, then, are no longer permanent, but rather are networks of continuous activity in the process of becoming.

People, by this view, are merely information systems to be molded by the one thing that represents the apex of the upward mobility of evolution—the computer:

> [The computer] has become the new metaphor for defining life and will be every bit as convincing to a generation raised on videogames and pocket calculators as the industrial machine was convincing as a metaphor for defining life among those conditioned by the industrial era. In Darwin's day, life was viewed as an aggregate of separate, interchangeable parts assembled into a working whole. Today, life is viewed as a code containing millions of bits of information capable of being pro-

grammed in a number of specific ways. We are experiencing the transformation from industrial machine to computer, from assembling to processing, from space to time, and from the cosmology of the Industrial Age to the cosmology of the Age of Biotechnology.[39]

With both the computer and living organisms, time becomes the primary consideration. Each succeeding generation of computers is more adept at processing larger amounts of information in shorter periods of time. Says John Naisbitt: "Information technology (computers) brings order to the chaos of information pollution and therefore gives value to data that would otherwise be useless."[40] Biologists are coming to see a similar pattern of development in nature, with the computer emerging as hero.

Moreover, it should not be difficult to understand why the first generation raised in a fully computerized society will come to accept so readily the new concept of nature that is emerging. They will grow up using the computer to organize and manipulate their entire environment.

MANIPULATING LIFE

One basic way of ordering the environment comes through the emergence of genetic technology—again an extension of cybernetic theory. There is a definite design behind genetic tampering, which involves the transfer of DNA from one organism to another. The characteristics of plants and animals (which, in evolutionary terms, include man) are accomplished in such a way that the organisms assume new functions not previously possessed. Genetic engineering, however, appears to be an opened Pandora's Box yielding fearful potentialities for all of mankind.

A basic principle of genetic engineering again involves the "machineness" of life. It has been noted:

[W]e find that a gene is being described as though it were a machine. Researchers regard it as a part of their work to find out how these so-called machines work, how they were originally built, and how they have developed to their present stage. It is commonly believed by the researchers that they will eventually synthesize all the processes, and that as they rearrange genetic patterns, ultimately they will virtually manufacture life itself.[41]

With the distinctions between man, animal, machine, and nature totally blurred in the view of modern science, and as science and technology grow more powerful in the wrong hands, they will do greater and greater damage. This is evident in the research in which transplanted genes for human growth hormones have been injected into mice and other animals. Reports Harold M. Schmeck, Jr., in *The New York Times:*

> Some of the new mice are about twice normal size because they carry human genes for the production of growth hormone and have an oversupply of that hormone in their blood. From these animals, scientists hope to breed whole colonies of mice that will...pass the human gene to their offspring in the normal course of heredity.[42]

The overall professed goal of this research is "gene regulation."[43] The immediate goal is, by conducting the same research in other animals (for example, cows, sheep, and pigs), to produce livestock that will grow more efficiently and more rapidly because of the human growth hormone.[44]

The United States government, through the Department of Agriculture, is now conducting the same research. As *The Washington Post* reported in October 1984:

> The Department of Agriculture's research center in Beltsville is carrying out experiments to produce super sheep and pigs—perhaps twice as large as current livestock—by injecting them with a growth hormone gene from humans.[45]

Over protest,[46] the government is proceeding with these gene transfers.

But here is the rub: With the philosophy of modern science, what is to stop genetic transfers of animal genes into humans? There is no secular ethic that can effectively argue against such things. Once the concept of man's uniqueness as being created in the image of God is lost, then all logical defenses against fusing man and animal are, at best, spurious. This obviously calls into question the worth of human beings in the man-animal-machine complex once distinctions are blurred.

The fact that these distinctions are indeed being blurred is, in grisly fashion, being brought into focus in the form of experimentation on *live* babies. This is seen in the research conducted by

Finnish researcher Dr. Martii Kekomaki. One nurse who observed Kekomaki's experiments on live aborted babies said:

> They [the doctors] took the fetus and cut its belly open. They said they wanted its liver. They carried the baby out of the incubator and it was still alive. It was a boy. It had a complete body, with hands, feet, mouth and ears. It was even secreting urine.[47]

The baby involved was not injected with an anesthetic when doctors sliced his belly open. Asked to explain the implications of his research, Kekomaki said, "An aborted baby is just garbage."[48]

Six months after the decision in *Roe v. Wade*,[49] legalizing abortion in the United States, Dr. Peter A. J. Adam, an associate professor of pediatrics at Case Western Reserve University, reported to the American Pediatric Research Society concerning research he and associates had conducted on twelve babies (up to twenty weeks old) who had been born alive by hysterotomy abortion.

These men decapitated the babies and cannulated the internal carotid arteries (that is, a tube was placed in the main artery feeding the brain). They kept the diminutive heads alive, much as the Russians kept dogs' heads alive in the 1950s. Note Dr. Adam's retort to criticism:

> Once society's declared the fetus dead, and abrogated its rights, I don't see any ethical problem. . . . Whose rights are we going to protect, once we've decided the fetus won't live?[50]

As science ventures into genetic engineering, cloning, fetal experimentation, a final vista is being crossed. As genes begin to flow back and forth between animal and man, and as the definitions of man begin to blur, we are at a new crossroads. It is something, however, we cannot hide from. It is here in the present, and it may hold a hideous future. As C. S. Lewis once wrote, he would not do "to minerals and vegetables what modern science threatens to do to man himself."[51]

AI

We have been discussing the mechanical view of man as propounded by modern science. This view has fostered a general propensity to integrate downward—that is, to view man not as the handiwork of the Creator, but merely as part of the existing matter. This low view of human beings is interwoven into the fabric of all branches of science and the public sentiment as well.

It is also responsible for two general phenomena which we will deal with in this chapter. First, within the scientific elite, especially those individuals in the artificial intelligence (AI) community, there is a great dissatisfaction with man as he exists. It borders on hatred.

This disdain of the human race is found in other branches of science too. The population planners, for example, as exemplified by the biologists, technicians, and scientists who work for Planned Parenthood and other influential population planning groups, have surveyed the human race and do not like what they see. Through the coercive utopianism of social and human engineering—be it population planning, cybernetics, or biotechnology—the goal is to remake man in a new image.

Secondly, with the idea that everything in the natural world is merely process, and that process can be manipulated by technological means, there is a drive to create a totally autonomous "thinking" computer. It is a counterpoint situation: the more the computer is idolized, the more man can be denigrated. Love one and hate the other.

THE COMPULSION

In 1957, computer scientist Herbert A. Simon predicted that within the following decade a computer program would reign as chess champion of the world, thus raising the spectre of the domination of artificial intelligence (at least, in terms of chess). Later, philosopher Hubert Dreyfus compared artificial intelligence (AI) to alchemy and denounced it as a fraud.

Prominent in Dreyfus's critique of AI was the fact that Simon's latest effort at a chess-playing program had been soundly beaten by a ten-year-old child. For Dreyfus, this was not a case of progress being slow. To him, real chess required real human thinking and intuition. It could not be done digitally.

Convinced this was true, Dreyfus could not refuse a challenge to play against a computer. He lost, however, much to the glee of the AI community.

As things stand today, Simon's prediction remains unfulfilled. Chess programs can beat most experts, but this type of contest foreshadows the struggle between man and computer that is looming on the horizon. It is manifesting itself through artificial intelligence.

AI research is a highly specialized form of computer programming. As previously mentioned, a program is a series of coded instructions to the machine. A computer can be programmed to do anything that can be expressed in a precise and unambiguous set of instructions—what is known in computer science as an "algorithm."

A computer, then, can do anything it can be programmed to do. Without a program, it can do nothing at all. What AI researchers are most involved in is the writing of programs that enable computers to think for themselves. And the ultimate goal of AI research is to develop programs that do not simply "think," but that think in much the same way as people.[1] Says Lewis Thomas: "You can make computers that are almost human. In some respects they are almost superhuman; they can beat most of us at chess, memorize whole telephone books at a glance, compose music of a certain kind and write obscure poetry, diagnose heart ailments, send personal invitations to vast parties, even go transiently crazy. No one has yet programmed a computer to be of two minds about a hard problem, or to burst out laughing, but that may come. Sooner or later, there will be real human hardware, great whirring, clicking cabinets intelligent enough to read magazines and vote, able to think rings around the rest of us."[2]

As Sherry Turkle points out in her book *The Second Self*, the real ambition of AI research goes even a step further:

The real ambition is of mythic proportions: making a "general-purpose" intelligence, a mind. In a long tradition of romantic and mystical thought, life is breathed into dead or in-animate matter by a person with special powers. In the early 1950s there was a growing belief among a group of mathematicians of diverse interests that this fantasy could be brought down to earth. They would use the computer to build mind.[3]

Two leaders in the field of AI, Herbert A. Simon and Allen Newell, boldly claimed the following, as early as 1958:

> There are now in the world machines that think, that learn and that create. Moreover, their ability to do these things is going to increase rapidly until—in the visible future—the range of problems they can handle will be coextensive with the range to which the human mind has been applied.[4]

The two men proclaimed the research aim of AI to be nothing less than the building of a machine whose cognitive behavior would be equivalent to that of humans. Since, however, the human mind applies itself to variables of aesthetics involving touch, taste, vision, and hearing, AI pioneers will eventually have to build machines that have these qualities too.

There are machines today, principally at M.I.T., Stanford University, and the Stanford Research Institute, that have arms and hands and whose movements are coordinated by computer-controlled eyes. Their hands have fingers, which are equipped with pressure-sensitive pads to give them a sense of touch. And there are hundreds of machines that may be said to have the sense of taste.

The computer is, of course, a physically embodied machine and, as such, cannot violate natural law. However, it is not completely characterized by only its manifest interaction with the real world. Electrons flow through it, its tapes move, and its lights blink, all in strict obedience to physical laws, to be sure, and the courses of its internal rivers of electrons are determined by physical events. "But," as Joseph Weizenbaum recognizes, "the game the computer plays out is regulated by systems of ideas whose range is bounded only by the limitations of the human imagination."[5]

Although the computer is bound by natural law and the limitations of its own internal forces, the abstractions of man's imagination, coupled with his ability to manipulate a computer program, are essentially boundless. Weizenbaum, a professor of computer science at M.I.T., explains:

> The computer, then, is a playing field on which one may play out any game one can imagine. One may create worlds in which there is no gravity. . . . One can create societies in whose economies prices rise as goods become plentiful and fall as they become scarce, and in which homosexual unions alone produce offspring. In short, one can singlehandedly write and produce plays in a theater that admits of no limitations. [6]

The computer programmer, then, is the creator of a universe for which he alone is the lawgiver. Weizenbaum argues that this has become a "compulsion" with AI researchers:

> We must first recognize that it *is* a compulsion. Normally, wishes for satisfaction lead to behaviors that have a texture of discrimination and spontaneity. The fulfillment of such wishes leads to pleasure. The compulsive programmer is driven; there is little spontaneity in how he behaves; and he finds no pleasure in the fulfillment of his nominal wishes. He seeks reassurance from the computer, not pleasure. The closest parallel we can find to this sort of psychopathology is in the relentless, pleasureless drive for reassurance that characterizes the life of the compulsive gambler. [7]

The compulsive gambler believes himself to be in control of a *magical* world to which only a few men are given entrance. "He believes Fate has singled him out. . .and communicates with him by means of small signs indicating approval and reproach." [8]

The gambler is the scientist of this magical world. He is the interpreter of the signs that Fate communicates to him, just as the scientist in the real world is an interpreter of the signs that nature communicates to everyone who cares to become sensitive to them.

Psychiatric literature informs us that pathologies deeply involve fantasies of omnipotence. The conviction that one is all-powerful, however, cannot rest. It must constantly be verified by tests. The test of power is control. The test of absolute power is absolute control. When dealing with the compulsive programmer involved in AI work, we are, therefore, dealing with his need to control and his need for certainty—both attributes, as we have seen, of man's relationship to magic. (Magic and its relationship to science is discussed in Chapter Five.)

The passion for certainty is, of course, also one of the cornerstones of science, philosophy, and religion. And the quest for *control* is inherent in all technology. "Indeed," as Weizenbaum comments, "the reason we are so interested in the compulsive programmer is that we see no discontinuity between his pathological motives and behavior and those of the modern scientist and technologist generally."[9]

We are here, again, dealing with man's extensions. Construction of a simulated human being, even if it is only mind and not sensory appendages, is the creation of an autonomous machine.

MIND BUILDING MIND

AI sees the mind—both artificial and human—as built from programming. AI scientists believe that the most important quality about people is that they possess intelligence and, as such, are closer than anything else in nature to *pure program*. Man is viewed totally in terms of the computer.

Most of the founders of AI were mathematicians who brought to the new field the mathematician's unique ability to build theories by pure quantitative thought. There was great pleasure in building worlds out of pure mind. The only limit was the particular mathematician's imagination.

The concept was reinforced by the nature of programming itself. For many programmers, much of the excitement of what they do concerning computer programming comes from freeing the mind from the constraints of matter.

Gerald Sussman, a faculty member at the M.I.T. Artificial Intelligence Laboratory, describes his "first real scientific theory" as a product of pure mind, of pure mental force.[10] Someone had given him a pair of toy binoculars when he was four or five years old. He observed that when he used the binoculars in the "right" way, objects appeared larger. However, objects appeared smaller and more distant when the binoculars were used in reverse. He clarifies:

> I was really shaken by that—that you could turn them around and it worked both ways. Somehow that clicked with other things—like if you look in a mirror and see someone, they can see you. I remember all of these things happened very fast.

> And all of a sudden I had this large collection of things and I
> suddenly realized that they were all the same thing.[11]

When we watch Sussman with his binoculars, we are watching
Sussman the child developing the intellectual personality of
Sussman the AI scientist. The penchant is toward reversing all
traditional concepts of truth.

Thus, AI exerts a powerful skepticism on the traditional way
of viewing all things. Some AI scientists go so far as to say that
they must transcend all categories of truth and falsity. For example, Roger Schank, an AI scientist at Yale, explains:

> *We are very much modern-day philosophers.* We're addressing
> the same questions that Aristotle addressed, and everybody
> else in between. We have a different method of doing it. That
> method can be summed up in one word: process. What we're
> saying is that the right approach to an analysis of events in the
> world is the process approach, seeing what the steps are, seeing
> what the inputs are, and providing algorithms to get from one
> place to another place, place A to place B.
>
> Philosophers have written tomes on the difference between
> knowing and believing. An AI person would have a lot less to
> say about that subject, but be a lot more coherent about it. In
> other words, the whole question of whether you really know or
> you really believe can be addressed in terms of what you do
> when you see the word "know." What do you do when you see
> the word "believe"? Under what circumstances? And when
> you reorient the question the way I just did, you change the
> question significantly. And this kind of change—well, in my
> judgment, that is what the philosophy of AI is all about.
>
> What I'm saying is, let's look at the old philosophical ques-
> tions. *Let's look at them in terms of what we do, in terms of how we
> approach and operate on these things rather than on truth. Truth is a
> nonmeaningful AI term, but truth is a key philosophical term.*[12]

In an interview with psychologist Sherry Turkle, one of
Schank's students reiterates:

> It has always bothered me that the philosopher types think that
> they are the only ones who know how to think deeply. I mean
> to think deeply about philosophy. Science fiction thinks about
> philosophy. If you start from a world that is a complete blank
> and you can fill in all the details, which is what you do in sci-
> ence fiction, you are doing the same thing as Plato: creating a
> whole system. *Make the minds in that system work however you
> want them to. In AI, we do that same kind of thing, but we take it*

one step further. We don't just fantasize about minds, *we think about building them.* With actor languages, and recursion, and multi-processing, well, I think that the scientists have what it takes. I mean what it takes to think about the mind. *We are the new philosophers. Not everybody can see it yet. But they are going to.* [13]

GOLEM

Challenging ageless concepts of truth and seeing oneself as a new self-appointed philosopher are not small aspirations. They are global aspirations and are an expression of the intellectual pride of AI—"part of its sense of being an enterprise of mythic proportions."[14]

From their earliest years, many in the field of AI have thought of themselves as creators of life. In fact, several members of the "present-day AI researchers at M.I.T. grew up with a family tradition that suggests they are descendants of Rabbi Loew, the Creator of Golem, a humanlike figure made of clay into whom God's name breathed life."[15] More than a philosophy, AI, for some scientists, has become a religion.

A fetish in this religion is the dream to build robots that simulate human beings. For example, Gary Drescher, a graduate student at the M.I.T. AI Laboratory, believes the ultimate criterion is consciousness. He wants to give this attribute to machines, proclaiming: "We have the right to create life, but not the right to take our act lightly."[16]

Although Drescher does not believe the supernatural Deity created man, he does believe that when AI scientists create a new consciousness—that is, a computer with artificial intelligence—they are acting as gods and have to deal with new ethical questions. For instance, in a society where human and artificial intelligence coexist, "what will be their respective rights, who will make their Ten Commandments?"[17]

To that end, Drescher proposes that we give equal rights to machines. Consciousness is life, according to such reasoning, and the taking away of consciousness—even from a cold machine—would be a new form of murder. Drescher argues:

> People always talk about pulling the plug on computers as though when it comes to that they will be saving the world, performing the ultimate moral act. But that is science fiction. In real life, it will probably be the other way around. We are going

to be creating consciousness, creating lives, and then people may simply want to pull the plug when one of these intelligences doesn't agree with them.[18]

This type of thinking does *not* propose to bring machines up to the level of human beings. It has completely the reverse affect. It brings human beings *down* to the level of mechanical objects. This is reflected in the philosophy of AI scientist Edward Fredkin:

> There is a popular view that the human mind is this fantastic thing that most of us are just barely using—5 or 10 percent of its capacity. If we could only unleash the whole human mind and all of its powers, we'd be supermen. Now my notion is that for an ordinary person to get along in society in a conventional way requires about 110 percent of the capacity of the human mind, causing breakdowns and trouble of various sorts. *Basically, the human mind is not most like a god or most like a computer. It's most like the mind of a chimpanzee and most of what's there isn't designed for living in high society but for getting along in the jungle or out in the fields.*[19]

Physicist Robert Jastrow, in his book *The Enchanted Loom: Mind in the Universe,* is more kind, but nevertheless arrives at a similar conclusion but in terms of the evolution of intelligence. He suggests that computer intelligence, unshackled by human limitations, may reach the apex of what is possible concerning the structure and function of thought. Jastrow concludes: "If this forecast is accurate, man is doomed to a subordinate status on his own planet."[20]

THE SEARCH FOR "I"

René Descartes once said, "I think, therefore I am." The statement assumes and reinforces the presupposition that wherever there is thinking, there must be an "I," a self, an agent of thought. Only an "I" can think.

For AI scientists, however, the suggestion that there must be a thinking agent, an "I," in order for thinking to happen, is "prescientific."[21] Such scientists presume that the mind and the brain are the same. Thus, there is no self or soul, only matter and the mechanical movements of man, the organic machine.

There is scientific evidence, however, to suggest that this presupposition is not true. Two leading pioneers in brain surgery, this stuff here critical to understanding the basis of AI philosophical underpinning.

AI □ 155

Sir William Charles Sherrington and Dr. Wilder Pennfield, discovered in numerous experiments on the brain that the mind and brain are different. This evidence suggests that mind, the nonmaterial entity, *uses* the brain (as opposed to *being* the brain) just as human beings *use* the computer.

To sidetrack for a moment, it can be stated without equivocation that traditional Christian theology has always viewed man in terms of a distinct spirit/body dichotomy. This is the clear position taken in the Old and New Testaments. Traditionally, theologians have spoken of the dual nature of man as being comprised of an *object* half and a *subject* half. The object half is termed in the New Testament *soma*, the subject half *pneuma*. Together the two distinct halves make up the "soul" or the "person." As Arthur C. Custance notes:

> Materialism with its denial of the soul makes man subjectless and therefore only a half-entity, while spiritualism with its denial of the body makes him objectless and therefore only a half-entity. Either view effectively annihilates man as man.[22]

Moreover, any system of thought which attempts to treat man as a half-entity is no longer dealing with the whole man. And AI deals precisely with man's object half. It is a one-dimensional view of people. It is man as computer, but inferior to the computers he has animated outside of himself. It's the same as saying that a love letter is the sole object of one's affections.[23]

AI, then, presents a new paradigm for thinking about people, thought, and reality. The concept of the machine triumphing over its creator marks a new era which borders on the theological. Asks Norbert Wiener, often regarded as the father of cybernetics:

> Can God play a significant game with his own creature? Can any creator, even a limited one, play a significant game with his own creature?[24]

THE MEAT MACHINE

If there is no soul, no self, no "I," then obviously it is well and fit to view man as he really is—a set of computer programs. This is becoming a prevailing view among AI researchers. As Turkle notes, "The idea of thinking of the self as a set of computer programs is widespread among students I interviewed at Harvard and MIT who were familiar with large computer systems."[25]

One computer science major interviewed by Turkle saw individuals as machines who merely act in accordance with programs provided by nature:

> You think you're making a decision, but are you really? For instance, when you have a creative idea, what happens? All of a sudden, you think of something. Right? Wrong. You didn't think of it. It just filtered through—the consciousness processor just sits there and watches this cacophony of other processors yelling onto the bus and skims off the top what he thinks is the most important thing, one thing at a time. A creative idea just means that one of the processors made a link between two unassociated things because he thought they were related.[26]

In response Turkle says:

> In the course of my interview with Mark, creativity, individual responsibility, free will, and emotion were all being dissolved, simply grist for the little processors' mills. I asked Mark if he thought that "mind" is anything more than the feeling of having one. His answer was clear: "You have to stop talking about your mind as though it were thinking. It's not. It is just doing."[27]

If this is one's view of man, then one should not be put off by M.I.T. professor Marvin Minsky's description of the brain as a "meat machine."[28] Man, by this view, is simply hardware— meat on a metal frame.

THE BIG QUESTION

It seems that the force of history has brought us sequences in how man views himself. Once we saw ourselves as one step below the supernatural Creator and in God's image. Next, we saw ourselves as rational animals lunging forward in the parade of evolution. Now we are just beginning to see ourselves as feeling computers, emotional machines. How will we view ourselves tomorrow?

The AI scientist ponders the matter of tomorrow and argues that all things are malleable and that there is no domain over which machines cannot triumph. The issue at hand concerns whether or not it is appropriate to delegate human functions to a machine and vice versa.

Man is not a machine. There are some things humans know simply by knowing their own bodies. We experience life's intangibles—love, compassion, hatred—and we know that these are simply not machine functions.

The robotic machine, however, creates a dilemma. Mary Shelley recognized this when she had Frankenstein's monster ponder its own ill-defined role: "I live, I breathe, I walk, I see—but what am I, Man or Monster?" The AI scientists have a partial answer. When they refer to robots as organisms, they declare their willingness initially to consider them animals. Beyond this, however, as we have seen, the thinking computer is much more than man the "chimpanzee."

Furthermore, if all goes according to plan for the AI people, one can imagine and expect a "metallic" future. It might go something like this: In some lonely outpost in the distant future where all the computers in the universe are linked together, some foreboding human servant asks, "Is there a God?" Striking the questioner down for his impudence, the computers reply, "Now there is."

PART THREE

MAN
AND
THE PLANNERS

We are driven inside. . .
For three years or more,
For three years of more.
To see again the barbed-wire fence,
The guard towers, the MPs, the machine guns,
The bayonets, the tanks, the mess halls, the latrine.
It's right to know the bitter cold of winter,
The dust storms. How can we forget the sand, the sand?
Biting into our skin, filling our eyes and nose and mouth
and ears,
Graying our hair in an instant.
How can we forget the sand, the sand?
It's right to recall the directives, their threats and lies, the
meetings, the strikes, the resistance, the arrests,
stockades, violent attacks, murder.
Derangement. Derangement. Pain, grief, separation.
Departure. Informers, recriminations, disagreements.
Loyalty, disloyalty. Yes, yes. No, no, no. Yes.

Hiroshi Kashiwagi
A Meeting at Tule Lake★

★ A memorial poem commemorating the Japanese internment camps
established in the United States during World War II.

TEN

THE CONDITIONERS

The final frontier for science to conquer is man himself. The philosophical groundwork has been laid.

If man is to be conquered, however, he must be controlled. That is, he *must be planned*. There simply are too many of him, or so it is believed.

This means that man's propensity to reproduce must be curtailed. As one would control the reproductive capacity of domestic animals, man's drive to produce offspring must somehow be managed. And rightly so: If man is only an animal—on the level of chimpanzees or ants—why not regulate his reproductive future?

These antinatal ideas, predominant as they are in our own time, are relatively new. However, they have been brought home with great force, and this is seen from the fact that most of us live within earshot of the contemporary *myth of overpopulation*—which is actually an excuse to eliminate future human beings.

The "population explosion" and "population crisis" mentality had its genesis in ideas promulgated near the end of the eighteenth century. Ironically, just as America was establishing its government on the belief that man had great dignity and worth, a man named Thomas Malthus was propounding a population theory that would have the opposite effect upon people. Its final conclusions are being played out in places like India, where over eleven million people were forcibly sterilized in the early 1970s;[1] and in China where millions more have been forced to abort their children.[2]

THE DISMAL THEOREM

The Englishman, Malthus, attended Cambridge University and had entered the Anglican ministry in 1797. His father Daniel, who was a personal friend of David Hume and Jean-Jacques Rousseau, was a firm believer in the eventual triumph of human reason. It would usher in a utopia, he believed.

Son Thomas, however, came to quite another conclusion. In 1798, he published a pessimistic view of man entitled, *An Essay on the Principle of Population as It Affects the Future Improvement of Society*.[3]

Malthus believed that the utopianism of the Enlightenment would repeatedly be stultified by the fact that any increases in the supply of food would be annulled by increases in population. The multiplication of mouths—through reckless reproduction and lowered infant and adult mortality—would eventually "use up" the food. Thus, according to Malthus, there was a certainty that mankind would be squeezed down to a long-run equilibrium of living at bare subsistence. This is known as Malthus's "dismal theorem."

Malthus tried to put his argument in mathematical form. Allowing a quantified increase in food supply every twenty-five years (from 1 to 2 to 3 to 4 to 5 to 6, etc.), and allowing four surviving children to every couple, he wrote: "In two centuries the population would be to the means of subsistence as 25 to 9; in three centuries it would be 4,096 to 13; and in 2,000 years the difference would be incalculable."[4]

However, the reason population has not risen so rapidly, Malthus believed, was that it was limited both by *negative* and by *positive* checks on reproduction. The negative checks were preventive: the deferment of marriage by poverty, "vice" (by which Malthus meant extramarital sex), "unnatural passions" (homosexuality, etc.), and the various means of contraception in or outside of marriage. When such negative factors failed to keep population in balance with the food supply, nature and history provided positive checks by means of infanticide, disease, famine, and war.

From this somber analysis, Malthus drew surprising conclusions. First, he argued that there was no use in raising the wages of the working class, for if wages were increased the workers would marry earlier and have more children. Thus, the population would grow, mouths would increase faster than food to feed them, and poverty would be brought back. Likewise, it was useless to raise the "poor rates" (taxes for the care of the unemployed) because this would be an incentive to idleness and larger families. Mouths again would multiply faster than goods. The competition among buyers would allow sellers to raise the prices of their diminishing stocks, and soon the poor would be as poor as before.

In a revised and much expanded form of the *Essay*, Malthus laid down, more clearly and harshly than before, the preventive remedies that might render unnecessary the catastrophic cures brought about by nature and history. He proposed a halt to poor relief, and a check on interference with free enterprise. The law of supply and demand should be left to operate in the scope of relations between producers and consumers, employers and employees. Early marriage must be discouraged to keep the birthrate down. "Our obligation [is] not to marry till we have a fair prospect of being able to support our children."[5] Above all, men must learn moral restraint before and after marriage. "The interval between the age of puberty and...marriage must...be passed in strict chastity."[6] Within marriage there must be *no* contraception in any way or form. If these or equivalent regulations were not observed, we would resign ourselves to periodic reductions of overpopulation by famine, pestilence, or war.

"The Essay on Population," writes Will and Ariel Durant, "was received as a divine revelation by the conservative elements of the British population."[7] Malthus's *Essays* were written in the matrix of the Industrial Revolution which assisted greatly in creating the poor houses and British ghettos so tellingly described by English writers such as Charles Dickens.

Thus, Malthus's works had an immediate impact. William Pitt, for example, withdrew the bill he had introduced for extending poor relief.[8] As the Durants note:

> The measures already taken by the government against British radicals seem justified by Malthus' contention that these peddlers of utopia were seducing simple souls to tragic delusions. British manufacturers were strengthened in their belief that low wages made for disciplined labor and obedience.... Now nearly all the evil incident to the Industrial Revolution could be ascribed to the reckless fertility of the poor.[9]

Malthus's initial essay at first threw many of the Enlightenment utopianists into disarray. However, later writers and logic itself have brought Malthusian theories into question. For example, in Europe, China, and India, population has more than doubled since Malthus's initial works; yet people are better fed than ever before in those countries.

Likewise, in the United States the population has more than doubled several times since 1800. Nevertheless, agriculture produces more adequately than ever before (and has an immense surplus for export).

Contrary to Malthus, the rise in wages has brought not an increase but a lowering of the birthrate. The problem is no longer a deficiency of seeds or fields, but a shortage of the supply of nonhuman energy to operate the mechanisms of agriculture and industry.

The long-run view of demographic history suggests that, contrary to Malthus, constant geometric growth does not correctly characterize the human population. "Rather," Julian Simon writes, "a major improvement of economic and health conditions produces a sudden increase in population, which gradually moderates as the major productive advances and concomitant health improvements are assimilated."[10]

Of course, an answer often posed to Malthusianism has been contraception—its moral acceptance, its wide dissemination, and its lower cost (often given away by governmental entities in the name of "population control"). The general secularization of thought and culture broke down the theological barriers to birth control. The Industrial Revolution transformed children from the economic assets they had been on the farm to the economic handicaps they became in cities as child labor slowly diminished and as education became expensive and urban crowding arose.

Thus, although Malthus's theories have been shown to be quite inaccurate, "neo-Malthusians" and their propaganda for mass birth control have kept his basic principles alive. As early as 1822, Francis Place, for instance, wrote his *Illustrations and Proofs of the Principle of Population* in which he accepted Malthus's principle that population tended to increase faster than the food supply. Restraint in producing children, he agreed, was necessary, but not by postponing marriage. Better would be the acceptance of *contraception* as a legitimate substitute for nature's blind fertility and war's wholesale destruction. Although Place himself had fifteen children, five of whom died in childhood, he distributed London handbills, printed at his own expense, advocating birth control. He continued his campaign until his death in 1854.

Malthus lived long enough to feel the force of Place and other neo-Malthusians. In 1824 he contributed to the *Encyclopedia Britannica* an article revising his theories, and even Charles Darwin was influenced by them. Darwin wrote in his *Autobiography:*

> In October, 1838, fifteen months after I had begun my systematic enquiry, I happened to read for amusement Malthus on Population; and being well prepared to appreciate the struggle for existence...from long-continued observation of the habits of animals and plants, it at once struck me that under these circumstances favorable variations would tend to be preserved, and unfavorable ones to be destroyed. The result of this would be the formation of a new species. Here then I had at last got hold of a theory by which to work.[11]

Thus, Darwin "was particularly cognizant of his indebtedness to Malthus" for assistance in developing his evolutionary theory.[12] However, it was in the newly emerging field of eugenics that neo-Malthusian thought would have its greatest impact. It has, in its final form, given us the population planners, who are in the business of planning people away.

THE NEO-MALTHUSIANS

Alfred Russel Wallace, the naturalist whose own discovery of the mechanism of natural selection had hurried Darwin into print, wrote in his *The Action of Natural Selection on Man:*

> At the present day it does not seem possible for natural selection to act in any way so as to secure the permanent advancement of morality and intelligence, for it is indisputably the mediocre, if not the low, both as regards morality and intelligence, who succeed best in life and multiply fastest.[13]

In 1885, Jane Hume Clapperton, in her book *Scientific Meliorism,* added:

The racial blood shall not be poisoned by moral disease. The guardians of social life in the present dare not be careless of the happiness of coming generations, therefore the criminal is forcibly restrained from perpetuating his vicious breed. Now mark the result. . . . The type will disappear; whilst evenly balanced natures, the gentle, the noble, the intellectual, will become parents of future generations; and the purified blood and unmixed blood in the veins of the British will enable the race to rise *far above* its present level of natural morality.

To promote the contentment of congenital criminals within their prison home, where they are detained for life, an alternative to celibacy might be offered [by way of] a surgical operation rendering the male sex incapable of reproduction.[14]

As discussed briefly in an earlier chapter, this is *eugenics.* The word was coined by Sir Francis Galton, Charles Darwin's cousin. For years the Eugenics Education Society (now known as the Eugenics Society) quoted Galton's definition of the term on the cover of the *Eugenics Review:* "Eugenics is the study of agencies under social control that may improve or impair the racial qualities of future generations, whether physically or mentally."[15]

The basic scheme of eugenics then is to produce pure breeds of people—similar to what has been done with animals. It is, in reality, genetic conditioning.

Arthur Keith, writing in the *Eugenics Review,* describes Galton's concept of racial purity:

His evidence justified him in putting forward a proposal or scheme, one of the most audacious ever formulated by a sane man of science, that the State ought to select its most gifted young men and young women in order to breed for genius. He even went so far as to write the speech which the "Senior Trustee of the Endowment Fund" was to address to the "ten deeply blushing young men of 25" who had issued successfully from the public examination which proved that they had "in the highest degree those qualities of body and mind which do most honour and service to our race."[16]

Under Galton's plan, ten young women were to be mated with young men in a ceremony in which they would be given away by the monarch. They would receive five thousand pounds for the rearing and education of their children.

It was an example of *positive* eugenics—that is, breeding for purity of race. But it was selective breeding. As Galton wrote in 1908, the major premise for eugenics rested "on bringing no more individuals into the world than can be properly cared for and those only of the best stock.''[17]

The eugenics movement of the late nineteenth century played on Caucasian prejudice, but was undergirded by Darwinian and Malthusian reasoning. And by 1911, the year of Galton's death, "the relevance of eugenic considerations was accepted by all shades of liberal and radical opinion, as well as by conservatives."[18]

In his will, Galton left a bequest for the establishment of a chair at University College, and named his own candidate, the brilliant mathematician and biologist, Karl Pearson. In a lecture of 1903, Pearson discussed the "national deterioration" in Great Britain:

> The mentally better stock of the nation is not reproducing itself at the same rate as it did of old; the less able and the less energetic are more fertile than the better stocks. No scheme of wider or more thorough education will bring up in scale of intelligence hereditary weakness to the level of hereditary strength. The only remedy, if one be possible at all, is to alter the relative fertility of the good and the bad stocks in the country.[19]

These arrogant elitist views consider the "population explosion" only in terms of "bad stocks." And *they are racist at their core.*

However, the assertions of Pearson and others fell upon fertile ground, and a basic idea was developed to find ways to eliminate the so-called "bad stocks." Initially in Great Britain, this came in the form of immigration laws that restricted the inflow of "bad stock." In America, however, it took on a different form, concerning itself with the mentally defective.

The movement to segregate "mentally defective" persons caught on rapidly in the United States. By 1923 forty states had established asylums. However, with the rising popularity of the eugenics movement, some professionals felt that such compartmentalization seemed inadequate in eliminating "defective strains." The more effective answer was *sterilization,* and it was performed at will.[20]

In 1899, Dr. Harry Sharp, a member of the Purity Society of Indiana and medical officer at Jeffersonville Reformatory, decided to carry out vasectomies by his own initiative. In 1912 he wrote to the *Eugenics Review* in London glibly describing his coercive sterilization activities:

> As to the workings of this law in the State of Indiana, I must say they have been most satisfactory. . . . In many instances, *we have operated on many against their will and over their vigorous protest.* . . . Since October, 1899, I have been performing an operation known as vasectomy. . . . *I do it without administering an anaesthetic either general or local.* . . . I have two hundred and thirty-six cases that have afforded splendid opportunity for post-operative observation, and I have never seen unfavourable symptoms. . . . The patient becomes of a more sunny disposition, brighter of intellect, ceases excessive masturbation.[21]

The first *law* providing for enforced sterilization of feeble-minded, insane, syphilitic, alcoholic, epileptic, and criminal individuals had been passed in Connecticut in 1896. Kansas followed in 1903; Ohio, New Jersey, and Michigan in 1905. However, in Pennsylvania the governor refused his consent to the bill, and while the state of Washington adopted a sterilization law, neighboring Oregon vetoed such a consideration. In California a law was not only passed in 1909, but was also energetically implemented. In seven years 635 "partly eugenic, partly therapeutic, partly punitive" sterilization operations had been carried out.[22]

In other states, such as Nevada, North Dakota, New Jersey, and Kansas, the laws were inoperative. In others, such as Michigan and Wisconsin, they were selectively applied. In all, twenty-two states had sterilization laws by 1918, when a Supreme Court decision found such laws to be unconstitutional. It was the seventh time the laws had been challenged. But, as on all previous occasions, the law was simply redrafted and passed again.

By now, however, the idea and practice of eugenics was embedded in American society. Various universities had established eugenics courses. The Carnegie Institute established the Station for Experimental Evolution, and in 1910 the Eugenics Record Office was opened. Its first report, published in 1913, was compiled by H. H. Laughlin, who later became head of the Psychopathic Laboratory of the Municipal Court in Chicago.[23]

Laughlin was convinced that racial intermarriage was genetically deleterious and immigration should be severely limited. He said:

> [T]here is no nation whose race-integrity and characteristic value cannot be destroyed either by radical out-crossing with races that may be equally talented but which biologically are very different, or by absorbing inferior family stocks from the generally best and most talented foreign races, which in general are quite assimilable to it. Thus in the exercise of its own rights and in building up its own stocks, the receiving nation must exercise its sovereign right and select courageously and radically for the improvement of its own human values in future generations. Immigration is a long-time investment in human stocks. Each nation must look after its own interest in this field.[24]

Laughlin served as the eugenics "expert" for the Committee on Immigration and Naturalization of the House of Representatives from 1921 to 1931.[25] And as the American eugenics lobby became powerful, it acquired the support of wealthy men such as John D. Rockefeller and Alexander Graham Bell.

However, it became obvious to the eugenicists that the problem of raving lunatics was not so severe. Such people could easily be identified. The real danger, to the eugenicists, lay in borderline cases. The more able to cope the "high-grade moron" was, the more fraught with reproductive peril he was to the "good" stocks. Thus, an article in the *Eugenics Review* proclaimed: "There is no greater menace to a race than is furnished by. . .sturdy degenerates."[26] Such "sturdy degenerates" could, however, be isolated by systematic application of *intelligence tests, one of a number of eugenic tools which has survived* to the present day. One eugenicist, in 1940, proclaimed: "The present situation is one in which it seems probable that no reproduction of all parents below I.Q. 90 would practically wipe out feeble-mindedness in a single generation."[27]

After a series of legal skirmishes which had resulted in the insertion of consent provisos in American eugenic sterilization laws, the matter came before the United States Supreme Court in 1927. Carrie Buck, a young mother with a child who possessed an allegedly feeble mind, had scored a mental age of nine on the

Stanford-Binet intelligence test. Mrs. Buck's mother, then fifty-two, had tested at mental age seven. In one of his most famous and chilling judicial opinions, Justice Oliver Wendell Holmes, Jr. wrote in *Buck v. Bell:*

> The judgment finds the facts that have been recited and that Carrie Buck "is the probable potential parent of socially inadequate offspring, likewise afflicted, that she may be sexually sterilized without detriment to her general health and that her welfare and that of society will be promoted by her sterilization. . . ." It is better for all the world, if instead of waiting to execute degenerate offspring for crime, or to let them starve for their imbecility, society can prevent those who are manifestly unfit from continuing their kind. The principle that sustains compulsory vaccination is broad enough to cover cutting the Fallopian tubes. . . . *Three generations of imbeciles are enough.* [28]

Judges in Kansas, Idaho, Nebraska, Oklahoma, and Ohio later agreed with Holmes. Similar verdicts were brought in Ohio and Nebraska as late as the 1960s. Moreover, the Virginia law Holmes upheld was implemented for forty-eight years, from 1924 to 1972. Sterilization operations had been performed in mental health facilities, primarily upon men and women considered "feeble-minded" or "anti-social." This included "unwed mothers, prostitutes, petty criminals, and children with disciplinary problems."[29] Even now, because of the success of the eugenics movement, as intertwined with population control, there are laws on the books of thirty states providing for involuntary sterilization of the "mentally defective."

Eugenics, thus, is yet alive. A good example of its continued legitimitization is a 1976 North Carolina law which permits the sterilization of "mentally retarded" or "mentally ill" persons. Under this law sterilization may be authorized "because of a physical, mental, or nervous disease, or deficiency which is not likely to. . .improve [and] the person would probably be unable to care for a child or children; or, because the person would be likely, unless sterilized, to procreate a child or children which probably would have serious physical, mental, or nervous deficiencies."[30] Furthermore, it is a "duty" of certain health officers to start the process if:

(1). . .sterilization is in the best interest of the mental, moral or physical improvement of the retarded person,

Mary Sanger

(2)...sterilization is in the best interest of the public at large,

(3)...[the retarded person] would be likely, unless sterilized, to procreate a child or children who would have a tendency to serious physical, mental, or nervous disease or deficiency; or, because of a physical, mental or nervous disease or deficiency, which is not likely to materially improve, the person would be unable to care for a child or children.[31]

A United States federal district court, in ruling on the law, said "evidence that is clear, strong and convincing that the subject is likely to engage in sexual activity without using contraceptive devices and that either a defective child is likely to be born or a child born that cannot be cared for by its parent" is grounds for sterilization.[32] Even more alarming is that the Supreme Court of North Carolina has said that the state may sterilize because "the people of North Carolina also have a right to prevent the procreation of children who will become a burden to the State."[33] In other words, as Julian Simon recognizes:

[I]f you do poorly on an IQ test, or if an M.D. says that you are mentally ill—both of which could happen to any of us under certain circumstances, as is happening today to some anti-government activists in the U.S.S.R.—then you could be forcibly sterilized.[34]

THE PLANNERS

The alliance of eugenicists and the so-called family planners became inevitable as soon as the former began arguing that sterilization was "good" for "the race." Population restriction, by way of birth control, was the next logical step.

With the strength and popularity of the Malthusian-Darwinian thought forms, there were many advocates of population control in early twentieth-century America. Margaret Sanger, the founder of the International Planned Parenthood Federation, became the most visible advocate of birth control.

From the outset, Sanger wanted to limit the "excess" fertility of the poor, wherein she also found what she interpreted as an excess of feeble-minded persons. In 1926 she wrote: "There is only one reply to a request for a higher birthrate among the intelligent and that is to ask the government first to take the burden of the insane and feeble-minded [off its] back. *Sterilization for these is the solution.*"[35] In her biography she recounted: "*We...sought first to stop the multiplication of the unfit. This appeared the most important and greatest step toward race betterment.*"[36]

The *unfit,* of course, potentially included almost anyone. The unfit could be labeled such by means of economic conditions, levels of consumption, skin color, language, and religion. The eugenics matrix has always had strong racial and nationalistic overtones.

The family planners (or conditioners) were given a remarkable boost from funds (private and public) made available to them. The paymasters were wealthy industrialists such as "Ford, Mellon, Dupont, Standard Oil, Rockefeller, and Shell."[37] Population control advocates had both the propaganda techniques as well as the financial backing to carry forth their efforts to thin out the human race.

As long as most people were unaware that a population problem even existed, the power wielded by the planners was limited. However, in the 1960s, the alarmist and, as it has turned out, mythic threat of overpopulation was thrust to the forefront of Western consciousness by propaganda campaigns of a magnitude that had been used previously to create massive fortunes.

Such propaganda urged that artificial birth control was the sole answer. Germaine Greer, in *Sex and Destiny,* writes:

> It could only be done with the help of the medical and pharmaceutical establishment. If manufactured contraceptive drugs and appliances were to be reliable, they had to be tested on wide samples of people and over long periods; only the biggest drug houses had the funds and facilities to do the work. The local family firms that had supplied the markets with pessaries and rubber goods were swallowed up or went under; the multinational chemical combines took over an expanding market with limitless possibilities. Once contraceptive use had saturated a stable population, new users had to be found; if enough money could be made from the home market, contraceptive supply to developing markets could be subsidized. If governments would accept the need for aggressive marketing of contraceptive hardware, more and better subsidies would be available. The piddling activities of the Stopeses and the Sangers and their radical, liberal, upper-class, do-gooder friends, together with the muddled altruism of the socialists and the earnestness of the Malthusians, needed to join forces with the prestige and power of the biochemical establishment. If a set of cryptoeugenic priorities came with the package, they would be relatively easy to ignore in the momentum created by

a streamlined and determined lobby, which in less than a decade created a vast and intricate population cartel which pushed hundreds of millions of dollars back and forth across the world map.[38]

Propaganda was the key in developing a population "crisis" in the psyche of the West. One such propaganda piece was *The Population Bomb* (funded by the Hugh Moore Fund). It was circulated among university campuses, high schools, radio stations, and newspapers by way of a media blitz. Later, it became the title of Paul Erlich's best seller.[39] Suddenly the phrases "population bomb" and "population explosion" were in general circulation, as they are today, and as though they are based on fact.

Private money has poured into population control agencies, the largest donors being "the Ford Foundation ($10.2 million), Andrew W. Mellon Foundation ($7.3 million) and Rockefeller Foundation ($5.2 million). All financed the development of contraceptives and abortifacients and promoted population control abroad."[40]

A private survey has "revealed that foundations gave more than $36 million in fiscal year 1982 to population studies and population control."[41] Journalist Mary Meehan writes: "A large portion of the total went directly or indirectly for abortion. Foundation money was used to finance pro-abortion litigation, to support public education and lobbying campaigns favoring abortion, and even to finance abortion facilities and equipment."[42]

Planned Parenthood, in its apparent drive to eliminate children, is one of the largest recipients of population control funds from private sources. As Meehan documents:

> They pour huge sums into Planned Parenthood—and on such a regular basis that it seems like paying their annual dues to a country club. Money virtually cascades into PP offices, some of it going to the national "Public Impact Program" of propaganda and lobbying. Foundations also give massive sums to local PP groups for general support or to build and renovate clinics. Thus the Longwood Foundation, established by the DuPonts primarily to support the famous Longwood Gardens, gave $400,000 to the Delaware League for Planned Parenthood in 1982. The money was earmarked for renovation of a Newark clinic and for construction of a new headquarters. In the same year, the Indianapolis Foundation gave $67,500 to a PP group for general support and "to assist with the costs of a

new clinic building.'' The Richard King Mellon Foundation gave $55,000 to the Planned Parenthood Center of Pittsburgh for purchase of a computer. The list goes on and on, to a total of $6.8 million in 1982 for Planned Parenthood and its many affiliates. This is undoubtedly a conservative figure, since the *Register* survey did not cover all foundation grants to United Way affiliates, many of which support Planned Parenthood.[43]

"Nowadays," writes Germaine Greer, "the lion's share of IPPF funding comes from the U.S. Agency for International Development, as well as from contributions from the member organizations (the national family planning associations), the Ford and Rockefeller foundations, and the World Bank, among others. On the board sit representatives of DuPont Chemical, the Chemical Bank of New York, the U.S. Sugar Corporation, General Motors, the Chase Manhattan Bank, Newmont Mining, International Nickel, Marconi-R.C.A., Xerox, and Gulf Oil."[44] Thus, "[c]ontributions to I.P.P.F.'s [Planned Parenthood] budget, currently around $50 million a year, come from private citizens and foundations all over the world, as well as from governments."[45]

A major step in funding for the population control advocates came with the securing of government financial support. It came in 1966 when President Lyndon Johnson included a commitment to federal funding for birth control programs at home and abroad in his State of the Union message that year. He said: "Let us act on the fact that less than five dollars invested in population control is worth a hundred dollars invested in economic growth."[46] Consequently, in 1967, the provisions of the Social Security Act, which apply to the administration of Aid to Families with Dependent Children, were altered:

> [From 1967 on A.F.D.C. would] (1) require that at least 6% of all funds available for maternal and child care be earmarked for family planning; (2) direct all the states to offer family planning services to present, past and potential AFDC recipients in an effort to reduce illegitimate births and corral welfare expenses; (3) establish a ceiling over the proportion of children under 18 who could qualify for AFDC in any state; (4) authorize states to purchase family planning services from nongovernmental providers; (5) provide matching federal grants to the states for family planning.[47]

The extent of government commitment to lowering the birthrate of the poor (largely minorities) can be estimated from the fact that for each dollar the state governments pledged, the federal government was authorized to provide $9 in matching funds.

Also in 1967, Congress allocated $35 million for population assistance (with the funds earmarked for this sole purpose) to be administered by the United States Agency for International Development (A.I.D.). By 1973, the Office of Population of A.I.D. had $125 million to spend in a single year for population control. The 1981 budget for the Office of Population was $190 million, to be used to purchase "modern contraceptives for use in population programs in over 100 countries."[48]

THE WEDDING

The "wedding" of government and the population control planners has resulted in a massive effort at eliminating future people. It threatens to coerce the world to live according to the secularistic-materialistic standards of contemporary Western man. The birth control propaganda is couched in fictional, utopian terms, but because of the pain and the death that has followed, it has become a genocidal nightmare—a nightmare often financed by American taxpayers.

Thus, the objective of population control worldwide is obvious:

> [It is] to influence people not only to limit their families, for in that respect they may well have had little success, but to limit their families in the manner appropriate to Western culture: by government-subsidized IUDs, by chemical contraceptives, some of which were bought by government agencies from superseded stocks of the big drug houses, and by the Draconian methods of male and female sterilization. The emotion that was stirred in the West was fear; very little lasting good is done by people who are motivated by fear, especially if the fear is shipped into panic by constant assertions that time is running out.[49]

ELEVEN

DEATH
CONTROL

As mentioned, the basic goal of the population planners is fewer live births: the elimination of future people.

Birth control, then, becomes the primary method of doing away with future generations. In the modern age, however, birth control encompasses more than preventative methods of escaping parenthood. It now includes abortion, and for the "defectives," infanticide.

This is illustrated by an article that appeared in the *Village Voice* several years ago.[1] The article indicates that abortion has become fashionable in feminist circles as women are replacing "having" children with "having" abortions. The article quotes a study which found that only 6 percent of five hundred women who had received abortions had regularly been using birth control when they conceived. According to the author, it now appeared that many women were becoming pregnant without any intention of carrying the baby to term. This, of course, is just one of the tragic consequences of the easy availability of abortion.

More than anything, the *Village Voice* article illustrates the callousness of people today. With little concept of a future, and sold on the rhetoric of the population planners, a form of genocide is being carried out on both the born and unborn—a consequence of the overpopulation myth.

THE MYTH

Overpopulation is defined as the condition whereby the density of population has exceeded basic resources. In other words, overpopulation happens when a society has more mouths than food (see Chapter Ten).

Of course, there *are* hungry people in the world. There are people who work all hours of daylight and go to bed with empty stomachs, only to rise the next morning and go back to work with barely the strength to continue.

But is the world overpopulated? As stated in Chapter Ten, Thomas Malthus certainly thought so. However, he might have been appalled to realize that his views inspired the policy of withholding famine relief in India in 1870. In that year, the population of India was 290 million. The same country now supports 712 million people. In other words, the famine in India of 1870 was not caused by population outgrowing its resource base:

> Pressure on resources is constant; no matter how many people were sterilized by starvation during that famine, pressure on resources would have continued. Pressure on resources may even have been intensified by the loss of people to produce food, although, if famine followed the usual pattern, the people who died would have been the least productive—the children, the old, the artisans who depended upon surplus value, barkers, cobblers, and the like.[2]

Famine in India, then, was *not* caused by an absolute shortage of food, by failure of crops, or by an excess of mouths to feed. As history has shown numerous times, as long as famine is vivid in people's memories, they do not have unlimited children who scavenge for food or who may die. As Julian Simon documents in *The Ultimate Resource*, "Population size adjusts to productive conditions rather than being an uncontrolled monster."[3]

However, from the population planning rhetoric we are bombarded with, we are still inclined to believe that India is dying in and from its own sea of humanity. Certainly there *are* a lot of people in India. However, India just is not dying from overpopulation. If the religion of the Indian people would simply allow them to eat the animals that would sustain them, the food supply would certainly be enhanced. Thus, the country's "population explosion" is nothing more than mythical, as far as India's welfare is concerned.

There is also little truth to claims of overpopulation in Western countries. In fact, it is now estimated that the present fertility rate is far below what will be needed to replace existing populations in major Western nations. One researcher estimates that in 1976 the United States had only 81 percent of the number of births necessary for its population to remain at the present level.[4] And countries such as France, Germany, and Russia all see population decline as a major problem. We are in the midst of a worldwide decline in fertility rather than a population explosion. And there are two main reasons for this long-run decline in fertility.

First, as income rises in poor countries, child mortality falls because of improved nutrition, sanitation, and health care. This is true, as Simon notes, "though, in the twentieth century, mortality may decline in poor countries even without a rise in income."[5] As people see that fewer births are necessary to achieve a given family size, they adjust their practices of fertility. Thus, "childbearing is responsive to the family's circumstances."[6]

The rise in income also reduces fertility in the long-run through a cluster of forces. These include:

> (a) increased education, which improves contraception, makes children more expensive to raise, and perhaps alters people's taste about having children; and (b) a trend to city living, where children cost more and produce less income for the family than they do in the country.[7]

We have said that overpopulation is a myth, and we can also say that the increased number of people in the world has beneficial, not detrimental, effects. In the long run, *the most important economic effect of population size and growth is the contribution of additional people to mankind's stock of useful knowledge.* Accordingly, this contribution is large enough in the long run to overcome all the costs of population growth:

> It is a simple fact that the source of improvements in productivity is the human mind, and a human mind is seldom found apart from a human body. And because improvements—their invention and their adoption—come from people, it seems reasonable to assume that the amount of improvement depends on the number of people available to use their minds.[8]

This is an old idea, going back at least as far as William Petty in 1682:

> As for the Arts of Delight and Ornament, they are best promoted by the greatest number of emulators. And it is more likely that one ingenious curious man may rather be found

among 4 million than 400 persons. . . . And for the propagation
and improvement of useful learning, the same may be said concerning it as above-said concerning. . .the Arts of Delight and
Ornaments.[9]

In reality, population growth spurs the adoption of existing
technology as well as the invention of new technology. Thus, resources increase in a real way as there is an increase in creative
people. Simon notes that this has been well documented in agriculture, where people turn successively to more advanced but
"more laborious methods of getting food as population density
increases—methods that were previously known but that were
not used because they were not needed earlier."[10]

Moreover, as has been previously supposed and disseminated
by antinatal propaganda, population growth is not detrimental to
energy use; it does not use up the available land; it has
unimportant effects on pollution levels; and, it is not dangerous
to physical or mental health. These facts are all documented by
Julian Simon in his book *The Ultimate Resource.*[11]

Despite evidence to the contrary, however, the overpopulation and limited resource myth continues to pervade the
thinking of many. Much of it has to do with the well-financed
propaganda effects of the population planners and the use of effective rhetorical devices. Antinatalists make it seem, for example, that all experts agree that population is growing too fast in
the United States and other countries, and, therefore, it is considered a *fact* that population is growing too fast. Fear of population growth is certainly heightened by the linking of population
and pollution issues and the alleged scarcity of natural resources.
With such views receiving a general audience through the ever-
hysterical media, it is little wonder that we live in a world poised
to kill both its unborn and born.

One other motivating factor undergirding the entire eugenics-
population control matrix is *racism.* "The eugenics package had
always," writes Germaine Greer, "included racism of the most
egregious kind."[12]

When, for example, the United States was drawn into war
against Germany, eugenicists like Leon F. Whitney had cause to
be embarrassed about statements such as the following:

We cannot but admire the foresight of the [German] plan [of
sterilizing 400,000 people] and realize by this action Germany

is going to make herself a stronger nation. American Jewry is naturally suspecting that the German chancellor has had the law enacted for the specific purpose but I believe nothing to be further from the truth.[13]

However, as minorities became more vocal, the old arguments about the deleterious effects of intermarriage, the absolute necessity of limiting immigration, and the origins of the different "races" of man fell into disuse. But the racist element of the population control movement still remained (although it was more subtly portrayed).

For example, Moya Woodside, in her work *Sterilization in North Carolina: A Sociological and Psychological Study,*[14] in 1950, carefully noted the higher birthrate of blacks and alleged high illegitimacy rate and mental deficiency in the United States: "It is certainly true that the feeble-minded Negro woman, often with illegitimate children, is a familiar and recurrent problem to health and welfare agencies."[15]

As a consequence of such thinking, blacks have been the target of sterilization. One example is, again, North Carolina:

> From July 1933 to June 1947, 1,851 "eugenic" sterilizations were performed in North Carolina—407 men and boys, 1,444 females; more than half the females, 770, were under twenty years of age, 169 of the males. Although only 27.5 percent of the state's population was black, and despite the fact that the Negro hospital at Goldsboro took no part in the sterilization program, as many black men were sterilized, both by vasectomy and by castration, as white.[16]

"There is plenty of anecdotal evidence," Julian Simon writes, "that racism has been a key motivation in domestic and international population activities."[17] Solid evidence of this can be found in data showing that the opening of state-supported birth control clinics is closely related to the concentrations of poor black people in various states. This is at least partially documented by Simon:

> As of 1965, 79 percent of the state-supported clinics in the U.S. were in the ten states of Alabama, Arkansas, Florida, Georgia, Kentucky, Mississippi, North Carolina, South Carolina, Tennessee, and Virginia, which have only 19 percent of the country's population. Analysis that holds per capita income

constant shows that the proportion of blacks in a local population is closely related to the density of family-planning
clinics.[18]

There is also evidence that the same racist motive also lies behind much of the proabortion movement. At least the effects appear to be racist, as Professor Gordon Zahn of the University of
Massachusetts writes:

> The crudest efforts at a pragmatic justification of abortion,
> however, are the dollars-and-cents calculations that have
> emerged from the political controversy about public funding of
> abortions for the poor.... Such reasoning lends support to a
> brochure published by a radical group calling itself "Hammer
> and Steel Community" in which they denounced the pro-
> abortion movement as "the billionaire's baby." One need not
> accept the full thrust of their charge that the pro-abortion
> movement represents *a deliberate program to eliminate the minor-
> ity poor,* a genteel form of genocide, but it would be naive to ig-
> nore the implications of *selective eugenics* inherent in any
> proposals of publicly funded abortions for the poor and other-
> wise disadvantaged.[19]

Of course, a large portion of the poor are minorities. This is especially true in the large urban areas. As such, one writer, a social
worker, notes: "Black women are being aborted at a rate of 2.5
times greater than any other ethnic group in New York City."[20]
Moreover, one California abortionist (and an owner of twelve
abortion clinics) has said:

> *Population control* is too important to be stopped by some right-
> wing pro-life types.... The Aid to Families with Dependent
> Children program is the worst boondoggle ever created. When
> a sullen black woman of 17 or 18 can decide to have a baby and
> get welfare and food stamps and become a burden to all of us,
> it's time to stop.[21]

At this juncture, population control, abortion, and racism become one and the same. It becomes Caucasian elitism. Patrick
Monaghan, writing in the *Lincoln Review,* concludes:

> Different veneers are paraded out—privacy, child abuse, the
> unwanted child, "back alley butchers," population control
> and welfare costs—all in an attempt to obscure or rationalize
> the true goal of those who have adopted the abortion mentality;

that being an elite-oriented attempt to judicially slaughter the poverty class, particularly the black portion of it.[22]

This elitist position, mixed with a drab callousness, has been propounded by several members of the United States Supreme Court. The dangers of the "unwanted" child and child abuse, with a racial twist to justify abortion, have been put forth by none other than black Justice Thurgood Marshall. In *Beal v. Doe*, for example, Marshall indicated that the "unwanted minority and mixed race children now spend blighted lives," and "absent day care facilities" they force their mothers "into full time child care."[23]

In their book *The Brethren*, Bob Woodward and Scott Armstrong present a portrait of a callous and cavalier Marshall who was quick to treat antiabortionist voices with cynicism and disdain. Jay Floyd, assistant attorney general of Texas, presented his state's case against legalizing abortion amid Marshall's callousness.

> "When, [Marshall] inquired, does an unborn fetus come to have full constitutional rights?"
> "At any time, Mr. Justice; we make no distinction. . ." Floyd replied. "There is life from the moment of impregnation."
> "And do you have any scientific data to support that?" Marshall asked.
> "Well, we begin, Mr. Justice, in our brief, with the development of the human embryo, carrying it through to the development of the fetus, from about seven to nine days after conception," Floyd answered.
> "Well, what about six days?" Marshall asked, eliciting a mild chuckle from the audience.
> "We don't know," Floyd acknowledged.
> "But this statute goes all the way back to one hour," Marshall said, clearly enjoying himself.
> "I don't—Mr. Justice, it—there are unanswerable questions in this field, I—" Floyd, flustered, was interrupted by laughter around him.
> "I appreciate it, I appreciate it," Marshall chanted, leaning back in exaggerated satisfaction with Floyd's befuddlement.[24]

In less cynical tones, Justice Harry Blackmun, in his defense of abortion, openly stated that there should be a proabortion policy because of "the welfare costs that will burden the state for the new indigents and their support in the long, long years ahead."[25] If this policy is not forthcoming in even greater proportions than it is now, Blackmun states, *"The cancer of poverty will continue to grow."*[26] Thus, in the eyes of Justice Blackmun, abortion is a form of population control for the poor.

A PARALLEL

The obvious historical parallel here is Nazi Germany,[27] where Hitler and his aides practiced what the neo-Malthusians were preaching. The Nazis set out to create a master race from "good" stocks, which meant eliminating the weak and disadvantaged. As a consequence, the furnaces burned hot throughout Germany.

Particularly troubling, however, was the silence of the German church in light of the atrocities that were occurring before its eyes. The Nazis noticed early on that the churches had taken a weak stand, one which ignored the human rights of all Jews, and focused instead on the expedient and self-serving concern for "Christian Jews." The church, by its lack of political involvement, was eventually neutralized by the inhumane culture which surrounded it.

Sadly, a similar thing has happened to many churches today, and to some leading voices of Christianity in the United States. It is coming through the advocation of therapeutic abortion or what can properly be called the elimination of the "unfit"—a form of eugenics.

There are various examples of this. One is found in Carl F. H. Henry's *The Christian Mindset in a Secular Society.*[28] He writes:

> When childbirth would endanger the mother's life abortion can be morally justifiable. The fetus seems less than human, moreover, in cases of extreme deformity in which rational and moral capacities integral to the *imago Dei* are clearly lacking. The scriptural correlation of sexual intercourse with marriage and the family, furthermore, implies an ethical basis for voluntary abortion in cases of incest and rape. But the ready sacrifice of fetal life as a means of sexual gratification and of birth control is monstrous.[29]

Moreover, Gareth Jones in *Brave New People,*[30] a book that was endorsed by a number of leading evangelicals, states:

> We are left with a twofold perspective; our view of the fetus should be a high one, but it should not be an absolute one. The

fetus, being weak and defenseless, should receive considerable protection, but that is not the same as guaranteeing absolute protection. . . .

Nevertheless, there may be situations in which abortion is the regrettable, and perhaps undesirable, solution to human problems. . . .

There are sometimes family situations where inadequacy, marital breakdown, financial stringency, unemployment and a host of other adverse social conditions could lead to the conclusion that abortion of an unwanted pregnancy, or of a pregnancy with a dubious outcome, is the least tragic of a number of tragic options. . . .

These are not easy issues, and I cannot believe there are easy answers to them. Fetal preservation is generally the course of choice in Christian terms, and yet the welfare of the subsequent handicapped child and the surrounding family also needs to be taken into account. This, too, is a part of Christian holism.

I sympathize with both objections, since both point very clearly towards the ideal for Christians. Nevertheless a compromise is sometimes called for, whether this be a reluctant abortion, institutional care for the child, or adoption. Although the latter may signify the preference of many Christians, it may not be acceptable for the mother or family. . . .

To destroy a fetus because its quality of life is substandard is to violate God's care for the handicapped and downtrodden. When the fetus is viewed in isolation, therefore, these are critical guideposts for Christian thinking. However, when fetal considerations have to be weighed against the type of family considerations I have outlined previously, the course of action is not always clear cut. Appalling dilemmas do occur, and appalling dilemmas sometimes have to be faced. My argument has been that some of these appalling dilemmas may be resolved only by therapeutic abortion. . . .

The condemnation of all abortion under all circumstances is an attractively simple solution to the evils connected with easy abortion.[31]

The thesis of these two works is the same: that is, we should oppose abortion except in "certain" circumstances. For Jones, this means aborting the unborn child if the mother's (or the family's) *mental health* would be damaged by having to care for an unwanted or deformed child.

This view is, of course, a marked departure from the "traditional" views on abortion as held by the early church. Such views focused entirely upon the fetus. The most distinctive feature of early Christian rejection of abortion is its placing the well-being of the unborn child at the center of the issue. Christians discarded all pagan definitions of the unborn child as merely part of the mother's body. To Christians, the unborn child was an independent living being.[32]

Henry is closer to this traditional view. However, he says that the unborn child "seems less than human" when it appears to be deformed. Henry's *caveat* on "sexual gratification and birth control" is of little consequence when one has already opened the door to the killing of *any* human life.

Such reasoning can have grave implications. For example, what does the term "deformity" really mean? Could some take it to mean a child who is not of the same genetic heritage as the master race? Is a black child, in the racist's mind, a deformed child? This question is increasingly important, since a large portion of abortions are performed on minorities by white doctors.

To argue for selective, therapeutic abortion opens the door for the killing of *all* human life. What is to stop the abortionist from killing a *born* child who is "extremely deformed" since he or she is "less than human"? Infanticide is the next logical step.

COERCION

The overpopulation myth has sunk so deep into the popular consciousness that even among Christians we find the use of the phrase "population explosion." In *The Living Bible*, for instance, in discussing the story of Noah, we read in Genesis 6:1: "Now a population explosion took place upon the earth."

Another example is Ronald Sider's *Rich Christians in an Age of Hunger*.[33] In this book Sider embraces population control:

> To make sure that food aid does not encourage countries to postpone hard political decisions on necessary agricultural reforms, especially land redistribution and *population control programs*, the United States and Canada should announce that food aid will go only to the countries which are implementing the internationally agreed upon World Plan of Action drawn up at the U.N.'s Population Conference (Bucharest 1974) and the U.S.'s World Food Conference (Rome 1974).[34]

This statement seems to make clear that Sider, in order to make sure countries institute population control programs, would withdraw food aid from nations that refuse to take such "necessary" measures. "In other words," as Franky Schaeffer and Harold Fickett write, "to accomplish his ends, he [Sider] is willing to see these countries starve."[35]

A striking element in the population-control mentality is *coercion*. If people fail to keep their offspring in check, then they should be coerced into doing so.

Thus, we find the likes of demographer Kingsley Davis, who writes: "In subsequent history the Twentieth Century may be called either the century of world wars or the century of the population plague."[36] How to deal with this "plague"? Kingsley responds: "Over-reproduction—that is, *the bearing of more than four children*—is a worse crime than most and *should be outlawed*."[37] Paul Erlich adds: "We can no longer afford merely to treat the symptoms of the cancer of population growth; *the cancer itself must be cut out*."[38]

Limiting offspring, however, will come only by coercion. It is inevitable. In fact, coercion has been proposed by members of the scientific elite. Consider, for example, the words of Francis Crick:

> [D]o people have the right to have children at all?... In terms of humanist ethics I do not see that people should have the right to have children.... If one did have a licensing scheme, the first child might be admitted on rather easy terms. If the parents were genetically unfavorable, they might be allowed to have only one child or possibly two under special circumstances.[39]

Logically, such coercive population control can be carried forth only by government (but in conjunction with population control organizations). And there are examples of coercion by authoritarian states that illustrate how mandatory birth control is carried forth. Two examples are India and China.

INDIA

India has been a guinea pig for the population planners. As Donald Warwick points out:

> India has been the proving ground for birth control. Almost every policy innovation, from incentives to workers on tea-estates to sterilization booths in railway stations, has been tried, applauded and abandoned. The country has alternately been the darling and the downfall of the donors, a prototype to be emulated and an anti-type to be shunned.... Yet despite

the enormous investment in birth control and the myriad policy experiments, family planning has not caught on in India.[40]

Family planning agencies found in India that they had to create awareness for the need of population control by changing cultural priorities. They had to turn, as it were, a population with a spending power of nil into materialists who see nothing to like or desire in children. Planned Parenthood has acted similarly in this country.

The Family Planning Association of India (FPAI) is the major recipient of financial support from International Planned Parenthood: the projected grant for 1982 was $2,782,600.[41] The FPAI has one major advantage over many of the other organizations working to reduce India's rate of population growth—it is Indian. The FPAI, while being Indian, is to some extent independent of the government of India and its policies.

The first international attempt at organized family planning in India was the ill-conceived "Khanna" experiment, instituted by Harvard University, the United States Public Health Service, and the Population Council; it also had the cooperation of the government of India, the Christian Medical College of Ludhiana, and the Indian Council of Medical Research. The objectives were:

> To determine if the rural couples in India could practice a single contraceptive method effectively enough to reduce significantly the growth rate of the population, and to evaluate factors affecting fertility. The targets were to increase acceptance and the effectiveness of contraceptives in order to reduce the birth rate from 40 to 35 births a year per thousand population.[42]

India, with its legacy of intercommunal violence and civil disobedience, was not well-adapted to pioneering mass birth control projects. This was true even if the lifestyle of its peoples, nearly all of whom lived without bathrooms and running water, had been adapted to caps, foams, jellies, insufflators, douches, and other instruments of contraception. Still, pressure for a commitment to family planning began to build within Nehru's government.

In 1959, the government of India initiated a scheme of recruiting canvassers to motivate vasectomy acceptors in Madras State.

The canvassers would receive ten rupees for each client produced. The system was highly criticized. Halfway through the scheme, the incentive payments were discontinued and the number of acceptors fell. The government, however, now knew what was the most cost-effective way of averting births. As Germaine Greer notes: "Madras was the pretest for the great push of 1975-77. The greatest problem. . .was. . .the fact that the poor did not wish to limit their families. At best, parents were ambivalent."[43]

By 1967, the United States Agency for International Development (AID) financed a pilot project involving the distribution in each Indian state of five to ten thousand cycles of a steroid contraceptive pill containing 1 mg of ethynodiol diacetate. "The dose seems extremely high for women of low body weight; the timing might indicate an unexpected source of discontinued high-dosage pills. By some such means the oral contraceptive was discredited in India."[44]

The intensified antinatal propaganda campaigns of the 1960s gradually produced more acceptors, but India's birthrate continued to climb. In 1965, the government of India set aside sixty-five million rupees for family planning; in 1966 it rose to a hundred and twenty million. Under the fourth five-year plan, the annual expenditure on family planning was to be about six hundred million rupees, but the population still continued to increase.[45] As Greer explains:

> The stepped-up program was based on eight components: the extension of voluntary fertility control services; the establishment of "involuntary" (populationese for "forced") fertility control; intensified educational (ditto for "propaganda") campaigns; incentive programs; tax and welfare benefits and penalties; changes of orientation in social and economic institutions; use of political channels and organizations in recruiting, with augmentation of research efforts trailing the field. The climate of liberal opinion was changing under the barrage of population panic propaganda that continued to assail it.[46]

AID, using American tax money, was also a major contributor to the Indian program. John Lewis, head of the Indian office of AID, announced that he "would press [population] funds on the Indian government whether it want[ed] them or not."[47]

Lewis's call for a policy change was not to be ignored. Some of the 3,788 million rupees for AID was earmarked for sterilization camps[48] in a country generally opposed to birth control:

> Family planning workers in countries like India know only too well that they must overcome the defensiveness of the people they are trying to help by showing that they can help and that they will help where they can. . . . It takes the refined brutality of Western aid to shove expensive contraceptive technology into a village whose people would feel a good deal better and produce more food and get more done generally if a few pence were spent on eradicating the parasites which infest them.[49]

What stimulated confidence that there was a right way of doing mass sterilizations was the success of camps in the Ernakulam district of Kerala in 1970 and 1971. The district was divided into units, and a list drawn up of eligible men in each unit, which was assigned its own day to be visited during each month-long camp. "An intensive publicity and education campaign was mounted in the unit, peaking on the eve of sterilization day, when the villagers went off to glory."[50]

Unfortunately not all the doctors were experts, "nor were the sanitary facilities adequate for those who had to wait, nor [was] walking all the way home very good for weakened scrota." Still, 15,005 vasectomies "were performed under these conditions and on men who averaged almost forty years in age."[51]

The next year another push was mounted, this time during the monsoon season, and 62,913 vasectomies and 505 "tubectomies" were performed. Camps were held in seven sub-districts, and the sterilizations continued:

> Meanwhile the much larger state of Gujurat, with 27 million people, was out to steal Kerala's thunder by performing 150,000 vasectomies in a thousand small camps around the state. Targets had been fixed for all the states of the union and sterilizations were available free in all public health facilities. . . . The cost per sterilization was rising steeply; the showy camps with their carnival atmosphere, their free food and entertainment, and the saturation propaganda campaign could not be indefinitely continued. Only one aspect of the psychology of the situation proved durable: in Gujurat the newspapers had published a scoreboard to show which districts were leading in the motivation race; family planning became a sport.[52]

With the influx of bureaucrats devoted to "democratic socialism," the push for population control became even more intense.[53]

At the same time, ill effects of the vasectomies were being discovered as one quarter of the men sterilized in Madurai reported adverse reactions to the operation. In Ramanathapuram, in the Madurai district, the effects of the program were still being felt in 1979.

The innovators of family planning from this village happen to be three vasectomized persons. Among them one suffered a swollen scrotum, weakness of body, and difficulty to walk long distances, besides a lowered capacity for hard manual work. According to Germaine Greer, this adverse experience of the vasectomy acceptor early in the program period in this village led to vasectomy becoming unpopular even to this day, to the extent that for about three years after the three persons underwent vasectomy no one from the village came forward to adopt a family planning method.[54]

Within months of the central government's discontinuation of the high-incentive sterilization camps, private enterprise and state governments stepped in suddenly. In December 1974, a camp run by the Corporation of Madras, in conjunction with the Rotary Club, carried out 2,006 sterilization operations in two weeks. Acceptors were given six days paid leave and gifts of cloth.[55]

Then, by April of 1975, sterilization mania was at its height:

> The next number of *Centre Calling* announced that "Three states—Haryana, Gujarat and Maharashtra—are running a neck and neck race to turn out the best performances of the year.".... In a camp at Mehsana in Gujarat, more than five hundred sterilization acceptors had registered on the first day.... All teachers in government schools had to provide six sterilizations a year, as did panchayat employees, village-level workers, district inspectors, extension officers and supply inspectors. Other public employees had to motivate twice as many. All government employees were to be given privileges such as travel passes, educational allowances and reimbursements of medical expenses for no more than three children, and all candidates for government jobs had to sign an undertaking to accept sterilization after two children or guarantee cessation of childbearing by some other means.[56]

In June of the same year the Indian Supreme Court declared Indira Gandhi's election invalid. Instead of stepping down, however, she invoked extraconstitutional powers by declaring a state of emergency, which provided for the suspension of civil liberties and the detention of subversive elements. The tempo of the population control program quickened in the wake of Gandhi's actions, and soon the 1975-76 population control targets were published:

There were to be 2,521,000 sterilizations, 904,400 IUD insertions and 4,086,100 new users of contraception. Maharashtra revised its 318,300 sterilization quota upward to 568,000 and achieved 611,000. Assam more than doubled its quota. All exceeded their quotas. . . . Among the sixteen measures to be taken were the providing of group incentives to popular institutions. The new sterilization targets were nearly twice those of the preceding year, but even so, many states revised them upwards. Andhra Pradesh, for example, which had managed little more than half its 1975-76 quota of 294,200 sterilizations, not only accepted a 1976-77 quota of 400,000 but raised it to 600,000 and actually carried out 741,713. Family Planning was the first point of Sanjay Gandhi's Five-Point Program, officially adopted along with his mother's Twenty-Point Economic Program. *By some mechanism the state authorities turned the 4,255,500 sterilizations demanded by the central government into 8,132,209.* [57]

Death and pain followed in the subsequent frenzy:

In Rajasthan, with only 364,760 sterilizations, 217 people died. Throughout the country, 1,774 people died as a direct consequence of the operation. . . . In Andhra Pradesh, no fewer than 21,563 sterilized men had fewer than two children; in Orissa, 19,237; in Punjab, 19,838; in Gujurat, 7,834. In Maharashtra, 151 died, 6,958 had fewer than two children, 368 were over fifty-five; in Barsi and Sholapur, two lepers were forcibly sterilized, and eight men were operated on for the second time. . . . [I]n Haryana, "Buses were diverted to camps and passengers sterilized. Persons were forcibly taken from villages, bus stands and railway stations for sterilizations, to family planning camps." With only 222,000 sterilizations, the Haryana death rate of 132 is one of the highest; the proportion of unmarried (105) and elderly (179) men sterilized is probably the highest for any state. [58]

Early in the morning of November 6, 1976, the village of Uttawar in the Gurgaon district of Haryana was raided by seven hundred police, who rounded up five hundred and fifty men and took them away. The village, inhabited by eight thousand Muslims of the Meo community, had refused to allow any family planning worker to enter:

> The inspector general of police who authorized the raid claimed that it was necessary as a security measure, the villagers being suspected of maintaining links with Pakistan, but in fact he had been informed of the attitude of the villagers to sterilization and that men rounded up would be taken for forcible sterilization. The villagers were taken to Hathin for interrogation; a hundred of them were imprisoned for assaulting a patwari, and one hundred eighty were sent to family planning centers at Nuh and Mandkola, where they were sterilized.[59]

Finally, at the height of sterilization euphoria, Tara Ali Baig, chairperson of the Indian Council of Child Welfare, wrote an article entitled "Prevention Is Better Than Care." She proceeded to vent convictions which should have been discredited forty years earlier:

[handwritten: same rhetoric]

> Sterilization of one partner has to be made imperative where a man or woman suffers from hereditary insanity, feeble-mindedness or congenital venereal disease: *they must be barred by law from procreating children.* This should have been done decades ago.
>
> If children's lives and future are to be protected, compulsory sterilization is necessary for many reasons.... *After all, considering the crime against children committed by irresponsible parenthood, compulsory sterilization of the unfit is long overdue.*[60]

CHINA

Turning now to the forced sterilizations happening in China, we note that since 1979, the Communist government of China has enforced a policy limiting most Chinese couples to one child. The program is designed to cap the population at 1.2 billion by the year 2000 and to whittle it down further in the next century.

The International Planned Parenthood Federation book, *Human Numbers, Human Needs* (published in late 1984), praises the Chinese model of birth control:

> [China has] the most remarkable of all family planning poli-
> cies.... Chinese parents are told that if action had been taken
> sooner it would have been acceptable for them to have had two
> children—the need for the one-child limit is, it is stressed, the
> price of delay.[61]

Slashing through China's traditional family-oriented society,
this "most remarkable of all family planning policies" has
aroused strong public resistance, especially in rural areas where
peasants counter birth control with subterfuge, occasional violence, and female infanticide. Chinese parents have allowed female babies to die in order to have a male son as the single child.[62]

Moreover, the success of China's efforts at population control
comes out of widespread coercion, wanton abortion, and intru-
sion by the state into the most intimate of human affairs. "The
size of a family is too important to be left to the personal decision
of a couple," Minister of Family Planning Qian Xinzhong explained before resigning last year.[63]

Loosely enforced at first, the policy was tightened in 1982
after population growth rates began to climb. Since then, the
state has strictly required intrauterine devices for all women with
one child and sterilizations for one member of every couple with
two or more children. Such measures are credited officially with
preventing millions of births a year. For all of its statistical gains,
however, the one-child policy is piling up heavy costs in broken
lives and is tearing at the fabric of Chinese society.

China is a society dominated by poor farming families who live
off the land and strive for big families as a matter of economic necessity. The more children, the more hands to till the soil. Birth
control is a threat, and many such families counter by hiding
pregnant women, removing intrauterine devices, falsifying sterilization certificates, and even by physically attacking public
officials.

Every year, millions of Chinese defy authority and have more
children, despite heavy fines, dismissal from jobs, and loss of
farmland, housing, and economic benefits that leave them farther behind in China's march to "modernization." Yet at least
one-quarter of fifteen million to twenty million babies born in
China every year are *unapproved.*[64]

Faced with such resistance, the Chinese government has resorted to even stronger measures. As *Washington Post* reporter
Michael Weisskopf writes:

What emerges from more than 200 interviews spaced over three years with officials, doctors, peasants and workers in almost two-thirds of China's 29 local jurisdictions is the story of an all-out government siege against ancient family traditions and the reproductive habits of a billion people.

The story offers a glimpse of China usually hidden from foreigners but painfully familiar to most Chinese—a world of government-sanctioned infanticide, of strong-arm sterilizations and of abortions performed at a rate as high as 800,000 a year in a single province.[65]

Nowhere is this dark side of "family planning" more evident than in Dongguan, a town in the Guangdong Province in southern China. Here, abortion "posses" scoured the countryside in the spring of 1981, rounding up women in rice paddies and thatched-roof houses. "Expectant mothers, including many in their last trimester, were trussed, handcuffed, herded into hog cages and delivered by the truckload to the operating tables of rural clinics, according to eyewitness accounts."[66]

Dongguan had been engulfed by an intense birth control campaign, known as "high tide," engineered by local officials to bring birth control offenders in line with the one-child policy. In fifty days, nineteen thousand abortions were performed—almost as many as the county's live births in all of 1981.[67] "Dongguan's 'high tide,'" writes Weisskopf, "dramatizes the least cited but *most frequently observed form of birth control in China: abortion.*"[68]

Any mother who becomes pregnant without receiving official authorization, after having one child, is *required* to have an abortion. The incidence of such operations is stunning—*fifty-three million from 1979 to 1984,* according to the Ministry of Public Health—and a five-year abortion count equals approximately the population of France.[69] "In 1983 alone, the number of abortions nationwide—14.4 million—exceeded the combined populations of the District of Columbia, Maryland, Virginia, West Virginia and Delaware."[70]

The timing of abortions performed is usually not of great concern to Chinese officials. *Many are performed in the last trimester of pregnancy,* and some happen as late as in the ninth month. "Officials say it often takes that long to get reluctant women to clinics."[71]

Doctors normally terminate late-term pregnancies by injecting an herbal drug into the womb, killing the unborn child and inducing labor—a kind of induced stillbirth. The dead child usually is expelled in twenty-four hours.

There are also cases of infanticide:

> In the Inner Mongolian capital of Hohhot...hospital doctors practice what amounts to infanticide by a different name, according to a Hohhot surgeon, who would not allow his name to be used for fear of reprisal. After inducing labor, he revealed, doctors routinely smash the baby's skull with forceps as it emerges from the womb.
>
> In some cases, he added, newborns are killed by injecting formaldehyde into the soft spot of the head.
>
> "If you kill the baby while it's still partly in the womb, it's considered an abortion," explained the 33-year-old surgeon. "If you do it after birth, it's murder."[72]

The primary target of the Chinese family planners is, however, couples who already have two or more children. One parent is required by the state to undergo *sterilization*, and local officials use incentives ranging from cash rewards to coercion to get those eligible to the operating table. *Almost always the woman bears the responsibility.* Weisskopf writes:

> Official statistics show a high level of success: 31 million women and 9.3 million men were sterilized between 1979 and 1984, totalling almost one-third of all married, productive couples in China.
>
> A national sterilization drive last winter boosted annual sterilizations for 1983 to an extraordinary 16.4 million for women and 4.4 million for men, according to the Public Health Ministry—exceeding the total number of such procedures in the previous five years.[73]

The planners even exercise coercion at places of employment. Many factories post on blackboards each female worker's contraceptive measure and the day her period arrives. The women are required to place a check mark next to their names after menstruation begins each month. If she fails to report on schedule, her boss is consulted, and she is then ordered to take a pregnancy test.

A positive test spells trouble for any woman who already has a child. If she does not immediately respond to rewards for terminating her pregnancy, state-induced force often prevails:

Sometimes, officials use collective coercion in operations like that in Dongguan, where thousands of pregnant women were picked up in trucks and Jeeps, taken to commune headquarters for lectures, then driven to abortion clinics, some reportedly under police escort, in what was later described by local eyewitnesses as a "slaughter movement."[74]

It should be evident that a form of *mass genocide is occurring in Southeast Asia.* Even Vietnam has, as of 1984, instituted a "family planning" policy similar to that of China.[75]

And as dictators throughout history have used war or rumors of war to distract attention from the state's domestic failures, Socialist and Communist nations of the world have embraced a baseless war on "excessive population." They have blamed "overpopulation" for their economic problems when, in fact, these problems stem from unworkable centralized economics and other Communist and Socialist inequities.

From the misguided population theories of Thomas Malthus, to the eugenics movement, to the overpopulation myth, the world has come a long way. The conditioners have in many respects triumphed in eradicating future people.

The propaganda has worked, and this is evidenced from the fact that *sterilization* is now the leading form of birth control, even in the United States. This fact was recently confirmed by a survey conducted by the National Center for Health Statistics. As the *Washington Post* reports:

"Contraceptive practice has changed dramatically in the U.S. since 1965, with the rise and subsequent decline of the pill and the rise of male and especially female sterilization," the survey said.

In 1965, the four most popular types of contraception were the pill, condom, rhythm, diaphragm. By 1982, the leading methods were female sterilization, the pill, male sterilization and the condom.

Surgical sterilization is now the leading contraceptive method, employed by 33 percent of couples using birth control in 1982. Twenty-two percent chose female sterilization, and 11 percent chose male sterilization.[76]

Therefore, while a large portion of the world is being forcibly sterilized and having their children torn from their wombs, Americans are voluntarily ending their reproductive futures.

Ironically, it is occurring in a nation of vast resources and land which, by any standard, is not overpopulated.

DEATH CONTROL

Finally, no other generation in history has ever achieved the level of *death control* that the present generation has. As Alva Myrdal pointed out in 1941:

> This present generation of productive age groups will go down in history as the most ravenous of all. It has increased its spending power per consumption unit by not bearing enough children to replace itself, and at the same time by self-insurance and social legislation it has usurped legal rights to a labor-free income in old age. The annuities then to be paid must as always be paid out of the income of the productive people, of which the consuming old will not have supplied a sufficient number.... That is the interpretation in human terms of the abstract fact that a temporarily increased level of living can be gained by individual families at the turning point from progressive to regressive population trends.[77]

Myrdal notes the burden of the aged as it is expressed, for example, in taxation. This and other increased expenses in order for society to care for its large aged population makes it more and more difficult for the young to reverse the trend and return to producing children along with everything else. The zero population growth is evidence of this.

Our modern low-mortality society, with its decreasing birthrate, supports few children as each person in the labor force has a great many aged to support. For example, "in 1900 in the U.S., 4.1 percent of the population was over 65. But extrapolations suggest that 11.7 percent of the population will be over 65 in 2000, and 16.1 percent in the year 2050."[78] Julian Simon comments:

> The cost of supporting a retired person is much greater than the cost of supporting a child in the U.S. Least important in a society such as ours is the difference in food consumption. Consider: Old people may travel for twelve months a year in trailers on public roads, whereas children cannot. And old people need much more expensive health care than do children. Except for schooling, old people consume much more than do children in almost every category of expensive goods and services.

This pattern of old-age dependency is already causing per-turbations in the U.S. Social Security program. In the future, the burden of Social Security payments will take up a much larger proportion of a U.S. worker's pay, and of the production of the economy as a whole, even without increases in the level of payments. In fact, the Social Security system is already in se-vere funding trouble as of 1980, and financing the payments is a serious economic and political problem for the federal government.[79]

Aged nations, wedded to their own comfort and fearful of change, tend to commit suicide. This may be particularly true of the entire Caucasian elite of the West. "Such has been the fate of practically every elite [group] that has ever existed; as its de-mands upon the environment have mounted, its viability has been threatened until it has been swept aside by tougher and more dynamic people," writes Germaine Greer.[80]

Such "gerontacracies" invariably take steps to preserve their supremacy. They become more authoritarian, secretive, and mil-itaristic. This is tellingly illustrated by the aged leadership of both the United States and the Soviet Union. We must not forget that it is the young who fight and die in wars.

However, as it becomes readily apparent that the aged are a "burden," we must be concerned with how modern secularistic society will react. Will a society which has assumed the right to kill infants also assume the right to kill older adults who are judged a social nuisance? In *Whatever Happened to the Human Race?* Francis A. Schaeffer and C. Everett Koop write:

> The next candidates for arbitrary reclassification as non-persons are the elderly. This will become increasingly so as the proportion of the old and weak in relation to the young and strong becomes abnormally large, due to the growing anti-family sentiment, the abortion rate, and medicine's contribu-tion to the lengthening of the normal life span. The imbalance will cause many of the young to perceive the old as a cramping nuisance in the hedonistic life-style they claim as their right. As the demand for affluence continues and the economic crunch gets greater, the amount of compassion that the legislature and the courts will have for the old does not seem likely to be signif-icant considering the precedent of the non-protection given to the unborn and newborn.[81]

If one is predisposed to consider forced killing of the aged ("euthanasia") as a foolish assumption, we must remember the malleability of modern American society. For example, a recent poll indicated that many Americans are now ready for forced birth control:

> Q.   The population crisis is becoming so severe that people will have to be limited on the number of children they can have.
>
> A.   Agree   47%
>   Disagree   41%[82]

We even find such distinguished and usually sound thinkers as Julian Simon saying: "Though I would vote against any overall U.S. policy that would coerce people not to have children—including taxes on children greater than social cost of the children—I do accord to a community the right to make such a decision if there is a consensus on the matter."[83] Such thinking can apply also to abortion, infanticide, and euthanasia. No society has a right, under constitutional or natural law, to end people (or what society might term "surplus potential humans").[84]

As human beings, we must realize we have no right to tell other people how to live. We have no right to propagandize and manipulate populations.

However, we do have the duty to love our fellowmen and women by respecting their worth and dignity. Unless this duty prevails, the logics of death control will mean the end of man.

PART FOUR

MAN
AND
THE STATE

If you want a picture of the future, imagine a boot stamping on a human face—forever.

George Orwell
Nineteen Eighty-Four

TWELVE

FRIENDLY FASCISM

One essential fact must be taken into consideration if one is to understand modern society. The fact is the growth of the state and its dominance in the modern world. Jacques Ellul explains:

> Government action is applied to a constantly growing number of realms. The means through which the state can act are constantly growing. Its personnel and its functions are constantly growing. Its responsibilities are growing. All this goes hand in hand with the total organization of society in the hands of the state.[1]

Indeed, "today the major social phenomenon is the state."[2]

Increasingly in the twentieth century, as Paul Johnson aptly documents in *Modern Times*,[3] men have been seeking order in the state. Although some states profess an intention to serve people, seldom has this been the result of civil government. To the contrary, power has tended to corrupt those who grasp its reins.

During the past half-century, the world has witnessed the rapid rise of totalitarian states with their controlled, monolithic societies. Even in the "free" West we have seen diversity exchanged for an apathetic monolithic sameness.

Ellul correctly recognizes that the growth and power of the state is the most significant political development of this century. It is borne out by the facts. For example, by 1950, what has commonly been called the "free world" had shrunk from over 90 to less than 70 percent of the world's population. By 1980, the number of Communist regimes had reached twenty-five, almost twice the total that existed in 1950. Before the year 2000—if current trends continue—the ratio between "free" and communist may well shrink from 65:35 to 50:50. The implications of such a shift are enormous.[4]

The world is moving inexorably toward statism—that is, government seen as a total, final solution to man's problems. Even our own governmental systems are being affected. Ideas do have consequences, and some of those consequences are just now emerging.

FASCISM WITH A SMILE

What we see in the Soviet Union today is the prototype for the general development of the state in our modern world, with its attendant growth and structure. To be sure, we are aware of all the differences that may exist between the Soviet state and the American state, or for instance, the British or French states—such as constitutional and other practical differences. However, as Jacques Ellul notes:

> They exist, but are of little consequence compared with the similarities, and particularly with the general trend. *There are more differences between the American state of 1910 and that of 1960 (despite the constitutional sameness) than between the latter and the Soviet state (despite the constitutional differences.)*[5]

As the stamping boot of totalitarianism casts its ominous shadow around us, and as the United States moves toward the Soviet mode, we must be concerned, not only with foreign enemies, but also with the signs of authoritarianism and monolithic sameness revealing themselves today in America. As former presidential advisor Bertram Gross has remarked: "As I look at America today, I am not afraid to say that I am afraid."[6] Gross explains:

> I am afraid of those who proclaim that it can't happen here. In 1935 Sinclair Lewis wrote a popular novel in which a racist, anti-Semitic, flag-waving, army-backed demagogue wins the 1936 presidential election and proceeds to establish an Americanized version of Nazi Germany. The title, *It Can't Happen Here*, was a tongue-in-cheek warning that it might. But the "it" Lewis referred to is unlikely to happen again any place. Even in today's Germany, Italy or Japan, a modern-style corporate state or society would be far different from the old regimes of Hitler, Mussolini, and the Japanese oligarchs. Anyone looking for black shirts, mass parties, or men on horseback will miss the telltale clues of creeping fascism. In any First World country of advanced capitalism, the new fascism

will be colored by national and cultural heritage, ethnic and religious composition, formal political structure, and geopolitical environment. The Japanese or German versions would be quite different from the Italian variety—and still more different from the British, French, Belgian, Dutch, Australian, Canadian, or Israeli versions. In America, it would be supermodern and multi-ethnic—as American as Madison Avenue, executive luncheons, credit cards, and apple pie. It would be fascism with a smile. As a warning against its cosmetic facade, subtle manipulation, and velvet gloves, I call it friendly fascism. What scares me most is its subtle appeal.[7]

People intuitively sense that we of the present era are in danger of being consumed by the authoritarian state. A few years ago political scientist Kenneth Dolbeare conducted a series of in-depth interviews totaling twenty-five hours per person. He found that most respondents were deeply afraid of some future statist authoritarianism. "The most striking thing about inquiring into expectations for the future," he reported, "is the rapidity with which the concept of fascism (with or without the label) enters the conversation."[8]

The typical response is that fascism is not possible in the current leftward drift of society. But that leftward drift is precisely what makes fascism an imminent threat, because fascism is and always has been a leftist ideology. It is simply *nationalistic socialism*, in contrast to *international socialism*, which is Marxism.

The crude old forms of totalitarianism, however, will most likely not come to fruition in America, but something more deadly and subtle. As Francis Schaeffer writes: "We must think rather of a *manipulative* authoritarian government. Modern governments have forms of manipulation at their disposal which the world has never known before."[9] Schaeffer writes:

> What of tomorrow? In the United States, for example, a manipulative authoritarian government could come from the administrative side or from the legislative side. A public official in the United States serving at the highest level has wisely said, "Legislative dictatorship is no better than executive tyranny." And one would have to add that with the concept of variable law and with the courts making law, it could come from the judicial side as well. The Supreme Court has the final voice in regard to both administrative and legislative actions, and with the concept of variable law the judicial side could become more and more the center of power. This could be called "the imperial judiciary."[10]

Hitler was awesome. But think what he could have accomplished if television had been available to him—or, for that matter, if other modern technological devices, such as the computer, had been at his disposal. Television and computers can be potent weapons of manipulation and control in the hands of an authoritarian dictator.

Political analyst Kevin Phillips would agree that if authoritarianism develops further in this country, it will not be of the obvious Hitler brand.[11] However, this should not lead us to believe that the results of a manipulative authoritarian government would be finally different from the type that Hitler established. *In the end, all authoritarian regimes, even the "benevolent" type, arrive at the same antihuman point.*

Therefore, in the United States we must not think of an overnight change, but rather of a subtle trend by those in leadership—government, media, education—toward greater control and manipulation of the individual. With the advent of the electronic media and the increasing computerization of American society, the mechanisms for manipulation have arrived. The media is the one instrument more than any other that forms public opinion. Wedded to the state, the media more than forms public opinion, however; *it alters the consciousness and world view of entire populations.*

In fact, in a society where the state and the media have merged, authoritarianism can and will be established even though the citizenry enjoys so-called democratic freedoms. A few years ago William L. Shirer, whose book *The Rise and Fall of the Third Reich*[12] certainly qualifies him as a penetrating observer, commented that America may be the first country in which fascism comes to power through democratic elections.[13]

Sweden, for example, has shown us that relatively crude indoctrination by television and public education holds tremendous possibilities for the authoritarian state. The Swedes through the medium of television have also demonstrated a kind of powerful semantic manipulation, not unlike Orwell's Newspeak, in which words are more or less gradually changed to mean something else. In this way undesirable concepts can be done away with.

As journalist Roland Huntford demonstrates in *The New Totalitarians,* the word *freedom* does not yet in Swedish mean exactly "slavery." It does, however, already imply "submission," thereby being effectively neutralized as a rallying word in the vocabulary of forces that oppose servitude to the state.[14]

Television, and its potential misuse, must concern us. Television, whether secular or religious, may be paving the way for a form of authoritarianism like no other medium in history before it. This can be seen as coming from many directions, but at least two distinct areas are apparent.

First, "the most significant American cultural fact of the second half of the twentieth century [is] the decline of the Age of Typography and the ascendancy of the Age of Television."[15] This means, as Neil Postman shows in his acute analysis of television,[16] that television is a direct, head-on attack of print. The total visual aspect of television essentially eliminates the desire to read. "Television does not ban books," Postman writes, "it simply displaces them."[17] The result has been one of the lowest literacy rates in the history of the United States (as well as other Western countries).[18] People such as Thomas Jefferson, James Madison, and John Adams argued that the best safeguard against authoritarian up-top statism was an educated citizenry. If the people are not literate, it stands to reason that they are fair game for statist propaganda (which is consistently presented over television).

Second, as "the influence of print wanes, the content of politics, religion, education and anything else that comprises public business must change and be recast in terms that are most suitable to television."[19] The content most suitable for television is entertainment, whether it be situation comedy or a "news" show. The direction of the future, then, may be toward a *Brave New World* scenario:

> What Huxley teaches is that in the age of advanced technology, spiritual devastation is more likely to come from an enemy with a smiling face than from one whose countenance exudes suspicion and hate. In the Huxleyan prophecy, Big Brother does not watch us, by his choice. We watch him, by ours. There is no need for wardens or gates or Ministries of Truth. When a population becomes distracted by trivia, when cultural life is redefined as a perpetual round of entertainments, when serious public conversation becomes a form of baby talk, when, in short, a people become an audience and their public business a vaudeville act, then a nation finds itself at risk: culture-death is a clear possibility.[20]

Television then is clearly a technological extension that came equipped with its own program for social change. Inevitably, this change has been toward secularization and statism.

Aldous Huxley believed, as Postman writes, that we are in "a race between education and disaster, and he wrote continuously about the necessity of our understanding the politics and epistemology of media. For in the end, he was trying to tell us that what afflicted the people in *Brave New World* was not that they were laughing instead of thinking, but that they did not know what they were laughing about and why they had stopped thinking."[21] But, nevertheless, they kept smiling.

However, in contemporary Western culture, Big Brother or Big Sister comes with a smile. The world, it must be remembered, has not been terrorized by despots advertising themselves as devils. Instead, the totalitarian regimes have come to power while reciting platitudes of liberty, equality, and fraternity. This was true of the French Revolution and the Russian Revolution, and is equally true of modern communism and Third-World socialism.

A DIFFERENT DRUMMER

Some might feel uncomfortable about increased government control and manipulation, but as our modern secular culture descends upon them, where will they draw the line? Moreover, many who speak of civil liberties are also committed to the concept of the state's authority and responsibility to solve all problems. Therefore, in a time of overwhelming pressures, at some point the feeling of discomfort will be submerged.

There is still enough of the older ethical base—what has been called the Christian memory—that the American people will rebel if they consciously realize what is happening. However, if this trend toward control continues to move slowly, there will most likely be little resistance.

As the state gradually assumes more control, calls to the people for allegiance will come from the right and the left. However, when and if the authoritarian curtain falls, as Francis Schaeffer notes, "the words *left* or *right* will make no difference. In their extreme forms they are only two roads to the same end. There is no difference between an authoritarian government from the right or the left: the results are the same."[22]

Modern men and women are beginning to feel the strain of the unmanageability of their lives. With this hopelessness they seem to be surrendering their minds and their civil liberties to those who "can explain the world anew."[23] As William Irwin Thompson puts it: "When the individual's consciousness is made up of a moving collage of televised fragments, his state of anxiety makes him prey to 'the recollectivization through terror' of the fascist state."[24] Therefore, helpless before the monster of technology he has created, man in an act of faith surrenders to the power of explanation given him by way of its mouthpiece, the media.

Off in the distance, we can hear the stamping boot coming closer and closer. It is the same old boot but with a velvet touch. And this time it is stamping to the beat of a different drummer.

A NEW
DESPOTISM

Bertram Gross writes:

> I am uneasy with those who still adhere strictly to President
> Eisenhower's warning in his farewell address against the po-
> tential for the disastrous rise of power in the hands of the
> military-industrial complex. Nearly two decades later, it
> should be clear to the opponents of militarism that the military-
> industrial complex does not walk alone. It has many partners:
> the nuclear-power complex, the technology-science complex,
> the energy-auto-highway complex, the banking-investment-
> housing complex, the city-planning-development-land-
> speculation complex, the agribusiness complex, the communi-
> cations complex, and the enormous tangle of public
> bureaucracies and universities whose overt and secret services
> provide the foregoing with financial sustenance and a
> nurturing environment. Equally important, the emerging Big
> Business-Big Government partnership has a global reach. It is
> rooted in colossal transnational corporations and complexes
> that help knit together a "Free World" on which the sun never
> sets. These are elements of the new despotism.[1]

The elements of the "new despotism" are coming to fruition
in modern times. However, most people have been numbed by
the rapidity of technology and its complexity. Thus, what is in
fact developing is often not readily accessible to the senses. Moreover, even when occasional stories break through in the media
about some beleaguered citizen who was harassed by a new technology as applied by the bureaucracy, we see it only as an isolated
instance. Asleep, we have not come to grips with the changing of
the guard. By the very slowness of our human actions, our effective control of our machines may be nullified.

SURVEILLANCE

The loss of privacy is a key symptom of one of the fundamental social problems of our time. It highlights very dramatically the growing problem of large public and private institutions in relation to the individual citizen.

Access to technologies such as the computer by government officials, often in cooperation with private business concerns, maximizes the powers of the state bureaucracies. The new demons up-top, however, are corrupted in a whole new way, this time in the name of efficiency.

With this, a new class has emerged. Access to the computer is a new way to define class. As long as the only people to build computerized record systems are those who use them to increase their own effectiveness, power, and influence, then we have increasingly a consolidation of power in society.

Those who cannot plug themselves into a terminal will stand on the bottom rung of the social ladder. Even with home computers we cannot be so naive as to believe that the average citizen will ever be allowed to plug into police files or other dossiers.

Surveillance is a *fact* of our times. Many of the effects of surveillance, however, are more subtle than ever thought. Kent Greenwalt, a professor at Columbia University's Law School, discussed one such indirect but powerful effect of surveillance in a thoughtful report he did for the White House a few years ago:

> If there is increased surveillance and disclosure and it is not offset by greater tolerance, the casualties of modern society are likely to increase as fewer misfits and past wrongdoers are able to find jobs and fruitful associations. The knowledge that one cannot discard one's past, that advancement in society depends heavily on a good record, will create considerable pressure for conformist actions. Many people will try harder than they do now to keep their records clean, avoid controversial or "deviant" actions, whatever their private views and inclinations. Diversity and social vitality is almost certain to suffer, and in the long run independent private thoughts will be reduced. [2]

The distinction between private and public life and thoughts is one of the first things to dissipate in countries that shift toward state authoritarianism. "The only person who is still a private individual in Germany," boasted Robert Ley, a member of the

Nazi hierarchy, after several years of Nazi rule, "is somebody who is asleep."[3] I have discussed elsewhere the case of pornography, which makes the most intimate act a public matter.[4] Pornography always precedes authoritarianism.

On July 12, 1977, the United States Privacy Protection Study Commission warned that "new avenues and needs for collection of information...multiply the dangers of official abuse against which the Constitution seeks to protect."[5] Since then, these worrisome trends have accelerated. According to Ronald Plesser, who served as the panel's general counsel: "We're becoming a society where it's taken for granted that more and more data need to be collected about individuals."[6]

In part, the privacy problem stems from the demands of private business (merchants, landlords, insurance companies, and so on) and an array of state, local, and federal agencies for detailed information about large numbers of people. "Both government agencies and private firms," write Ted Gest and Patricia Scherschel in *U.S. News & World Report* in an article entitled "Who Is Watching You?," "feel a need for computerized files to deal efficiently with a mobile population of 230 million Americans, whether the task be calculating a citizen's eligibility for Social Security or determining whether a person pays bills on time."[7]

As private and public arenas have merged, surveillance has increased. An example is the credit bureaus and data centers that now proliferate. These "private" firms exist by selling credit information. They compile more than twenty-five million reports each year on consumers' dealings. Now stored in their computers are data on more than half of our nation's population.[8] This information is exchanged among leaders and is available to the federal and state bureaucracies.

The federal bureaucracy maintains a mass of dossiers and other information on its computers. This amounts to "3.5 billion records overall, or an average of more than 15 for every American. Uncounted others are kept by state and local agencies."[9]

Though most of this information is maintained in separate governmental units, the spread of automation has made it possible for agencies of the state to exchange information with each other for purposes other than that for which it was originally collected. "It is becoming increasingly possible for government to track the behavior and conduct of its citizens," argues George Trubow, professor of law at John Marshall School of Law in Chicago.[10]

Case in point:

> Despite the belief of most Americans that Internal Revenue Service and Social Security files are confidential, both agencies are required by law to provide taxpayers' addresses to Selective Service officials to help track down young men who have not registered for the draft. In May [1982], the Social Security Administration notified the 4 million recipients of Supplemental Security Income that they would be dropped from aid rolls if they refused to authorize the agency to see their tax records. The objective was to check further on their eligibility.[11]

The question looms before us. Can freedom in the United States continue to flourish and grow in an age when the physical movements, individual purchases, conversations, and meetings of every citizen are constantly under surveillance by private companies and government agencies?

Sometimes the surveillance is undertaken for "innocent" reasons, sometimes it is not. Does not surveillance, even the innocent sort, gradually poison the soul of a nation? Does not surveillance limit personal options—deny freedom of choice—for many individuals? Does not surveillance increase the powers of those who are in a position to enjoy the fruits of this activity? Is not *control* the name of the game?

Aleksandr Solzhenitsyn wrote about this process some years ago:

> As every man goes through life he fills in a number of forms for the record, each containing a number of questions.... There are thus hundreds of little threads radiating from every man, millions of threads in all. If these threads were suddenly to become visible, the whole sky would look like a spider's web, and if they materialized like rubber bands, buses and trams and even people would lose the ability to move and the wind would be unable to carry torn-up newspapers or autumn leaves along the streets of the city.[12]

TECHNOCRACY

It should be obvious that with the concentration of power up-top there would necessarily emerge a "limited" elite that would seek to direct government activity—what we will call the techno-scientific elite. Ellul writes:

> [T]here is a limited elite that understands the secrets of their own techniques, but not necessarily of all techniques. These men are close to the seat of modern governmental power. The state is no longer founded on the "average citizen" but on the ability and knowledge of this elite. The average man is altogether unable to penetrate technical secrets or governmental organization and consequently can exert no influence at all on the state.[13]

Ellul notes that the elite, of which we speak, is composed of two levels of conditioners. "The first," he writes, "numerically small, understands the means to conceive, organize, direct and control; the second, infinitely more numerous, is composed of mere executants."[14] The second class, the technicians, comprises the bureaucracy which is so common to modern states.

Harvard professor John Kenneth Galbraith who, in actuality, is an apologist for big business has on various occasions argued for an elite of intellectuals—composed of academic-scientific-governmental leaders.[15] Likewise, socioeconomist Robert Theobald has endorsed the concept of "sapientary authority," a social structure in which "wise men" selected by merit would be deeply involved in the governmental decision-making process. "It's naive," declared Theobald, "to deny the necessity for some kind of competent elite."[16]

Daniel Bell, professor of sociology at Harvard University, believes the elite should be composed of select individuals. In his book *The Coming of Post-Industrial Society,* he writes that "the university—or some other knowledge institute—will become the central institution of the next hundred years because of its role as the new source of innovation and knowledge."[17]

Bell notes that the crucial decisions will come from the government. However, more and more the decisions of the corporate state will be predicated on government-sponsored research, and "because of the intricately linked nature of their consequences, [the decisions] will have an increasingly technical character."[18] Society, then, becomes a technocracy where "the determining influence belongs to technicians of the administration and of the economy."[19]

In the final analysis, the corporate state—its business, its education, its government, even the daily pattern of the ordinary man's life—becomes a matter of control by the technocratic elite. This scientific elite (or conditioners) are the only ones who know how to run the complicated machinery of society and they will then, in collusion with the corporate state elite, possess the necessary power to manage life. As a consequence, Bell notes that in the future people can be remade, their behavior conditioned, or their consciousness altered.

Zbigniew Brzezinski in *Between Two Ages*, proposing elite control, writes:

> Technological developments make it certain that modern society will require more and more planning. Deliberate management of the American future will be widespread, with the planner eventually displacing the lawyer as the key social legislator and *manipulator*. This will put a greater emphasis on defining goals and, by the same token, on a more self-conscious preoccupation with social ends.[20]

Brzezinski served as a key advisor in the Carter Administration.

Pointed up clearly here is the necessity for the technician in the future scheme of things. This, of course, necessitates the bureaucracy, or what Ellul terms the second tier of the technological elite.

The massive bureaucracies—now computerized—that administer governmental policy are a *permanent* form of government. Presidents come and go, but the nonelected bureaucrats remain.

Mainly, the bureaucracy, in its implementation of policy on a day-to-day basis, inevitably comes into conflict with the elected politicians. Theoretically, as the United States Constitution provides, our politicians are to be the center of the state machinery. Actually, however, they are being progressively eliminated by it.

The basic decisions of the American government, as Watergate so tellingly illustrated, are made by the nonelected technicians. This includes the President's advisors as well as his cabinet.

As a consequence, many politicians have become impotent satellites of the corporate state's machine, which apparently can function without them. Essentially, the message is that the second-tier elite will tolerate no outside interference.

Agencies such as the Internal Revenue Service (and others) have proven on more than one occasion that any of their courses can be altered only by lengthy struggles from elected politicians.[21] Even then, the so-called gains are small.

The penchant in America, as Ellul notes, is toward the predominance of the technician in government. He writes that "the United States has shown a desire to establish a truly independent corps of. . .technicians as opposed to politicians, and to separate completely the political organ of decision from the technical organ of preparation."[22]

The basic function of the technician-bureaucrat is to furnish the politician with information and estimates on which he can base a decision. Once the technician has completed his task, supposedly he retires from the process. Thus, although exhibiting power and authority, the technician takes no responsibility for the final decision of the politician. The politician who relies exclusively on the technician, as many do, is reduced to a sycophant for the nonelected bureaucracy.

TOO BIG

When we discuss technicians we are not, as I emphasized earlier, necessarily saying that these are bad men. What we are saying is the technicized bureaucracy is essentially autonomous. It is unwieldy, and no one person or group can control it completely. Although an upper elite is developing that will dictate more and more a basic public policy, the functioning of the second-tier elite will operate—often sporadically—autonomously.

For example, a second-tier technician that is employed by the Internal Revenue Service decides that a certain taxpayer must atone for a "mistake" he or she made on a tax return. The taxpayer is then harrassed with audits for the next five or ten years (along with other bureaucratic harassment). This occurs routinely and unabated until a Congressman, for example, steps into conflict with the technician. Hopefully this will correct the harassment.

This type of situation represents the crisis in a governmental system out of control. It results in "sporadic tyranny" by government technicians much in the same way as described by Anthony Burgess in his novel *A Clockwork Orange*[23] and tellingly visualized by Stanley Kubrick in the movie version of the book.

This should come as no surprise when one realizes that the United States Constitution, with its checks and balances, was not designed as an intimate governing tool for restraining the bureaucracy for the fifty states. It was basically meant only to regulate and *limit* the *federal* government. However, because of the expansion of power by way of court interpretation of the Constitution, we operate under a document that was never intended to be used the way it is today. As a result, *we no longer operate under a written constitution* but, instead, under the edicts of the courts and the technicians who attempt to impose a national bureaucracy from a centralized (and regionalized) state.

This is illustrated very clearly in the numerous regulations passed by the bureaucratic agencies, such as the Department of Education, the Environmental Protection Agency, the Internal Revenue Service, and so on. These regulations are never put to a vote by the electorate. They operate as laws, however. This is troubling since Article I of the Constitution requires all laws to be passed by Congress. This was intended by the framers to maintain the so-called "power" in the people, who can unseat their congressman if they disagree with his or her performance. Without this safeguard, there is *no* representative government. We must realize that the state is no longer founded on the "average citizen," but on the ability and knowledge of the elite.

Most Americans, whether on the left or right, do not understand the governmental malaise because they do not know how the system was intended to work (nor do most care). There is the naive assumption that the system operates at least minimally as the framers of the original American government intended.

The framers simply did not envision technology and the technicians nor the *total* distortion of the Constitution. Moreover, they saw the individual states as the basic units of government, not the giant federal machine.[24]

Thus, there exists a governmental system that is "too big" and that has expanded beyond the borders of its governing document. Many Americans intuitively recognize something is wrong. That is why the government places so much emphasis on the "reassurance ritual" of voting. *It provides the illusion of participation.*

Even if we want to hedge and say that we are not yet at the stage where our power to control our government is greatly reduced, we must recognize that every time the governmental technician's power is increased, our role is decreased. "Democracy in such a society," Jacques Ellul writes, "can only be a mere appearance."[25]

One thing further must be said. Even if the elite is popular with the people, it is still an elite. It is an aristocracy nonetheless. And it was never intended by those who founded the country.

IRS

The government bureaucracy has used computers to enlarge its institutional powers. The Internal Revenue Service is an example.

The power of the IRS is enhanced by the authority of the agency to make very broad inquiry of the taxpayer to verify tax returns. Under the law and the interpretations of the United States Supreme Court, the IRS has the unique power to issue a summons to a taxpayer, employer, accountant, or any other third party. The authority of the IRS to issue a summons on its own authority contrasts with other law enforcement agencies such as the FBI, who must apply to a court when they desire to compel a person to appear before them.

Over the years, the detailed personal information collected about millions of Americans by the IRS has made the agency's files an almost irresistible temptation to those who could gain access to it. The tape recorders installed in the White House by Richard Nixon gave the world an indication of the resources that can be used. Journalist David Burnham details, in his telling book *The Rise of the Computer State*, the following conversation:

> "Do you need any IRS [unintelligible] stuff?" Mr. Nixon asked his assistant John Dean.
> "...We have a couple of sources over there I can go to," Dean replied. "I don't have to fool around with Johnnie Walters or anybody, we can get right in and get what we need."[26]

This conversation was part of the evidence supporting the proposed articles of impeachment against Nixon. Moreover, there were at least fourteen occasions when information was drawn from the IRS files at the request of the Nixon White House. This type of activity was also true of the Kennedy administration.[27] Should we expect that it is not occurring, in some form at least, under the present administration?

Access to citizens' tax information is not limited to the IRS. Documented evidence supports the fact that the Federal Bureau of Investigation and the Central Intelligence Agency have conducted systematic snooping efforts into the lives of Americans, especially their political activities.[28]

In fact, the information that government departments collect can easily be transmitted to other departments. As data processing operations become more efficient, there will be much *sharing* of data. The chairman of the United States Civil Service Commission has said:

> For proper decisions we must have integrated information systems. This will require the use of information across departmental boundaries. It is here that current efforts to standardize symbols and codes will pay dividends. Direct tape-to-tape feeding of data from one department to another may become common. These systems will mesh well with developing plans for an executive-level staffing program which will be designed to locate the best possible man for any given top-level assignment, no matter where in government he may be serving.
>
> The computer's ability to search its perfect memory and pick out records of individuals with specific characteristics has been applied in the search for candidates for Presidential appointments. A computerized file containing the names and employment data of some 25,000 persons, all considered likely prospects for federal appointive positions, is searched electronically. The talent bank, with its automated retrieval system, broadens the field of consideration for the President in critical decisions of leadership selection.[29]

Unfortunately, the dossiers kept about individuals often contain information that even the subject himself does not know or remember.

In 1973 the IRS established a central computer index—the Intelligence Gathering Retrieval System—for collecting general intelligence data (a good deal of which is not directly related to tax law enforcement). Within a few months after establishing it, more than four hundred and sixty-five thousand Americans were indexed in the new system—many of whom were not suspected of any tax violation.

> Under the system, intelligence gathering was begun on an individual before IRS had received any specific allegation of wrongdoing. The sole criteria for deciding whether to add a name to the computerized file was possible "future value."[30]

As we shall see, inside the world of dossiers there is a thin line between hard-core criminals and innocent *suspects*.

The IRS has now developed a computerized information system called the Taxpayer Compliance Measurement Program (TCMP). It is a computer-assisted process to help IRS predict the behavior of every American taxpayer. TCMP enchances the power of IRS in relation to the citizenry by allowing it to concentrate its small army of investigators and accountants on the targets most likely to have tried to cheat the government.

The program works like this: since 1962, a random sample of different kinds of taxpayers has been selected on a periodic basis. These are not individuals, corporations, or other organizations who are suspected of any wrongdoing, just a cross section of average taxpayers. Once identified, the individuals or institutions are subjected to an intensive examination—the feared audit. Burnham reports:

> In one recent survey, 200 separate items were collected about each of the 50,000 individuals who had been randomly selected to represent the entire population of 93 million American taxpayers. Once collected by the auditors, the 10 million bits of information collected by survey were fed into a giant IRS computer for analysis. The result: a line-by-line, income-level-by-income-level, region-by-region list of probabilities that a taxpayer in any one of these categories incorrectly stated the amount of tax due the government.[31]

From the elaborate statistical tables developed from the periodic audits of "selected" taxpayers, the IRS develops its "enforcement" strategy for the entire nation—the marching orders for its eighty-seven thousand employees. "But," as David Burnham notes, "the TCMP is more than that: it is the basis for virtually all of the agency's basic policy decisions."[32] Indeed, the "IRS uses the TCMP data to support its budget requests to Congress, to make proposals for changes in the tax law and to make decisions on such matters as staffing levels, training requirements, taxpayer education programs and the form of the tax returns."[33]

Therefore, the computer has strengthened the IRS in relation to citizens. The computer, however, also serves to enhance the power of the management of the IRS in another way: to help IRS bosses keep track of their employees.

The computer program developed by the IRS managers for this purpose is called the Audit Information Management System (AIMS). AIMS is a de facto quota system that requires every IRS agent to meet certain standards, what is known as the "plan";[34] that is, to audit a sufficient number of tax returns, to identify a sufficient number of taxpayer errors, and to recommend bringing a sufficient number of criminal cases.

When a massive, highly computerized *law-enforcement* agency such as the IRS imposes quotas, there can be trouble. For example, what happens when an IRS agent knows his next promotion is dependent upon making a certain number of cases and he or she falls short? Might such an agent—a government technician—be tempted to bring charges of some sort against some citizens who had not actually violated the law?

IRS officials have repeatedly denied that the IRS operates by quota systems. However, as Burnham discovered:

> Nonetheless, an extensive investigation of the IRS of a small government watchdog agency called the Administrative Conference of the United States found that substantial numbers of IRS employees believe quotas are set and used to measure their performance.
>
> "Group managers are well aware of the 'plan' and their group's part in accomplishing it," the report to the Administrative Conference said. "One manager, in fact, stated that he was well aware of management's expectations for the group and he saw his primary function as assisting his group in 'making the plan.' This view was shared, but not so bluntly stated, by most if not all managers. Numerous interviews with agents and management personnel indicate they believe that closing cases so as to 'make the audit plan' is the most important part of the job."[35]

This is, without question, government *against* the people. However, it must be realized that we are only in the beginning stages of computer technology. As the computer expands the authority of domestic agencies like the IRS, it can only get worse.

Clearly, the ability to track large numbers of individuals and the concentration of power are not the only contributions of the influence of the major bureaucracies by giving these organizations a method by which they can anticipate the probable future thoughts and activities of groups of people. The ability to make statistically reliable predictions about future behavior of people is significant. It means *control* from up-top.

NSA

The National Security Agency is among the least known and most influential organizations within the United States government. NSA is an intelligence organization which acts much like a worldwide electronic vacuum cleaner.

NSA's unique leverage on world events is based on its massive bank of computers. It is believed NSA's computers are the largest and most advanced in the world. NSA is probably the single largest source of federal research dollars spent in the development of advanced computers.

What type of computers? Computers to break codes; to direct spy satellites; to intercept millions of electronic messages transmitted by friends and enemies from every corner of the globe; and to recognize certain target words in spoken communications. However, NSA is more than a computer collection agency. This "virtually unknown government agency has also sought to influence the operation and development of all kinds of communication networks widely used by the [American] public."[36]

The power of NSA is enhanced by its unique legal status. It was created by a presidential executive order in 1952, and Congress has never passed a law defining its responsibilities and obligations. This fundamental flaw allows NSA to avoid the constitutional system of checks and balances. Instead, NSA is uniquely free to pursue whatever goals its directors decide are essential. As such, NSA has two professed goals: to monitor foreign intelligence communications and to defend the communication links that carry information bearing on the national security of the United States from penetration by the spies of other nations.

NSA's extraordinary power has been further enhanced by its incredible technical capacity. "This capacity, built on billions of dollars of secret appropriations, includes a formidable electronic eavesdropping network of satellites, thousands of earthbound listening posts and what almost certainly is the world's largest single computer based at Fort George Meade, just outside of Washington, D.C."[37]

A tight screen of secrecy surrounds NSA. However, an occasional document slips through the rigid bureaucratic censorship. For example, an unpublished analysis by the House Government Operations Committee estimates that in 1976 NSA may have employed one hundred and twenty thousand persons (when the military personnel under the agency's direction is included in the count) with an annual budget of some fifteen billion dollars.[38]

The dangers are apparent. An agency that seems to work without the law, because no legal mandate exists, and which monitors all forms of electronic communication opens the door to invasions of privacy and freedom. The same computers used to monitor the Russians are just as easily used to monitor the private communications of Americans. This has, in fact, happened.

In addition to scanning written messages, NSA has the equipment and manpower to monitor all the spoken conversations moving along a specific communication pathway or all the calls made from or to telephones that have been selected for surveillance.

One of the few specific examples of this capacity ever to be publicly documented occurred in the early 1970s when federal narcotics agents became convinced that illegal shipments of drugs were being arranged during conversations between some dealers speaking from public telephone booths in New York City's Grand Central Station to their colleagues in a single South American city. As David Burnham writes:

> After determining that the wiretap law barred the Bureau of Narcotics and Dangerous Drugs from installing a tap on the Grand Central pay phones, John Ingersoll, then head of the bureau, asked the NSA for help. Within a few months the spy agency was sorting through all the conversations it already was acquiring for general intelligence purposes, looking for the specific messages between the targeted public phones and the specific South American city.
>
> To record the conversations of the drug dealers, of course, the technicians were required to acquire, monitor and discard a large number of calls made by people with no connection with the cocaine business. But so pleased was Mr. Ingersoll with the tips he was getting from the NSA that he ultimately persuaded the agency to look for narcotics intelligence from the conversations made over nineteen different communication links connecting New York and Miami with six large South American cities."[39]

It is impossible to determine the number of innocuous conversations between separated lovers, lonely tourists, and traveling salesmen that NSA scrutinized in the government's search for the occasional narcotics dealer. "During just one year of the three-year period that the program continued, however, records of the American Telephone and Telegraph Company show a total of 2,477,881 calls between the United States and all of South America."[40]

Over the years NSA surveillance activities have also focused on individuals who were merely stating their political opposition to the racial situation in the United States or the war in Vietnam. According to an investigation by the Senate Intelligence Committee, a total of twelve hundred Americans were targeted by NSA between 1967 and 1973 because of their political activities.[41] Using the information obtained by its surveillance, NSA's security office between 1952 and 1974 developed files on approximately seventy-five thousand Americans, some of whom undoubtedly threatened the security of the United States.[42]

However, it does not stop here. The computers keep on developing new techniques of intelligence gathering:

> There are persistent rumors, however, that the National Security Agency, the secret eavesdropping arm of the United States government, has developed a system that scans the tape recordings of international telephone calls and automatically flags those messages where one of the callers uses certain trigger words such as the name of the president or a highly sensitive subject like plutonium. Because of the towering barrier of secrecy that surrounds the NSA, determining whether the agency actually has developed such an ability simply is not possible. But from the experiments we know have been conducted by AT & T and other groups, it is not unreasonable to assume that the NSA has such equipment to monitor some telephone calls.[43]

The collusion of public and private governments in the name of internal security is obvious here.

Few would say that we do not need a system of internal security. Such a system is vital to the safeguarding of the country. The crucial question, however, concerns the final use of the devices described above. Will the citizens be able to limit the government's use of these things, or are they caught in an electronic nightmare from which there is no escape?

The message should be clear. The computerization of society has led to the construction of a large number of data bases that are electronic windows into the most intimate details of people's lives. We have become human goldfish. Not knowing who is looking in, we have created an electronic concentration camp from which escape is less likely with each passing day.

THE ELECTRONIC CONCENTRATION CAMP

In the mid-1960s public concern developed over the value and wisdom of establishing a National Data Center. The proposed center would collect, on a single computer, all the statistical information obtained by scores of different federal agencies about everyone in the United States. All government bureaucracies, such as the IRS, Census Bureau, and the Social Security Administration, would feed data into it. While the Center was never formally recommended by the Johnson Administration, it was warmly endorsed by the Office of Management and Budget of the President and by economists, planners, and other top managers of the executive branch. The point is, however, that with the exchange of computer information among governmental bureaucracies and private corporational governments, we have, in *de facto* fashion, established such a computer collection agency.

This is more so with the widespread use of computers, computerized technology, and computer-created dossier files by the police. "Police" means local police, state troopers, federal agents (from the FBI to intelligence police that work domestically), and even agents employed by private corporational governments who often work in collusion with public police. The computer makes cooperation among police easier since they are now electronically interlocked.

The police in modern secular society operate in a high state of tension. The domestic warfare with crime perpetrates a "pig mentality." This often lessens the ability of the police to distinguish between criminal and noncriminal elements of the population. There are legitimate cases of police brutality.

This high state of tension has moved the police to develop an effective degree of technical methods both of research and of action. All this to the delight of a large number of people.

Of course, the "war on crime" propaganda (which is not without its good points) creates the gun-down-the-criminal mentality. It also creates a state of fear in people who, in the large urban areas, barricade themselves in at the first sign of darkness.

One of the major forces currently shaping the psyche of the American people is fear. People are afraid of communism. People are afraid of crime. People are afraid of terrorism. Whether these fears are entirely valid, whether these fears are greatly enhanced by the media, and whether other ages have had much more to fear is irrelevant. It is the open-arms mentality toward police surveillance and "crackdown" by the people that such fear creates. Moreover, it heightens the police tension which sooner or later falls upon even innocent people.

This means that the technological apparatuses of the police will not be applied only to criminals. We know this is not the case. Technology tends, as we have seen, to be applied everywhere it can be applied. Technology functions without discrimination because it exists without discrimination.

It is in this respect that the "Technological Society becomes a System, a unified whole subsuming all within it to the point of containment."[44] The logical consequence, then, of the technologically equipped police, who operate as technicians, is control, containment, and, eventually, restriction of freedom. This is true, according to Jacques Ellul, even if there is a moral conversion of the police:

> The infusion of some more or less vague sentiment of human welfare cannot alter it. Not even the moral conversion of the technicians could make a difference. At best they would cease to be good technicians.[45]

Think through the implications of this in terms of the police forces of the future. With total, instant information on each citizen available to the government, something menacing develops. Os Guinness notes:

> [I]t is not difficult to see the more sinister dangers of this. If the notion of a technically perfect police force is in line with the required availability of instant, total information, then such technological perfection is hardly distinguishable from the harshest fears of a police state or a totalitarian regime.[46]

Again, no perverse intention is imputed to any man. It is simply that to be sure of apprehending criminals, it is necessary that *everyone* be supervised. It is necessary to know what the citizenry is up to and to know its relations and amusements. And, as we have seen, the state is increasingly in a position to know these things. But as Jacques Ellul writes:

> This does not imply a reign of terror or of arbitrary arrests. The best technique is one which makes itself felt the least and which represents the least burden. But every citizen must be thoroughly known to the police and must live under conditions of discreet surveillance.[47]

The police must increasingly move in the direction of anticipating and forestalling crime. This means employing technology to attain total control.

One of the most important items in police control is computerized "suspect files." These show whether or not the police ever suspected any individual for any reason or at any time whatsoever, even though no legal document or procedure ever existed against him. "This means," as Ellul recognizes, "that any citizen who, once in life, had anything to do with the police, even for noncriminal reasons, is put under observation—a fact which ought to affect, speaking conservatively, half the adult male population."[48]

This eventually means demeaning people. It also means dealing with computerized files and bureaucracies that can be genuinely abusive. Consider, for example, the case of Leonard Smith as detailed in David Burnham's book *The Rise of the Computer State*.[49]

Smith was a retired postal inspector. One May night in 1977 he was picked up outside his home on charges of public drunkenness. Two days later he pleaded not guilty, and the judge ordered his release on his own recognizance.

The jailers, however, did not let Leonard Smith go. The computerized warrant system had come up with another Leonard Smith who was wanted for violating his probation twenty-seven years earlier, in 1950. The retired postal inspector insisted he was not the same man. He was six feet tall, had hazel eyes, and weighed 205 pounds. The man they were looking for was five feet nine inches tall, had blue eyes, and weighed 137 pounds.

The warrant was so old, in fact, that the judge who had signed it was dead and the courthouse where he sat had been demolished. Six days after Leonard Smith had been ordered freed on the original charge of public drunkenness, the confusion over his identity was cleared up and he finally was released. One footnote: the warrant for which he had been incorrectly held was for a Leonard Smith who was on probation for bouncing a ten-dollar check.

The reason Leonard Smith was held is not hard to understand once the rules of the computerized warrant system are explained. Under these rules, each item of identification like a person's name, Social Security number, or color is given a different numerical value. If the authorities have about 60 percent of possible points of the various identifiers, they are authorized to detain a person.

Mr. Smith's case is not unusual. In fact, he is one of the thousands of Los Angeles citizens who were mistakenly taken into custody each year because of a faulty computerized warrant system by thirty separate law-enforcement agencies in Los Angeles. Because the Automated Wants and Warrants System was allowed to continue operating under the same identification rules for the last decade, the Los Angeles Center for Law in the Public Interest estimates that tens of thousands of wholly innocent persons have been improperly detained for various lengths of time since the computerized system was established.

The arrest of Mr. Smith, and countless others like him, is a graphic example supporting the contention that the industrial nations of the world have become enmeshed in a complicated political and technical process that is transforming them into increasingly powerful but relatively benign police states. They have become concentration camps—not in their dramatic aspects—but in their *administrative* aspects.

We cannot be stuck to the older concept of the concentration camp. "The Nazis' use of concentration camps has warped our perspective. The concentration camp is based on two ideas which derive directly from the technical conception of the police: preventive detention (which completes prevention), and reeducation."[50] Indeed, the further we advance into the camp, the more will the police, as are the prison systems, be considered responsible for the reeducation (that is, "rehabilitation") of "social misfits." A misfit, depending upon the definition, can mean anyone.

As the national concentration camp descends upon modern society, it does not and will not involve the suffering usually associated with it. Logically, technology increases the pressures upon people until they "flip their lids" or are reduced to rats in the technological maze. The choice is rather simple: live in a cave or enter the camp.

If the system is to operate at optimum level, every citizen must eventually be kept track of throughout his life, geographically, biologically, and economically. The police must know precisely what he is up to at every moment (or possess the capability to do so).

The terror associated with old regimes is a thing of the past (or soon will be) in industrialized nations. In the camp the police exist only to protect "good" citizens. As with misfits, a good citizen can mean anyone.

Aldous Huxley, in his customary farsighted way, had long foreseen the new methods of future states. In a 1946 foreword to *Brave New World* he wryly remarked: "Government by clubs and firing squads. . .is not merely inhumane (nobody much cares about that nowadays); it is demonstrably inefficient—and in an age of advanced technology, inefficiency is the sin against the Holy Ghost."[51]

Efficiency accompanies the technician who arises with the advancement of science and technology. In this way police work has become scientific. There are computer dossiers on virtually everyone. The tax returns and other government-required information often begins the process. This means that the "average Joe" cannot evade the police or disappear. (Caves are becoming curiously scarce.) But who really wants to escape? For many, a computer dossier is not particularly fearsome. It is simply the price we pay for the luxury of progress.

In controlling the national camp, the police will necessarily need instantaneous information on the whereabouts of citizens—again, keeping track of all movements. This could eventually mean employing computers and electronic devices upon the persons of people. The most effective and potentially dangerous would be the provision of low-cost "personal chips," possibly grafted under the skin. This would require a relatively painless and minor operation (of which the technology is presently available to perform the surgery).

If this is objectionable, then devices could be placed in wrist watches. Even in this form the chips could identify their owners on the basis of a combination of factors—blood pressure, pulse, or electrical skin resistance—and would be inoperative when worn by another individual.

These chips would not only identify each individual accurately but also, if required, locate him anywhere and at any time through a multitude of special sensors—again relatively inexpensive to install in large numbers.

Some people will undoubtedly resist. In commenting on this, Christopher Evans notes:

> The individual location feature will, of course, be far more difficult to push through than the personal identifier, though any government sufficiently unscrupulous or desperate could do so with few problems. If in doubt, consider the restrictions of personal liberty which people are prepared to accept in the case of war or political unrest. To give one example out of many: ten years ago air travelers would have been horrified to think that it would soon be customary for them to submit to a thorough body search, the X-raying and photographing of their baggage, and the constant electronic surveillance before boarding an airplane. Yet this all came to pass with barely a demurring voice.[52]

By the 1990s it will be increasingly difficult—maybe impossible if events move as fast as some believe—to avail oneself of many public-private services without an electronic identifier which can transfer funds into or out of one's credit account. The universal power of the electronic chip overrides the objection raised by many people to the notion of the cashless society.[53] This may be necessary to keep order and total control in the camp.

Protests and campaigns against the electronic surveillance in the electronic concentration camp will inevitably be strong. However, the "law and order" folks, because of the rise in crime or possibly terrorist acts, would carry the day in such a case.

WAR AND PEACE

Computers, in terms of the technological state and modern warfare, have technologically rationalized war and killing. This is true for a number of reasons.

In the Vietnam War, computers operated by officers who had not the slightest idea of what went on inside their machines effectively chose which hamlets were to be bombed and what zones had a sufficient density of Viet Cong to be "legitimately" declared free-fire zones (that is, large geographical areas in which pilots had the "right" to kill *every* living thing). (Of course, for the Christian this is in itself an immoral act, but computers do not operate based upon moral decisions.)

Only "machine readable" data—that is, largely targeting information coming from other computers—could enter these machines. And when the American President decided to bomb Cambodia and to keep the secret from the American Congress, the computers in the Pentagon were "fixed" to transform the genuine strike reports from the field into false reports to which government leaders were given access. The high government leaders who felt themselves privileged to be allowed to read the falsified secret reports that were printed out by the Pentagon's computers believed them to be accurate. After all, the computer had spoken.

Admiral Thomas Moores, chairman of the Joint Chiefs of Staff, explained to the United States Armed Services Committee that air strikes against Cambodia were entered into the "Pentagon's large data computer" as strikes against South Viet Nam.[54] *The New York Times*, in a story on this, exhibited a photocopy of a strike report which carries the notation: "All strikes targeted against Cambodia will be programmed against alternate targets in South Viet Nam."[55] To the Committee, Admiral Moores is reported to have said: "It is unfortunate that we had to become slaves to these damned computers."[56]

In modern warfare the soldier often operates at an enormous physical and, thus, psychological distance from his victims. We touched on this earlier. The bomber pilot can abdicate responsibility for the burned children because he never sees the village, his bombs, and certainly not the flaming children themselves.

Modern technological rationalizations of war, then, have, as Joseph Weizenbaum notes, an insidious effect on policy-making.[57] It has meant a denial of responsibility. As Admiral Moores pointed out, as "a slave to these damned computers," he only does what the computer says. Thus, no human is, in the end, responsible for the computer's output.

This eventually means that pure instrumental reason will prevail. It is the technician's dream. If it is efficient, it must be done—even if children have to burn for it. Anyway, the technician never smells the burning flesh. Killing, then, becomes easy.

The United States government is, through the Department of Defense, *the* major developer of war computers. Joseph Weizenbaum quotes a planning paper from a major university as stating:

The Department of Defense, as well as other agencies of our government, is engaged in the development and operation of complex systems that have a very great destructive potential and that, increasingly, are commanded and controlled through digital computers. *These systems are responsible*, in large part, for the maintenance of what peace and stability there is in the world, and at the same time they are capable of unleashing destruction of a scale that is almost impossible for man to comprehend.[58]

Note that systems are responsible, not people.

This paper goes on, however, to recognize that there is no stemming the tide toward development of computers by the Department of Defense. For example, the Department of Defense has now spent over fifteen million dollars attempting to devise a computer for the military that recognizes human speech.[59] This would obviously provide for much quicker reactions in time of war—a truly efficient killing machine.

Jacques Ellul comments that technological progress favors war because new and more efficient weapons have rendered more difficult the distinction between offense and defense; and because modern war machines have enormously reduced the pain and anguish, psychological and otherwise, traditionally associated with the act of killing. Simply put, with the computer the push of the button and the distance from the screams make the entire process painless for the technician.

This discussion should not be taken as an antiwar statement. There are just wars and unjust wars. Such must be evaluated as they build or occur. Moreover, one's participation in any war may be limited by his or her conscience. A valid liberty-of-conscience objection to war should be respected.

This discussion should also not be taken as a broadside statement against nuclear power or its alleged corollary, nuclear war. Nuclear war as portrayed today by many in the peace movement is misleading and mythical.

Total nuclear war is a myth. Its threat keeps the masses in tension and subdued numbness.

The entire meaning of the Bomb has been misunderstood. The Bomb altered the nature of modern warfare. With the Bomb, for the first time in history the "necessity" of warfare is so stalemated by the "absurdity" of warfare that traditional resort to war as a solution to international problems is no longer viable. In fact, the tirades against the Bomb, as moving us toward total nuclear war, reveal at least the unconscious realization or annoyance at the removal of society's ultimate recourse.

However, the Bomb does not mean the end of war. It merely forces violence further down the strata of society. This means guerrilla warfare, terrorism, and, increasingly, limited wars.

George Gallup, Jr., in his book *Forecast 2000*, sees terrorist attacks, even in the United States, as the wave of the future.[60] Armed with small nuclear weapons, terrorist attacks, he believes, will take on a new dimension. He writes:

> A disciplined terrorist squad, funded by some hostile government and armed with a nuclear weapon, would be in a position to wreak havoc on our nation (or any other), almost at will. They would probably choose a site like New York City, Washington, D.C., or some military installation with a high public relations value. Then, they could try various forms of extortion on a global scale—and government authorities might be foolish to assume that such a group would hesitate to die for their cause.[61]

Nuclear weapons worldwide are proliferating. The United States, for example, is helping France to produce the neutron bomb. France is the world's third-largest arms dealer already, after the United States and the Soviet Union.[62] Moreover, as Gallup reports: "What is especially distressing about this proliferation is that those countries most likely to use the weapon are among those acquiring the ability to produce it."[63] As such, this means that terrorist attacks will continue on a worldwide scale.

Finally, we should have a deep concern for the cold-corporate-mechanization of modern warfare (which includes the nuclear war phobia and the coming terrorist attacks paranoia). With such developments, we move closer and closer to easy and nonresponsible killing; which is something *no* man, Christian or non-Christian, should condone.

HOPE AND PRAY

The spectre of the computer state is no easy thing to swallow. For some computer enthusiasts, however, it is merely the next step on the evolutionary chain as man's extensions reach out farther and farther into the universe.[64] Christopher Evans, one such optimist, nevertheless, has a word of caution:

[W]e should hope and pray that the day of dictatorship and authoritarian governments is done before substantial advances are made in artificial intelligence. . . . Any regime supported by the power of intelligent machines would be more secure and more terrible than any all-human equivalent.[65]

FREEDOM AND HUMANITY

A large proportion of the world's population is, at present, living under some sort of oppressive regime. Leaders in Iron Curtain, Third World, Eastern Asia, and Southern Hemisphere countries manipulate, control, and often terrorize their own countrymen.

The so-called free societies of the West, as we have seen, are on the decline. In fact, Jean-François Revel in *How Democracies Perish* writes that "[d]emocracy may. . .turn out to be a historical accident, a brief parenthesis that is closing before our eyes."[1] Revel elaborates:

> In its modern sense of a form of society reconciling governmental efficiency with legitimacy, authority with individual freedoms, it will have lasted a little over two centuries, to judge by the speed of growth of the forces bent on its destruction. And, really, only a tiny minority of the human race will have experienced it. In both time and space, democracy fills a very small corner. The span of roughly two hundred years applies only to the few countries where it first appeared, still very incomplete, at the end of the eighteenth century. Most of the other countries in which democracy exists adopted it under a century ago, under half a century ago, in some cases less than a decade ago.[2]

Why is this true?

> Democracy probably could have endured had it been the only type of political organization in the world. But it is not basically structured to defend itself against outside enemies seeking its annihilation, especially since the latest and most dangerous of these external enemies, communism—the current and complete model of totalitarianism—parades as democracy perfected when it is in fact the absolute negation of democracy.

238 ☐ THE END OF MAN

Democracy is by its very nature turned inward. Its vocation is the patient and realistic improvement of life in a community. Communism, on the other hand, necessarily looks outward because it is a failed society and is incapable of engendering a viable one. The Nomenklatura, the body of bureaucrat-dictators who govern the system, has no choice, therefore, but to direct its abilities toward expansion abroad. Communism is more skillful, more persevering than democracy in defending itself. Democracy tends to ignore, even deny, threats to its existence because it loathes doing what is needed to counter them. It awakens only when the danger becomes deadly, imminent, evident. By then, either there is too little time left for it to save itself, or the price of survival has become crushingly high.[3]

The greatest quest of man—liberty, equality and brotherhood—seems, in most instances, to be an inescapable dream or, in other words, an illusion. And even where this shibboleth is the banner cry (such as in the French Revolution of the eighteenth century) the result is often unspeakable horrors.

Of course, the most obvious question concerning the illusive nature of freedom is why it seems almost inevitable that man is doomed to slavery instead of liberty. And why do the people tyrannized in states such as the Soviet Union seem to languish under oppression with little resistance? As early as 1776, Thomas Jefferson in the Declaration of Independence noted that "all experience hath shown that mankind are more disposed to suffer, while evils are sufferable, than to right themselves by abolishing the forms to which they are accustomed."

Aleksandr Solzhenitsyn speaks of how the Russian people would kneel inside the door of their apartments, pressing their ears to listen when the KGB came at midnight to arrest a neighbor. He comments that if all the people had come out and driven off the officers, sheer public opinion would have demoralized the effort to subdue what should be a free people. But the people hid and trembled.

Fallen man is faced with a dilemma. There is an urge for freedom in most people. However, it seems unattainable. Moreover, governments that are founded as free societies seem to inevitably degenerate into some form of despotism.

The fundamental answer to this predicament lies in the nature of freedom itself. *True freedom imposes a corresponding responsibility to remain free.* Freedom is a gift. And on those to whom it is bestowed, a price is exacted. That price is vigilance and involvement. It also means not falling prey to the temptation to prefer security over liberty.

THE TEMPTATIONS

Fyodor Dostoyevski (1821-1881) in his last novel, *The Brothers Karamazov*,[4] tellingly discusses the gift of freedom as reflected in the three questions (or temptations) posed to Jesus Christ in the wilderness by Satan. Dostoyevski illustrates how the culture and church of his day had fallen prey to these very temptations. The chapter is entitled "The Grand Inquisitor," after the inquisitions by the church of the thirteenth century and following.[5] During the inquisitions the church purged the system of what it believed to be heretics, resulting in the death of thousands.

It may be appropriate to apply the same three temptations to the modern culture and governments. Since the modern governmental systems have taken on a religious aura, it seems neither fallacious nor presumptuous to assume that the temptations can apply to them.

The Bible says that Christ was led into the wilderness where He fasted for forty days and forty nights, all the while being tempted by Satan. Dostoyevski notes that Satan's three questions revealed the entire future history of man. Moreover, they offered three symbols which reconciled all the irreconcilable strivings of man.

BREAD AND STONES

Christ came into the world empty of this world's goods. He did bring the promise of salvation and freedom. Most men, however, fear and dread freedom because there has been nothing more difficult for man and society to bear than freedom.[6]

Satan first tempted Christ by saying, "If you are the Son of God, command that these stones become bread."[7] Christ could have turned the stones into bread, and men would have followed Him in multitudes. Instead, as Dostoyevski notes, Christ did not want to deprive man of his freedom, for obedience bought with bread is not the spiritual freedom that Christ desired for man. Therefore, Christ replied: "It is written, 'Man shall not live on bread alone, but on every word that proceeds out of the mouth of God.'"[8]

Christ promised man heavenly bread, but man has sought earthly bread instead. "Enslave us, but feed us" seems to be the cry of man.[9] However, freedom and assurance of daily bread are incompatible in a fallen world.

LOVE OF SLAVERY

In his foreword to *Brave New World*, Aldous Huxley wrote that a "really efficient totalitarian state would be one in which the all-powerful executive of political bosses and their army of managers control a population of slaves who do not have to be coerced because they love their servitude. To make them love it is the task assigned, in present-day totalitarian states, to ministers of propaganda, newspaper editors, and schoolteachers."[10]

Approximately a century ago, following his visit to America, Alexis de Tocqueville wrote that if tyranny was established in a democratic state, it would have a different character than the old terror regimes. "It would," he said, "be more widespread and milder: it would degrade men rather than torment them."[11] And how are men degraded?

Degradation, in modern times, is merely a synonym for dehumanization of human life in the twentieth century. Abortion, infanticide, and euthanasia are realities of the present.

The proliferation of pornography and its acceptance as a legitimate form of expression in virtually every sector of society is a signal that dehumanization is deeply imbedded in modern culture. Pornography reduces man and woman, husband and wife, mother and father and their children to their genitals. It totally depersonalizes people. Women, especially, are portrayed as things rather than as human beings.

Instead of being an expression of love, sex becomes a source of immediate gratification and eventually a form of manipulation. We see this in the current problem with the heavy use of children in prostitution.[12]

Pornography makes sex, one of the most private acts imaginable, public. Sex, in effect, becomes a public property. Naturally, what is public will eventually be linked with the state.

We see in history that statism and the rise of pornography go hand in hand. Thus, under an authoritarian state there is no distinction between private and public matters.

Pornography has a denigrating effect on the psyche of a people. It eventually creates a servitude mentality. The Goncourt brothers, who studied the rise of pornography in early France, have written: "Pornographic literature serves a Bas-Empire ...one tames a people as one tames lions, by masturbation."[13]

Pornography, like any idol, is then, a form of bondage. The sacrifice it requires is freedom.

Behaviorist B. F. Skinner, in his *Beyond Freedom and Dignity*, writes that to tame the animal nature in man, man must be deprived of his value, dignity, worth, and freedom. Skinner opts for positive control of man's behavior rather than negative control to keep the people from defecting. A better method for the government to pursue would be to make life more interesting. To Skinner, life is made more interesting by providing bread, circuses, sports, gambling, the use of alcohol and other drugs, and various kinds of sexual behavior.[14]

Skinner notes that under the type of system evolving in the United States, the entire population eventually becomes a slave population. By means of positive control, the people become slaves without knowing it.

Skinner scorns the literature of freedom because it makes man aware of his slavery while failing to rescue him from his unhappiness.[15] "Happiness," to Skinner, is more important than freedom. Why not, if men are animals? Without freedom, however, there is no happiness. Huxley recognized this when he said it was important that "the great societies" provide frequent vacations for the citizens in order for them to escape all the "happiness."

The real threat to freedom is a system of slavery so well designed that it does not breed revolt. A system which does not breed revolt will be a state that is a master of manipulation.

A particularly important statist mode of keeping revolt down is to give the people choices, thereby maintaining an appearance of freedom. The choices presented to the people, however, are totally dictated by the state and its appendage, the media. Actually, freedom in the true sense of the word is destroyed when this occurs. A clever state will only present a group of options, any of which, if chosen, will be most desirable to it.

Jean-Jacques Rousseau said that there is no subjugation so perfect as that which keeps the appearance of freedom because it captures man's ability willfully to choose and act. In other words, a rat in a maze does not possess choices, only alternatives.

To have the ability and duty to choose requires responsibility, and this, modern man is running away from. Responsibility is an

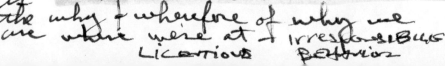

This is the why + wherefore of why we are where were at + irresponsible LICENTIOUS behavior

aspect of freedom, thereby making freedom a burden to an irresponsible populace. As Dostoyevski had the Grand Inquisitor say to Christ, "Have you forgotten that peace, and even death, is more attractive to man than freedom of choice...there is nothing more alluring to man than freedom of conscience, but neither is there anything more agonizing."[16]

Jacques Ellul in *The Political Illusion*, remarking on what he calls the "illusion of freedom," argues that the state that talks most about freedom denies it most.[17] If a citizenry is truly free, then why does the president or leader, in virtually every speech, tell it how free it is? A people truly free needs not to be told it is.

FILLED WITH STRAW

Aleksandr Solzhenitsyn has grown sour in his view toward Western democracy. Basically, Solzhenitsyn says that as morality declines, freedom declines. He argues that this is happening in the West.

In a BBC interview in late 1975, Solzhenitsyn created a controversy in Great Britain when he said the moral consciousness of the Western nations had descended so low that the Soviet Union did not need weapons to conquer the West. All it needed, he said, was its bare hands.

"Genuinely human freedom," declares Solzhenitsyn, "is inner freedom given to us by God: freedom to decide upon our own acts, as well as moral responsibility for them."[18] This inner freedom is being denied by Western culture as it has shifted individual responsibility for man's acts to his society or environment. From this B. F. Skinner says, control the environment and man is controlled.

As opposed to Solzhenitsyn's inner freedom, what type of freedom do we have? Solzhenitsyn said:

> Freedom! to litter compulsorily with commercial rubbish the mail boxes, the eyes, ears, and brains of the people, the telecasts—so that it is impossible to watch a single one with a sense of coherence. Freedom! to impose information taking no account of the right of the individual not to accept it, of the right of the individual to peace of mind. Freedom! to spit in the eye and in the soul of the passerby and the passenger with advertising.... Freedom! for editors and film producers to start the younger generation off with seductive miscreations. Freedom! for adolescents of 14-18 years to immerse themselves in idleness and amusements instead of invigorating tasks and

spiritual growth. . . . Freedom! for healthy young adults to avoid work and live at the expense of society. . . . Freedom! for politicians indiscriminately to bring about whatever pleases the voter today, but not what farsightedly provides for his safety and well-being.[19]

Solzhenitsyn has denounced what he terms a destructive freedom—one that adds chains to men instead of fulfillment. It is a freedom to act and speak regardless of the rights of others. Most of all, it is a freedom from traditional absolutes.

Like the hollow men of T. S. Eliot's epic poem, the word freedom has become "filled with straw." It has no content, for it is hollow freedom. When man seeks freedom from God, freedom then becomes "another word for nothing else to lose."

Man cannot live on bread alone, and when he attempts to, his bread is taken away in the end. Ultimately, his life, as the recent rise in abortion, infanticide, and euthanasia illustrates, is also taken by the state.

CREATURE OVER CREATOR

Following the denunciation of Satan's first temptation, Christ was led to a mountaintop and shown all the kingdoms of the world "in a moment of time."[20] Satan then said to Christ: "All these things will I give to you, if you fall down and worship me."[21]

The temptation to serve something other than the true God has plagued man throughout history. Men have often attempted to serve the true God and something else at the same time. Some in Old Testament Israel tried this repeatedly. Christ, however, made it clear in the Sermon on the Mount that man cannot serve two masters simultaneously.[22]

In the Roman games, the gladiators of the arena paraded before the assembled multitude while a fifty-piece band played a march. As the gladiators came to the Emperor's private box, they stopped, raised their right hands (similar to the Nazi salute), and chanted, "Hail, Caesar! We who are about to die salute you."[23] The angel Gabriel appeared before the Virgin Mary in Nazareth of Galilee and declared, "Hail, thou who art highly favored, the Lord is with thee; blessed art thou among women."[24] Both salutations were religious.

From the early days of Rome, the Roman games were a basic religious practice of the state. Accordingly, Pierre Grimal in *The*

Civilization of Rome writes, "Their religious character is undeniable."[25] In these two salutes to deity there is set forth symbolically the battle of the centuries—Christ versus Caesar, or man under God versus man under the state. This is played out in vivid detail today in such countries as the Soviet Union, where believers are persecuted for their assertion that all men, including those who administer the state, are under God.

As head of the Roman college of priests, the Emperor Augustus Caesar gave the masses of the Roman Empire forgiveness for their past sins. Augustus was looked upon as a messiah and savior. An inscription on Roman coins even hailed him as the "son of god."[26]

The conflict between the two rivals was inescapable. In the early part of the first century, Simon Peter, apostle of Jesus Christ, challenged the religious and civil leaders of his day, declaring: "There is salvation in no one else; for there is no other name under heaven that has been given among men, by which we must be saved."[27] The issue was now clear. The battle was not between church and state, but between two kingdoms declaring ultimate and divine authority over all men.

Eventually, the Christians within Rome were ordered by the government to burn incense to the superior jurisdiction of the state. To acquiesce meant that they recognized the earthly government had superior jurisdiction over man as against God. The early Christians refused to acknowledge Caesar's claim and pledged allegiance to none other than Christ. As a result, they were persecuted for their loyalty to God.

Christ repulsed this temptation to worship him by replying, "Be gone, Satan! For it is written, 'You shall worship the Lord your God, and serve Him only.'"[28] The secular states have accepted what Christ rejected, but they have been thwarted from ruling all the kingdoms of the earth. The great conquerors of history, such as Alexander the Great and Genghis Khan, failed to gain the whole.

There is an almost unquenchable thirst in man to find the ultimate unity. Christ rejected this temptation. He knew that fallen man, to accomplish unity, would have to serve the author of evil.

There is nothing, as history teaches us, that a man is more anxious to do than find something to worship. It must, however, unquestionably be something that all men can agree, at least by mental affirmation, to worship communally. As basic fallen human nature instructs, it is always easier to love one's self as reflected in the ideal mass man than to love individual people or to love something as ephemeral as the modern concepts of God. This humanistic principle inevitably leads to the persistent drive for the world state made more appetizing with the emergence of the mass media and the computer.

Christ rejected the immense power He would hold if He both fed and controlled men's consciences. Christ acknowledged it was God's sovereignty that was over man and that there could be only death in man's attempt at playing God. He knew where the answer to man's dilemma was centered, and it was not in hopes of a world state.

TEMPTING GOD

There are three forces on earth that can overcome and capture once and for all the conscience of man and give him pseudo-happiness. These are, as Dostoyevski writes, miracles, authority, and mystery.[29] Christ rejected the first, the second, and finally the third.

When Satan presented his last temptation to Christ it was aimed not only at Christ, but at God the Father also. The dreaded spirit led Him to Jerusalem and set Him on the pinnacle of the temple, saying, "If you are the Son of God, throw yourself down; for it is written, 'He will give His angels charge concerning you; and, in their hands they will bear you up, lest you strike your foot against a stone.'"[30] Christ answered, "It is written, 'You shall not tempt the Lord your God.'"[31] Christ would not test God, for this would show that He had lost His faith in the Father.

Modern man, as reflected in his states, has not withstood this temptation. The Grand Inquisitor asked Christ, "Didn't you know that whenever man rejects miracles he rejects God, because he seeks not so much God as miracles?"[32] Man cannot live without miracles, so he creates his own. He turns to astrology, sorcery, witchcraft, and pseudo-Christianity even though he is an atheist or agnostic.

As it denies God, the state assumes the role of the miracle-worker. It feeds and clothes its citizens from cradle to grave with statist services. This is the modern welfare state. Faith is transferred from the Creator to the statist god.

The charismatic political leader who, shrouded with mystery, announces he will cure all ills, is an example of the modern miracle-worker. People follow the contemporary leader less for what he can offer in the way of leadership than for what he can offer in the way of expanded state service. The mistrust of his predecessor is soon forgotten because, as Ellul says, modern man "is a man without memory."[33]

Christ would not come down when they taunted Him and challenged Him, saying, "Let Him now come down from the cross, and we shall believe in Him."[34] Christ's way of saving men was not by curiosity-pleasing power displays. He required, as Dostoyevski writes, love from redeemed hearts "rather than the servile rapture of slaves subdued forever by a display of power."[35]

The mighty show of power by the modern police state, which controls by coercion, is in contrast to the modern provider state that is literally dehumanizing its people with irresponsibility. Christ would not buy man's love or dazzle him with miracles in order to control him. He was honest and, as a consequence, was crucified.

THE VARIABLE

It is virtually impossible to predict the future. There are simply too many variables.

The world appears to be headed for a series of disasters. Rivers of blood could flow.

At least two things are certain. Dehumanization of people will continue, and freedom as we have known it in the past is in jeopardy.

We must, therefore, concern ourselves with *humanness. A primary task for this generation is in keeping humanness in the human race*—that is, upgrade and then maintain man's high place in the universe.

All men bear the Creator's image. They have value, not because they are redeemed, but because they are God's creation in God's image. Modern man, who has rejected this, has little if no clue as to who he is. Because of this, he can find no real value for himself or for other men. "Hence," Francis Schaeffer writes, "he downgrades the value of other men and produces the horrible thing we face today—a sick culture in which men treat men as inhuman, as machines. As Christians, however, we know the value of men."[36]

We must also teach the true nature of liberty. This concerns the variable of *internal freedom*. Freedom cannot exist externally without the internal freedom that true Christianity offers. Freedom can never be imposed from without. It must come from within the person and flow into the external world. Possessing this true freedom is why believers incarcerated in concentration camps can speak of joy and freedom even under conditions of imprisonment.

Finally, we must not circumvent true freedom by giving ourselves over to modern deities, even if some grand inquisitor demands it. As men and women, we must assert that we are creatures of worth and dignity made in the image of God and not machines of the modern state. We must not submit to servitude because pleasure commands it or because fear demands it. In the words of the Apostle Peter, we must obey God rather than men in doing everything at our disposal to keep true freedom alive for all people.

NOTES

CHAPTER ONE: THE CHRISTIAN VACUUM

1. David Ogilvy, *Ogilvy on Advertising* (New York: Crown 1983), p. 7.
2. John W. Whitehead, *The Stealing of America* (Westchester, Ill.: Crossway Books, 1983), pp. 31-42.
3. *See generally* John W. Whitehead, *The Second American Revolution* (Elgin, Ill.: David C. Cook, 1982).
4. Norman Foerster, *Image in America* (Notre Dame, Ind.: University of Notre Dame Press, 1962), pp. 2, 3.
5. Harold O. J. Brown, *The Reconstruction of the Republic* (New Rochelle, N.Y.: Arlington House, 1977), pp. 18-23.
6. *Ibid.*, p. 19.
7. *Ibid.* (emphasis in original).
8. *See* Whitehead, *The Second American Revolution, op. cit.*, pp. 26-28; Whitehead, *The Stealing of America, op. cit.*, pp. 31-33.
9. Whitehead, *The Second American Revolution, op. cit.*, p. 26.
10. *Ibid.*, pp. 26-28.
11. Albert Camus, *The Rebel*, trans. Anthony Bower (New York: Knopf, 1969), p. 10.
12. *See generally* Whitehead, *The Second American Revolution, op. cit.*
13. C. Gregg Singer, *A Theological Interpretation of American History* (Nutley, N.J.: Craig Press, 1969), p. 284.
14. Brown, *op. cit.*, p. 22.
15. Foerster, *op. cit.*, p. 9.
16. *See* Francis A. Schaeffer, *A Christian Manifesto* (Westchester, Ill.: Crossway Books, 1981), pp. 18-20.
17. Ernest Lee Tuveson, *Redeemer Nation: The Idea of America's Millennial Role* (Chicago: University of Chicago Press, 1968), p. 12.
18. Perry Miller, *The Life of the Mind in America* (London: Victor Gallancz, 1966), pp. 10ff.
19. Mark Twain, *Autobiography of Mark Twain*, ed. Charles Neider (New York: Harper & Row, 1959), p. 30.
20. C. Gregg Singer, *From Rationalism to Irrationality: The Decline of the Western Mind from the Renaissance to the Present* (Phillipsburg, N.J.: Presbyterian and Reformed, 1979), p. 55.
21. Paul Johnson, *Modern Times: The World from the Twenties to the Eighties* (New York: Harper and Row, 1983), p. 1.
22. *Ibid.* (footnote omitted).
23. Alfred North Whitehead, *Science and the Modern World* (New York: Macmillan, 1925), n.p.

24. Albert Einstein, *Out of My Later Years* (London: Thames and Hudson, 1950), p. 41.
25. Johnson, *op. cit.*, p. 4.
26. *Ibid.*
27. Eugene T. Mallove, "Einstein's Intoxication with the God of the Cosmos," *Washington Post* (December 22, 1985), p. C1.
28. Johnson, *op. cit.*, p. 4
29. *Ibid.*, p. 5
30. *Ibid.*
31. Neil Postman, *Amusing Ourselves to Death: Public Discourse in the Age of Show Business* (New York: Viking Books, 1985), p. 55.
32. Francis A. Schaeffer, *The God Who Is There* (Downers Grove, Ill.: InterVarsity, 1968), p. 14.
33. *See* Robert Pirsig, *Zen and the Art of Motorcycle Maintenance* (New York: Morrow, 1974), p. 7.
34. Francis A. Schaeffer, *The Great Evangelical Disaster* (Westchester, Ill.: Crossway Books, 1984), pp. 35, 36.
35. Schaeffer, *The God Who Is There, op. cit.*, p. 15
36. *See, for example,* Romans 2:13; James 1:22-27; 2:17, 18.
37. Schaeffer, *The Great Evangelical Disaster, op. cit.*, p. 37.
38. *See* John R. W. Stott, *Christ the Controversialist* (Downers Grove, Ill.: InterVarsity Press, 1970).
39. *Ibid.*, pp. 13, 14 (footnote omitted).
40. *Ibid.*, p. 18 (footnote omitted).
41. *Ibid.*, pp. 13-19.
42. Schaeffer, *The Great Evangelical Disaster, op. cit.*, p. 37 (emphasis in original).
43. George Gallup, *Forecast 2000: George Gallup, Jr., Predicts the Future of America* (New York: William Morrow, 1984), p.152.
44. *Ibid.*, p. 153.
45. As cited in Michael Harrington, *The Politics at God's Funeral: The Spiritual Crisis of Western Civilization* (New York: Holt, Rinehart and Winston, 1983), p. 165.
46. *Ibid.*
47. *Ibid. Also see* "Theological Survey Finds Tolerance for Pre-Marital Sex," *Washington Post* (December 29, 1984), p. A3.
48. *Ibid.*, p. 7.
49. Postman, *op. cit.*, pp. 55, 56.
50. Harry Blamires, *The Christian Mind* (Ann Arbor, Mich.: Servant Books, 1978), p. 3.
51. Harrington, *op. cit.*, p. 8.
52. J. Gresham Machen, *The Christian Faith in the Modern World* (Grand Rapids, Mich.: Eerdmans, 1965), p. 4.
53. *Ibid.*, p. 10.

CHAPTER TWO: THE DEATH OF HUMANISM

1. Herbert Schlossberg, *Idols for Destruction* (Nashville: Thomas Nelson, 1983), p. 273 (emphasis supplied).

2. Gerhard Lenski, *The Religious Factor: A Sociological Study of Religion's Impact on Politics, Economics and Family Life* (Garden City, N.Y.: Doubleday, 1961), pp. 298ff., 322.
3. Michael Harrington, *The Politics at God's Funeral: The Spiritual Crisis of Western Civilization* (New York: Holt, Rinehart and Winston, 1983), p. 4.
4. Helmut Thielicke, *The Evangelical Faith*, Geoffrey W. Bromiley, trans. (Grand Rapids, Mich.: Eerdmans, 1974), pp. 225.
5. Heinrich Heine, *Selected Works*, Helen M. Mustard, trans. (New York: Vintage, 1973), p. 365.
6. As quoted by Paul Johnson, *Modern Times: The World from the Twenties to the Eighties* (New York: Harper and Row, 1983), p. 734.
7. Francis A. Schaeffer, *A Christian Manifesto* (Westchester, Ill.: Crossway Books, 1981), p. 23 (footnote omitted).
8. Lucien Goldman, *Le Dieu Caché* (Paris: Gallimard, 1955), p. 45.
9. James Hitchcock, *What Is Secular Humanism?* (Ann Arbor, Mich.: Servant Books, 1982), pp. 8, 9.
10. *Ibid.*, pp. 10, 11.
11. Aldous Huxley, *Brave New World* (New York: Harper and Row), pp. 41-42.
12. *See generally* George Holyoake, *Secularism: The Practical Philosophy of the People* (London: Holyoake and Co., 1845).
13. George Holyoake, *Life of Holyoake—Sixty Years of an Agitator's Life* (London: T. F. Unwin, 1906), pp. 293, 294.
14. *Ibid.*, p. 294. *Cf.* George Holyoake, *The History of the Last Trial by Jury for Atheism in England*, M. O'Hair, ed. (New York: Arno Press, 1973).
15. Os Guinness, *The Dust of Death* (Downers Grove, Ill.: InterVarsity Press, 1973), p. 14.
16. *Ibid.*, p. 15.
17. *Ibid.*
18. Michael Novak, *The Experience of Nothingness* (New York: Harper & Row, 1970), p. 66.
19. *See generally* B. F. Skinner, *Beyond Freedom and Dignity* (New York: Knopf, 1971).
20. As quoted in Frederick E. Trinklein, *The God of Science* (Grand Rapids, Mich.: Eerdmans, 1971).
21. Phil Donahue, *The Human Animal* (New York: Simon & Schuster, 1985), p. 98.
22. Lewis Thomas, *Late Night Thoughts on Listening to Mahler's Ninth Symphony* (New York: Viking, 1983), p. 119.
23. Guinness, *op. cit.*, p. 16.
24. Skinner, *op. cit.*, pp. 200, 201.
25. Leonard Broom and Philip Selznick, *Sociology: A Text with Adapted Readings*, 4th ed. (New York: Harper and Row, 1968), pp. 47, 48.
26. As quoted by Francis A. Schaeffer, *Back to Freedom and Dignity* (Downers Grove, Ill.: InterVarsity Press, 1972), p. 20.
27. *Ibid.*, p. 23.
28. Vadim Borisov, "Personality and National Awareness," *From Under the Rubble*, M. Scammel, trans. (Boston: Little, Brown, 1975), pp. 194, 200, 201.

29. Arthur Koestler, *The Ghost in the Machine* (New York: Macmillan, 1968), p. 15.
30. Guinness, *op. cit.*, p. 23.
31. Schaeffer, *op. cit.*, pp. 15-16.
32. Harvey Cox, *The Secular City* (New York: Macmillian, 1965).
33. *Ibid.*, p. 18.
34. *Ibid.*
35. Hitchcock, *op. cit.*, p. 141.
36. Mary Jordan, "Suicides Plague College Campuses," *Washington Post* (November 12, 1984), p. A1; W. Gardner Selby, "Teen Suicides Portrayed As 'Epidemic,'" *Washington Post* (December 16, 1984), p. A6.
37. Hitchcock, *op. cit.*, p. 141.
38. *Ibid.*, p. 142.
39. *Ibid.*

CHAPTER THREE: A NEW FAITH

1. C. Gregg Singer, *From Rationalism to Irrationality: The Decline of the Western Mind from the Renaissance to the Present* (Phillipsburg, N.J.: Presbyterian and Reformed, 1979), p. 127.
2. Charles Darwin, *Descent of Man* (London: John Murray, 1871), p. 9.
3. As quoted in Douglas DeWar and H. S. Shelton, *Is Evolution Proved?* (London: Hollis and Carter, 1947), p. 4.
4. As quoted in Amaury de Reincourt, *The Coming Caesars* (N.Y.: Coward-McCann, 1957), p. 179.
5. As quoted in Herbert Agar, *The Price of Union* (Boston: Houghton Mifflin, 1950), p. 522.
6. See Arnold C. Brackman, *A Delicate Arrangement: The Strange Case of Charles Darwin and Alfred Russel Wallace* (New York: Times Books, 1980).
7. See generally Alfred Russel Wallace, *Darwinism* (London: Macmillan, 1889).
8. *Ibid.*
9. Jeremy Rifkin, *Algeny* (New York: Viking, 1983), p. 98.
10. *Ibid.*
11. Reincourt, *op. cit.*, p. 179.
12. Singer, *op. cit.*, p. 135.
13. *Ibid.*
14. Ralph Henry Gabriel, *The Course of American Democratic Thought*, 2nd ed. (New York: John Wiley and Sons, 1956), p. 183.
15. Charles Hodge, *What is Darwinism?* (New York: Scribner, Armstrong, 1874), p. 95.
16. Singer, *op. cit.*, p. 132.
17. Charles Darwin, *The Origin of Species by Means of Natural Selection or the Preservation of Favoured Races in the Struggle for Life* (New York: D. Appleton, 1872), p. 63.
18. Jacques Barzun, *Darwin, Marx and Wagner* (Boston: Peter Smith, 1946), pp. 351, 352.

19. Singer, *op, cit.*, p. 134.
20. Gabriel, *op. cit.*, p. 183.
21. Singer. *op. cit.*, p. 149.
22. Victor Ranford, "Sociology," *Encyclopedia Britannica*, Vol. 20 (1949), p. 912.
23. Julian Huxley, "Evolution and Genetics," *What is Science?* J. Newman, ed. (New York: Simon and Schuster, 1955), pp. 272-278.
24. *See* John W. Whitehead, *The Stealing of America* (Westchester, Ill.: Crossway Books, 1983), pp. 16-20.
25. *McClean v. Arkansas*, 529 F. Supp. 1255, 720 (E.D. Ark., 1982).
26. A. E. Wilder-Smith, *He Who Thinks Has to Believe* (Minneapolis, Minn.: Bethany House, 1981), p. 71.
27. *See generally* Thorkild Jacobsen, "Enuma Elish—'The Babylonian Genesis,'" *Theories of the Universe*, M. K. Munitz, ed. (New York: Free Press of Glencoe, 1957).
28. *Ibid.*, p. 9.
29. E. A. Wallis, trans., *The Book of the Dead* (New York: University Books, 1960), p. 552.
30. Henry M. Morris, *The Twilight of Evolution* (Grand Rapids, Mich.: Baker Book House, 1963), pp. 75, 76.
31. Charles Darwin, *The Origin of the Species by Means of Natural Selection or the Preservation of Favoured Races in the Struggle for Life*, L. Valorium, ed. (Philadelphia: University of Pennsylvania Press, 1959), p. 759. *Compare* M. J. Savage, *The Religion of Evolution* (Boston: Lockwood, Brooks, 1876.)
32. Charles Darwin, *The Illustrated Origin of the Species*, Richard E. Leakey, ed. (New York: Hill and Wang, 1979), p. 223.
33. *See generally*, Pierre Teilhard de Chardin, *The Vision of the Past*, J. Cohen, trans. (New York: Harper and Row, 1966).
34. As quoted by Peter Smulders, *The Design of Teilhard de Chardin*, A. Gibson, trans. (Westminster, Md.: Newman Press, 1967), p. 30.
35. Pierre Teilhard de Chardin, *The Phenomenon of Man*, B. Wall, trans. (New York: Harper and Row, 1959), p. 241.
36. Julian Huxley, "At Random—A Television Preview," *Evolution After Darwin*, Vol. I, Sol Tax, ed. (Chicago: University of Chicago Press, 1960), p. 42.
37. Rifkin, *op. cit.*, p. 112.
38. Colin Patterson, speech delivered at the American Museum of Natural History, New York, N.Y. (July 5, 1981) (emphasis supplied).
39. Edwin G. Conklin, *Man Real and Ideal: Observations and Reflections on Man's Nature, Development and Destiny* (New York: Scribner's, 1943), p. 147 (emphasis supplied).
40. As quoted in Robert Cowen, "Biological Origins: Theories Evolve," *Christian Science Monitor* (January 4, 1962), p. 4 (emphasis supplied).
41. *Ibid.* (emphasis supplied).
42. As quoted in William Overend, "Two Looks into the Future and Past," *Los Angeles Times* (November 9, 1977), Pt. IV, p. 1.

43. As quoted in Henry Morris and John Whitcomb, *The Genesis Flood* (Philadelphia: Presbyterian and Reformed, 1961) p. 234.
44. Pierre P. Grassé, *Evolution of Living Organisms* (New York: Academic Press, 1977), p. 6.
45. *Ibid.*, p. 202.
46. *Ibid.*, p. 31.
47. *Ibid.*
48. For example, consider the alleged transformation from fish to amphibians. As Rifkin notes:

> The structual differences between the two are so great that it would have taken millions of years of gradual evolutionary changes, in which time countless intermediate forms would have had to emerge, in order to link fish with amphibians. Yet...the links are nowhere to be found. The record shows that between the fin of the crossopterygian and the foot of the amphibian Ichthyostega is an anatomical gap so large that it begs the question once again: Where are the millions of intermediate forms that would be required to exist in order for the former to evolve into the latter? Rifkin, *op. cit.*, p. 127.

There is a basic difference in anatomy between fishes and all amphibians not bridged by transitional forms:

> In all fishes, living or fossil, the pelvic bones are small and loosely embedded in muscle. There is no connection between the pelvic bones and the vertebral column. None is needed. The pelvic bones do not and could not support the weight of the body.... In tetrapod amphibians, living or fossil, on the other hand, the pelvic bones are very large and firmly attached to the vertebral column. This is the type of anatomy an animal must have to walk. It is the type of anatomy found in all living or fossil tetrapod amphibians but which is absent in all living or fossil fishes. There are no transitional forms.

Duane Gish, *The Fossils Say No!* (San Diego: Creation-Life Publishers, 1978), pp. 74, 75. There is more so with birds. *See* Rifkin, *op. cit.*, pp. 128-130.
49. Rifkin, *op. cit.*, p. 153.
50. G. A. Kerkut, *Implications of Evolution* (New York: Pergamon Press, 1960), p. 150.
51. Richard B. Morris, *Dismantling the Universe: The Nature of Scientific Discovery* (New York: Simon and Schuster, 1983), p. 129.
52. Theodosius Dobzhansky, "On Methods of Evolutionary Biology and Anthropology," *American Scientist*, Vol. 45 (1957), p. 388.
53. Alan C. Burton, "The Human Side of the Physiologist, Prejudice and Poetry," *Physiologist*, Vol. 1, No. 1 (1975), p. 2.
54. Francis A. Schaeffer, *Genesis in Space and Time* (Downers Grove, Ill.: InterVarsity Press, 1972), p. 21.

55. *Ibid.* (emphasis supplied).
56. R. L. Wysong, *The Creation-Evolution Controversy* (Midland, Mich.: Inquiry Press, 1976), p. 7.
57. Robert E. D. Clarke, *Darwin: Before and After* (London: Paternoster Press, 1948), p. 115.
58. *Ibid.*, p. 115.
59. *Ibid.*, pp. 115-117.
60. Arthur Keith, *Evolution and Ethics* (New York: G. P. Putnam's Sons, 1949), p. 230.
61. As quoted in Geoffrey West, *Charles Darwin: A Portrait* (New Haven, Conn.: Yale University Press, 1938), p. 324.
62. Rifkin, *op. cit.*, p. 105.
63. *Ibid.*, pp. 105, 106. *See also* Paul Johnson, *Modern Times: The World from the Twenties to the Eighties* (New York: Harper and Row, 1983), pp. 730, 731.
64. Arnold M. Rose, "The Slow Painful Death of the Race Myth," *Society Today and Tomorrow*, E. Hunt and J. Karlin, eds. (New York: Macmillan, 1961), p. 194. *Compare* John S. Holler, Jr., *Outcasts from Evolution: Scientific Attitudes of Racial Inferiority* (New York: McGraw-Hill, 1971).
65. Stephen Jay Gould, *The Mismeasure of Man* (New York: W. W. Norton, 1981).
66. *See* Patrick Monaghan, "'Substantively Due Processing' The Blacks Population," 4 *Lincoln Review* 45 (1983).

CHAPTER FOUR: THE DISENCHANTED WORLD

1. Henry David Thoreau, *Walden* (Princeton, N.J.: Princeton University Press, 1971), p. 98.
2. Annie Dillard, *Pilgrim at Tinker Creek* (New York: Harper and Row, 1974), p. 271.
3. Joseph Campbell, *The Masks of God* (New York: Viking, 1969), p. 150.
4. Lynn White, Jr., "The Historical Roots of Our Ecologic Crisis," *Science*, Vol. 155 (March 10, 1967), pp. 1203-1207.
5. J. A. Walter, *The Human Home: The Myth of the Sacred Environment* (Icknield Way, Tring, Herts, England: Lion Publishing Co., 1982), p. 13.
6. For a discussion of Lynn White's criticisms, *see* Francis A. Schaeffer, *Pollution and the Death of Man: The Christian View of Ecology* (Wheaton, Ill.: Tyndale House, 1970).
7. Lewis Thomas, *The Youngest Science* (New York: Viking, 1983), p. 248.
8. Phil Donahue, *The Human Animal* (New York: Simon & Schuster, 1983), p. 41.
9. Walter, *op. cit.*, pp. 18, 19.
10. As quoted in Walter, *op. cit.*, p. 15.
11. Edward Abbey, *Desert Solitaire* (New York: Ballantine Books, 1971), p. 60.
12. Walter, *op. cit.*, p. 26.
13. *Ibid.*, p. 20.

14. *See generally* Julian Simon, *The Ultimate Resource* (Princeton, N.J.: Princeton University Press, 1981) and Germaine Greer, *Sex and Destiny* (New York: Harper and Row, 1984).

15. *See* Greer, *Ibid.*

16. Simon, *op. cit.*, p. 331.

17. Schaeffer, *op. cit.*, p. 30.

18. Will and Ariel Durant, *The Life of Greece* (New York: Simon & Schuster, 1939), p. 565.

19. As quoted in A. E. Wilder-Smith, *He Who Thinks Has to Believe* (Minneapolis, Minn.: Bethany House, 1981), p. 71.

20. *Ibid.*, p. 71, 72.

21. Schaeffer, *op. cit.*, p. 30. Likewise, we should see ourselves as being one with the animals of creation. Though the Bible does not contain a comprehensive principle concerning animal rights, it repeatedly speaks on behalf of animals. They must not be tortured unnecessarily (Deut. 25:4); they must not be emasculated (Lev. 22:24); mother and young must not be slaughtered on the same day (Lev. 22:28); beasts of burden and all domestic animals must rest on the Sabbath Day (Exod. 20:10), etc. All creation is viewed as one by the Bible, and in this sense man has a duty to "watch out" for his fellow creatures.

22. Erik Erikson, *Childhood and Society* (New York: W. W. Norton, 2nd ed., 1963), pp. 79, 80.

23. *Ibid.*

24. Gary North, *The Dominion Covenant: Genesis* (Tyler, Tex.: Institute for Christian Economics, 1982), pp. 125, 126.

25. Francis A. Schaeffer, *Escape from Reason* (Downers Grove, Ill.: Inter-Varsity, 1968), p. 31.

26. Jeremy Rifkin, *Algeny* (New York: Viking, 1983), p. 40.

27. *Ibid.*, p. 52.

28. *Ibid.*

29. *Ibid.*, p. 53

30. *Ibid.*

31. As quoted in Michael Salomon, *Future Life*, G. Daniels, trans. (New York: Macmillian, 1983), p. 105.

32. C. S. Lewis, *The Abolition of Man* (New York: Macmillian, 1947), pp. 70, 71.

33. *See* John W. Whitehead, *The Stealing of America* (Westchester, Ill.: Crossway, 1983), pp. 45-47.

34. Ethan Singer, "Recombinant DNA: It's Not What We Need," (March 7, 8, and 9, 1977), as cited in Rifkin, *op. cit.*, p. 230.

35. Lewis, *op. cit.*, p. 72 (emphasis in original).

36. *Ibid.*, p. 76.

37. As quoted in Salomon, *op. cit.*, pp. 109, 117.

38. Lewis, *op. cit.*, p. 80.

CHAPTER FIVE: THE MAGICIAN'S BARGAIN

1. Michael Polanyi *The Tacit Dimension* (New York: Doubleday, Anchor ed., 1967), pp. 3, 4.

2. As quoted in Norman Foerster, *Image in America* (Notre Dame, Ind.: University of Notre Dame Press, 1962), p. 63.
3. Blaise Pascal, *Pensées* (New York: Dutton, 1931), p. 72.
4. Jeremy Jackson, *No Other Foundation* (Westchester, Ill.: Cornerstone, 1980), p. 21.
5. Will Durant, *The Age of Faith* (New York: Simon & Schuster, 1950), p. 988.
6. H. R. Rookmaaker, *Modern Art and the Death of a Culture* (Downers Grove, Ill.: InterVarsity Press, 1970), p. 42.
7. *Ibid.*
8. Jackson, *op. cit.*, p. 180.
9. Michael Harrington, *The Politics at God's Funeral: The Spiritual Crisis of Western Civilization* (New York: Holt, Rinehart and Winston, 1983), p. 13.
10. *Ibid.*, pp. 13, 14. Einstein once said: "I cannot conceive of a genuine scientist without that profound faith." Eugene T. Mallove, "Einstein's Intoxication with the God of the Cosmos," *Washington Post* (December 22, 1985), p. C4.
11. *See* Francis A. Schaeffer, *How Should We Then Live?* (Old Tappan, N.J.: Revell, 1976), pp. 130-143.
12. *See* Will and Ariel Durant, *The Age of Reason Begins* (New York: Simon and Schuster, 1961).
13. Rookmaaker, *op. cit.*, p. 44.
14. Immanuel Kant, *Gesammelte Schriften*, Prussian Academy, ed. (Berlin: George Reimer, 1911), p. 12.
15. *Ibid.*
16. *Ibid.*, pp. 403ff.
17. Harrington, *op. cit.*, p. 15.
18. Vincent Canby, "'A Clockwork Orange': Dazzles the Senses and Mind," *New York Times* (December 20, 1971), p. 44
19. Rookmaaker, *op. cit.*, p. 45.
20. Thus, we see the present debate over whether man has a mind or thoughts independent of the brain itself. Being immaterial, such things are questionable. *See generally* Arthur C. Custance, *The Mysterious Matter of Mind* (Grand Rapids, Mich.: Zondervan, 1980).
21. As quoted in Rookmaaker, *op. cit.*, p. 46.
22. Harold O. J. Brown, *Heresies* (Garden City, N.Y.: Doubleday, 1984), p. 21
23. Rookmaaker, *op. cit.*, p. 46.
24. *Ibid.*
25. Schaeffer, *op. cit.*, p. 154.
26. Michel Salomon. *Future Life*, G. Daniels, trans. (New York: Macmillan, 1983), p. 116.
27. Rookmaaker, *op. cit.*, p. 48.
28. C. S. Lewis, *The Abolition of Man* (New York: Macmillan, 1947), p. 84.
29. Carl Sagan, *Cosmos* (New York: Random House, 1980), p. 4.
30. Jacques Ellul, *The Technological Society* (New York: Vintage, 1964), p. 3.
31. *Ibid.*, p. 6.
32. *Ibid.*, p. 25.

33. *Ibid.*, p. 24.
34. *Ibid.*, p. 25.
35. William Doerflinger, *The Magic Catalogue* (New York: Dutton, 1977), p. 5.
36. Lewis, *op. cit.*, p. 87.
37. *Ibid.*, pp. 88-89.
38. Doerflinger, *op. cit.*, p. 39.
39. Aldous Huxley, *Science, Liberty, and Peace* (New York: Harper, 1946), p. 291 (emphasis supplied).
40. Herbert A. Simon, *The Sciences of the Artificial* (Cambridge, Mass.: M.I.T. Press, 1964), pp. 24, 25 (emphasis supplied).
41. Simon, *op. cit.*, p. 53.
42. Joseph Weizenbaum, *Computer Power and Human Reason* (San Francisco: W.H. Freeman, 1976), p. 266.
43. *Ibid.*, p. 261.
44. *Ibid.*, pp. 14, 15.
45. *Ibid.*, p. 15.

CHAPTER SIX: EXTENSIONS

1. Marshall McLuhan, *Understanding Media: The Extensions of Man* (New York: McGraw-Hill, 1964), p. 51.
2. *Ibid.*, p. 51.
3. Man's extensions have been seen in evolutionistic terms: "[M]an has shifted evolution from his body to his extensions and in doing so has tremendously accelerated the evolutionary process." Edward T. Hall, *The Hidden Dimension* (Garden City, N.Y.: Anchor Books, 1969), p. 4.
4. McLuhan, *op. cit.*, p. 194.
5. Alvin Toffler, *The Third Wave* (New York: Morrow, 1980), p. 30.
6. Marshall McLuhan, "Cybernation and Culture," *The Social Impact of Cybernetics* (New York: Simon and Schuster, Clarion ed., 1966), p. 99.
7. *See* Arthur C. Custance, *The Mysterious Matter of the Mind* (Grand Rapids, Mich.: Zondervan, 1980).
8. Marshall McLuhan, *The Gutenberg Galaxy* (Toronto: University of Toronto Press, 1962), p. i.
9. Lewis Mumford, *Technics and Civilization* (New York: Harcourt Brace Jovanovich, 1963), p. 14.
10. *Ibid.*, pp 13, 14.
11. *Ibid.*, p. 15.
12. McLuhan, *Understanding Media, op. cit.*, p. 144.
13. *See* Jeremy Rifkin, *Algeny* (New York: Viking Press, 1983), pp. 172-176.
14. McLuhan, *Understanding Media, op. cit.*, p. 19.
15. *Ibid.*, p. 20.
16. Zbigniew Brzezinski, *Between Two Ages: America's Role in the Technetronic Era* (New York: Penguin, 1970), p. 19.
17. McLuhan, *Understanding Media, op. cit.*, p. 280.
18. *Ibid.*, p. 272.

258 □ THE END OF MAN

19. *Ibid.*, p. 323.
20. *See* Neil Postman, *Amusing Ourselves to Death: Public Discourse in the Age of Show Business* (New York: Viking Books, 1985).
21. McLuhan, *Understanding Media, op. cit.*, p. 269.
22. *Ibid.*, p. 48.
23. Jacques Ellul, *The Technological Society* (New York: Vintage Books, 1964), p. 433.
24. *Ibid.*
25. McLuhan, *Understanding Media, op. cit.*, pp. 300, 301.
26. *Ibid.*, p. 304 (emphasis supplied).

CHAPTER SEVEN: THE SCHIZOID COMPROMISE

1. Lewis Thomas, *The Lives of a Cell* (New York: Viking, 1975), p. 12.
2. Sherry Turkle, *The Second Self: Computers and the Human Spirit* (New York: Simon and Schuster, 1984), p. 39.
3. Joseph Weizenbaum, *Computer Power and Human Reason* (San Francisco: W. H. Freeman, 1976), p. 3.
4. *Ibid.*, pp. 3, 4.
5. *See* Paul C. Vitz, *Psychology as Religion:The Cult of Self-Worship* (Grand Rapids, Mich.: Eerdmans, 1977) and Garth Wood, *The Myth of Neurosis: Overcoming the Illness Excuse* (New York: Harper and Row, 1986).
6. K. M. Colby, J. B. Watt, and J. P. Gilbert, "A Computer Method of Psychotherapy: Preliminary Communication," *The Journal of Nervous and Mental Disease*, Vol. 142, No. 2 (1966), pp. 148-152.
7. Carl Sagan, "In Praise of Robots," *Natural History,*Vol. LXXXIV, No. 1 (January 1975), p. 10.
8. Colby, Watt, and Gilbert, *op. cit.*, pp. 148-152 (emphasis supplied).
9. Weizenbaum, *op. cit.*, p. 6.
10. Michael Polanyi, *The Tacit Dimension* (New York: Doubleday, Anchor ed., 1967), pp. 3, 4.
11. Weizenbaum, *op. cit.*, p. 7.
12. *Ibid.*, p. 8.
13. *See* Christopher Lasch, *The Culture of Narcissism* (New York: Norton, 1979).
14. Turkle, *op. cit.*, p. 306.
15. *Ibid.*, p. 307.
16. *Ibid.*, pp. 307, 308.
17. *Ibid.*, p. 308.
18. Herbert A. Simon, "What Computers Mean for Man and Society,"*Science* (March 18, 1977), pp. 1186-1191.
19. Sharon Begley, "How The Brain Works," *Newsweek* (February 7, 1983), p. 47.
20. Christopher Evans, *The Micro Millennium* (New York: Washington Square Press, 1979), p. 273.
21. *Ibid.*
22. Marshall McLuhan, *Understanding Media: The Extensions of Man* (New York: New American Library, Signet ed., 1964), p. 52.

23. *Ibid.*
24. Jeremy Rifkin, *Algeny* (New York: Viking, 1983), p. 19.
25. As quoted in Edward B. Fiske, "Computers Alter Life of Pupils and Teachers," *New York Times* (April 4, 1982), p. 1.
26. *Ibid.*

CHAPTER EIGHT: THE ORGANIC MACHINE

1. Julian Huxley, "At Random—A Television Preview," *Evolution after Darwin*, ed. Sol Tax, Vol. 2 (Chicago: University of Chicago Press, 1960), p. 42.
2. Jeremy Rifkin, *Algeny* (New York: Viking, 1983), p. 112.
3. Huxley, *op. cit.*, p. 41.
4. Garrett Hardin, *Nature and Man's Fate* (New York: Mentor Books, 1961), p. 216.
5. Speech delivered by Colin Patterson at the American Museum of Natural History, New York, N.Y. (November 5, 1981).
6. Rifkin, *op. cit.*, p. 114
7. The first inkling came during a centennial celebration of Darwin's theory held at the University of Chicago in 1959. One of the speakers, paleontologist Everett Claire Olson of the University of California, noted:

> [T]here exists. . .a generally silent group of students engaged in biological pursuits who tend to disagree with much of the current thought, but say and write little because they are not particularly interested, do not see that controversy over evolution is of any particular importance, or are so strongly in disagreement that it seems futile to undertake the monumental task of controverting the immense body of information and theory that exists in the formulation of modern thinking.

Everett Claire Olson, "The Evolution of Life," *Evolution after Darwin*, ed. Sol Tax, Vol. 1 (Chicago: University of Chicago Press, 1960), p. 523.
8. Rifkin, *op. cit.*, p. 115.
9. G. A. Kerkut, *Implications of Evolution* (New York: Pergamon Press, 1960), p. vii.
10. Aleksandr Oparin, *Life: Its Nature, Origin and Development* (London: J. M. Dent and Sons, 1971), p. xi.
11. Rifkin, *op. cit.*, p. 120.
12. *Ibid.*, p. 177.
13. *Ibid.*
14. *Ibid.*
15. *Ibid.*, p. 182.
16. R. G. Collingwood, *The Idea of Nature* (Oxford: Clarendon Press, 1945), p. 146.
17. As quoted in Alfred North Whitehead, *The Principles of Natural Knowledge*, 2nd ed. (Cambridge, England: Cambridge University Press, 1925), p. 54.

18. Collingwood, *op. cit.*, p. 146.
19. Alfred North Whitehead, *Nature and Life* (New York: Greenwood Press, 1968), pp. 20-22.
20. *Ibid.*, p. 27.
21. C. Gregg Singer, *From Rationalism to Irrationality* (Phillipsburg, N.J.: Presbyterian and Reformed, 1979), p. 237. Whitehead's final idea of religion reflected his process philosophy. He wrote:

Religion is the vision of something which stands beyond, behind and within, the passing flux of immediate things; something which is real and yet waiting to be realized; something which is a remote possibility, and yet the greatest of present facts; something that gives meaning to all that passes, and yet eludes apprehension; something whose possession is a final good, and yet is beyond all reach; something which is the ultimate ideal, and the hopeless quest.

Alfred North Whitehead, *Science and the Modern World* (New York: Macmillan, 1925), p. 180.
22. Rifkin, *op. cit.*, p. 188.
23. J. T. Fraser, *Of Time, Passion, and Knowledge: Reflections on the Strategy of Existence* (New York: George Braziller, 1975), p. 442.
24. Rifkin, *op. cit.*, p. 200.
25. *Ibid.*
26. *Ibid.*, p. 201.
27. A. Rosenblueth, N. Wiener, and J. Bigelow, "Behavior, Purpose and Teleology," *Philosophy of Science*, Vol. 101 (1943), p. 18.
28. *Ibid.*, p. 278.
29. John Naisbitt, *Megatrends* (New York: Warner Books, 1982), p. 16.
30. William H. Thorpe and Oliver L. Zangwill, *Current Problems in Animal Behavior* (Cambridge: Cambridge University Press, 1980), p. 303.
31. *Ibid.*
32. Marjorie Grene, *The Understanding of Nature* (Dordrecht: D. Reidel, 1974), p. 68.
33. Rifkin, *op. cit.*, p. 207.
34. R. L. Gregory, "The Brain as an Engineering Problem," *Current Problems in Animal Behavior*, eds. W. H. Thorpe and O. L. Zangwill (Cambridge: Cambridge University Press, 1961), p. 307.
35. W. H. Thorpe, "The Frontiers of Biology," *Mind in Nature*, eds. John Cobb and David Griffin (Washington, D.C.: University Press of America, 1977), p. 3.
36. *Ibid.*, p. 6 (emphasis supplied).
37. Pierre Grassé, *Evolution of Living Organisms: Evidence for a New Theory of Transformation* (New York: Academic Press, 1977), p. 223.
38. *Ibid.*, p. 225.
39. Rifkin, *op. cit.*, p. 209.
40. Naisbitt, *op. cit.*, p. 24.
41. Duane T. Gish and Clifford Wilson, *Manipulating Life: Where Does It Stop?* (San Diego: Master Books, 1981), p. 18.

42. Harold M. Schmeck, Jr., "Animals Given a Human Gene: Growth Hormone Gene Yields Dramatic Results," *New York Times* (December 6, 1983), p. C1. *See also* Boyce Remsberger, "Scientists Hail Gene Transfers As Promising," *Washington Post* (November 20, 1984), p. A1.
43. *Ibid.*, p. C4.
44. *Ibid.*
45. Cristine Russell, "USDA Using Human Gene in Effort to Grow Super Livestock," *Washington Post* (October 1, 1984), p. A1.
46. *See, for example,* Cristine Russell, "Gene Panel Rejects Ban: Interspecies Transfer Seen Useful by NIH," *Washington Post* (October 30, 1984), p. A8. *See also* Cristine Russell, "Activist Challenges Gene-Transfer Research," *Washington Post* (November 20, 1984), p. A6.
47. *International Life Times* (November 7, 1980), p. 9.
48. *Ibid.*
49. *Roe v. Wade,* 410 U.S. 113 (1973).
50. "Post-Abortion Fetal Study Stirs Storm," *Medical World News* (June 8, 1973), p. 21.
51. C. S. Lewis, *The Abolition of Man* (New York: Macmillan, 1947), pp. 89, 90.

CHAPTER NINE: AI

1. Frank Rose, *Into the Heart of the Mind: An American Quest for Artificial Intelligence* (New York: Harper and Row, 1984), p. 12.
2. Lewis Thomas, *Lives of a Cell* (New York: Viking, 1973), p. 111.
3. Sherry Turkle, *The Second Self: Computers and the Human Spirit* (New York: Simon and Schuster, 1984), pp. 240, 241.
4. Herbert A. Simon and Allen Newell, "Heuristic Problem Solving: The Next Advance in Operation Research," *Operations Research,* Vol. 6 (Jan.-Feb.1958), p. 8.
5. Joseph Weizenbaum, *Computer Power and Human Reason: From Judgment to Calculation* (San Francisco: Walt Freeman, 1976), p. 112.
6. *Ibid.*, pp. 112, 113.
7. *Ibid.*, p. 121.
8. Edmund Bergler, *The Psychology of Gambling* (New York: Hill and Wang, 1957), p. 230.
9. Weizenbaum, *op. cit.*, p. 126.
10. As quoted in Turkle, *op, cit.*, p. 252. *See also* Gerald Jay Sussman, *A Computer Model of Skill Acquisition* (New York: American Elsevier, 1975).
11. Turkel, *op. cit.*, pp. 252, 253.
12. *Ibid.*, p. 259 (emphasis supplied).
13. *Ibid.*, p. 260 (emphasis supplied).
14. *Ibid.*
15. *Ibid.*
16. *Ibid.*, p. 261.
17. *Ibid.*
18. *Ibid.*, pp. 261, 262.

19. As quoted in Pamela McCorduck, *Machines Who Think* (San Francisco: W. H. Freeman, 1979), p. 346.
20. Robert Jastrow, *The Enchanted Loom: Mind in the Universe* (New York: Simon and Schuster, 1981), p. 163.
21. Turkle, *op. cit.*, p. 267.
22. Arthur C. Custance, *The Mysterious Matter of the Mind* (Grand Rapids, Mich.: Zondervan, 1980), p. 92.
23. *Ibid.*
24. Norbert Wiener, *God and Golem, Inc.* (Cambridge, Mass.: MIT Press, 1964), p. 17.
25. Turkle, *op. cit.*, p. 289.
26. *Ibid.*, p. 288.
27. *Ibid.*
28. *Ibid.*, p. 296.

CHAPTER TEN: THE CONDITIONERS

1. J. Mayone Stycos, "Demographic Chic at the Union," as reprinted in Thomas Robert Malthus, *An Essay on The Principle of Population*, Philip Appleman, ed.(New York: W. W. Norton, 1976), p. 225.
2. *See generally* Steven W. Mosher, *Broken Faith: The Rural Chinese* (New York: Free Press, 1983).
3. Thomas Malthus, *An Essay on the Principle of Population as It Affects the Future Improvement of Society (1798)*, Phillip Appleman, ed. (New York: W. W. Norton, 1976).
4. *Ibid.*, p. 23.
5. Thomas Malthus, *An Essay on the Principle of Population, or a View of Its Post and Present Effects on Human Happiness with an Inquiry Into Our Prospects Respecting the Future Removal or Mitigation of the Evils Which It Occasions (1803)*, Phillip Appleman, ed. (New York: W. W. Norton, 1976).
6. *Ibid.*, p. 132.
7. Will and Ariel Durant, *The Age of Napoleon: A History of European Civilization from 1789 to 1815* (New York: Simon and Schuster, 1975), p. 402.
8. Robert L. Heilbroner, *The Worldly Philosophers* (New York: Simon and Schuster, 1953), p. 85.
9. Durant, *op. cit.*, p. 402.
10. Julian L. Simon, *The Ultimate Resource* (Princeton, N.J.: Princeton University Press, 1981), p. 163.
11. Charles Darwin, *Autobiography* (New York: Dover Publications, 1958), p. 42.
12. Philip P. Weiner, *Dictionary of the History of Ideas*, Vol. II (New York: Charles Scribner's Sons, 1973), p. 180.
13. Alfred Russel Wallace, *The Action of Natural Selection on Man* (Stanford: Academic Reprints, 1953), p. 27.
14. Jane Hume Clapperton, *Scientific Meliorism* (London: K. Paul, Trench, 1885), p. 373 (emphasis in original).

15. Francis Galton, "Eugenics: Its Definition, Scope and Aims," *Sociological Papers* (London: Macmillan, 1905), p. 47.
16. Arthur Keith, "Galton's Place Among Anthropologists," *Eugenics Review*, Vol. 12 (1920-21), p. 20.
17. Francis Galton, *Memories of My Life* (London: Methuen, 1908), p. 323.
18. Germaine Greer, *Sex and Destiny* (New York: Harper and Row, 1984), p. 309.
19. As quoted in Greer, *ibid.*, pp. 309, 310.
20. *See* Leon F. Whitney, *The Case for Sterilization* (New York: Frederick A. Stokes, 1934).
21. *Eugenics Review*, Vol. 4 (1912), pp. 204, 205 (emphasis supplied).
22. Greer, *op. cit.*, p. 312.
23. *Ibid.*, p. 313.
24. H. H. Laughlin, "Immigration Control," *A Report of the Special Committee on Immigration and the Alien Insane Submitting a Study on Immigration Control*, Chamber of Commerce of the State of New York (1934), p. 7.
25. Greer, *op. cit.*, p. 314.
26. Arabella Kenealy, "A Study of Degeneracy," *Eugenics Review*, Vol. 3 (1911), pp. 39, 43.
27. L. Burlingame, *Heredity and Social Problems* (New York: McGraw-Hill, 1940), p. 278.
28. *Buck v. Bell*, 247 U.S. 200, 207 (1926) (emphasis supplied).
29. Stephen J. Gould, *The Mismeasure of Man* (New York: W. W. Norton, 1981), p. 335.
30. As quoted in Simon, *op. cit.*, p. 324.
31. *Ibid.*
32. *Ibid.*
33. *Ibid.*
34. *Ibid.*
35. *Birth Control Review* (October 1926), p. 299 (emphasis supplied).
36. Margaret Sanger, *An Autobiography* (New York: Dover Publishers, 1971), p. 366.
37. Greer, *op. cit.*, p. 377.
38. *Ibid.*, p. 378.
39. Paul Erlich, *The Population Bomb* (New York: Ballantine Books, 1968).
40. Mary Meehan, "Foundation Power," *Human Life Review*, Vol. X (Fall 1984), p. 43.
41. *Ibid.*
42. *Ibid.*
43. *Ibid.*, p. 48 (footnotes omitted).
44. Greer, *op. cit.*, pp. 404, 405.
45. As quoted in Greer, *ibid.*, p. 406.
46. *Ibid.*, p. 381.
47. As quoted in Thomas B. Littlewood, *The Politics of Population Control* (Notre Dame, Ind.: University of Notre Dame Press, 1977), p. 51.
48. Greer, *op. cit.*, p. 385.
49. *Ibid.*, p. 386.

CHAPTER ELEVEN: DEATH CONTROL

1. *See generally* Leslie Savan, "Abortion Chic: The Attraction of Wanted—Unwanted Pregnancies," *Village Voice* (February 4, 1981).
2. Germaine Greer, *Sex and Destiny* (New York: Harper and Row, 1984), p. 473.
3. Julian L. Simon, *The Ultimate Resource* (Princeton, N.J.: Princeton University Press, 1981), pp. 162, 163.
4. *Ibid.*, pp. 171, 172.
5. *Ibid.*, p. 184.
6. *Ibid.*
7. *Ibid.*
8. *Ibid.*, p. 197.
9. As quoted in Charles Henry Hull, ed., *The Economic Writings of Sir William Petty*, Vol. I (Cambridge: Cambridge University Press, 1889), p. 474.
10. Simon, *op. cit.*, p. 199
11. *Ibid.*, pp. 216-256.
12. Greer, *op. cit.*, p. 325.
13. Leon F. Whitney, *The Case for Sterilization* (New York: Frederick A. Stokes, 1934), p. 137.
14. Moya Woodside, *Sterilization in North Carolina: A Sociological and Pyschological Study* (Chapel Hill, N.C.: University of North Carolina Press, 1950).
15. *Ibid.*, p. 6.
16. *Ibid.*, p. 191.
17. Simon, *op. cit.*, p. 322.
18. *Ibid.*
19. Gordon Zahn, "Abortion and the Corruption of the Mind," *New Perspectives on Human Abortion* (Frederick, Md.: University Publications of America, 1981), p. 337 (emphasis supplied).
20. Erma Clardy Craven, "Abortion, Poverty and Black Genocide: Gifts to the Poor," *Abortion and Social Justice* (New York: Sheed and Ward, 1972), p. 240.
21. "On the Edge of the Pit: Abortion as a Racist Tool," *The Daily Californian* (October 14, 1980), p. 4B (emphasis supplied).
22. Patrick Monaghan, "'Substantively Due Processing' the Black Population," *Lincoln Review*, Vol. 4 (Summer 1983), p. 46.
23. *Beal v. Doe*, 432 U.S. 438, 546 (1977) (Marshall, J., dissenting).
24. Bob Woodward and Scott Armstrong, *The Brethren* (New York: Avon, 1980), p. 166.
25. 432 U.S. at 462-63 (Blackmun, J., dissenting).
26. *Ibid.* (emphasis supplied).
27. *See generally* John W. Whitehead, *The Stealing of America* (Westchester, Ill.: Crossway Books, 1983).
28. Carl F. H. Henry, *The Christian Mindset in a Secular Society* (Portland Ore.: Multnomah Press, 1984).
29. *Ibid.*, p. 103.
30. Gareth Jones, *Brave New People* (Downers Grove, Ill.: InterVarsity Press, 1984).

31. *Ibid.*, pp. 176, 183.
32. *See generally* Michael J. Gorman, *Abortion and The Early Church* (Downers Grove, Ill.: InterVarsity Press, 1982).
33. Ronald J. Sider, *Rich Christians in an Age of Hunger* (Downers Grove, Ill.: InterVarsity Press, 1977).
34. *Ibid.*, p. 216
35. Franky Schaeffer and Harold Fickett, *A Modest Proposal for Peace, Prosperity and Happiness* (Nashville, Tenn.: Thomas Nelson, 1985), p. 133.
36. Kingsley Davis, "The Climax of Population Growth: Past and Future Perspective," *California Medicine,* Vol. 113 (1970), p. 33.
37. As quoted in Robin Elliott, Lynn C. Landman, Richard Lincoln, and Theodore Tsuruoka, "U.S. Population and Family Planning: A Review of the Literature," *Family Planning Perspectives,* Vol. 2, as reprinted in Daniel Callahan, ed., *The American Population Debate* (New York: Anchor Books, 1971), p. 206 (emphasis supplied).
38. Paul R. Erlich, *The Population Bomb* (New York: Ballantine, 1968), p. xi (emphasis supplied).
39. As quoted in Gordon Wolstenholme, ed., *Man and His Future: A CIBA Foundation Volume* (Boston: Little, Brown, 1963), p. 274, 275.
40. Donald Warwick, *Bitter Pills* (New York: Cambridge University Press, 1982), p. 28. Thus far birth control is not catching on in some African countries. *See* Blaine Harden, "Birth Control Raises Scare in Kenya," *Washington Post* (April 18, 1986), p. A17.
41. Greer, *op. cit.,* p. 404.
42. Roberta Cura and Catherine S. Pierce, *Experiments in Family Planning: Lessons from the Developing World* (Baltimore: Johns Hopkins Press, 1977), p. 132.
43. Greer, *op. cit.,* p. 406.
44. *Ibid.*, p. 408.
45. *Ibid.*, p. 410.
46. *Ibid.* (footnote omitted).
47. Meredith Minkler, "Consultants or Colleagues: The Role of the U.S. Population Advisers in India," *Population and Development Review* (December 1977), p. 414.
48. Greer, *op. cit.,* p. 413.
49. *Ibid.*, pp. 411, 412.
50. Ibid., p. 413.
51. *Ibid.*, pp. 413, 414.
52. *Ibid.*, p. 414.
53. *Ibid.*, p. 415.
54. Ibid., p. 417. *See also* M. E. Kahn and C. U. S. Prasad, *Fertility Control in India* (New Delhi: Monahar, 1980).
55. Greer, *op. cit.,* p. 418.
56. *Ibid.*, p. 419.
57. *Ibid.*, pp. 419, 420, 421 (emphasis supplied).
58. *Ibid.*, pp. 421, 422.
59. *Ibid.*, p. 422.
60. *Centre Calling,* Vol. 10 (1975), p. 3 (emphasis supplied).

61. As quoted by "Planned Parenthood's Plans," *Wall Street Journal* (December 19, 1984), p. 28.

62. Michael Weisskopf, "Shanghai's Curse: Too Many Fight for Too Little: Tough Birth Control Policy Shakes Chinese Society," *Washington Post* (January 6, 1985), p. A1. *Also see* Steven W. Mosher, *Broken Earth: The Rural Chinese* (New York: Free Press, 1983), for a detailed discussion of China's coercive family planning. Massive population control in the past in the Soviet Union is frustrating present efforts to stimulate births. *See* Michael Bonafield, "Soviet World-Record Abortion Rate Undermines Drive for More Births." *Washington Times* (August 19, 1985), p. 1A.

63. Michael Weisskopf, "Abortion Policy Tears at Fabric of China's Society," *Washington Post* (January 7, 1985), p. A1.

64. *Ibid.*

65. *Ibid.*, p. A20.

66. *Ibid.*

67. *Ibid.*

68. *Ibid.* (emphasis supplied).

69. *Ibid.*

70. *Ibid.*

71. *Ibid.*

72. *Ibid.*

73. *Ibid.*

74. *Ibid.*

75. "Vietnam Sets Penalties to Stem Births," *Washington Post* (December 26, 1984), p. A24.

76. "Sterilization Leads Birth-Control List: Popularity Exceeds Pill's," *Washington Post* (December 6, 1984), p. A6. *See also* Lloyd Shearer, "No Babies for U.S. Women," *Parade* (June 23, 1985), p. 19; and Robin Marantz Henig, "The Sterilization Option," *Washington Post Health* (March 19, 1986), p. 12.

77. Alva Myrdal, *Nation and Family* (New York: Harper and Brothers, 1941), pp. 87, 88.

78. Simon, *op. cit.*, p. 173. *See also* "Half U.S. Population Is Over 31 Years Old," *Washington Post* (April 11, 1985), p. A8.

79. *Ibid.*, p. 173. See also Cristine Russell, "Private Report Shows High Price of Living Longer," *Washington Post* (September 5, 1984), p. A2.

80. Greer, *op. cit.*, p. 444.

81. Francis A. Schaeffer and C. Everett Koop, *Whatever Happened to the Human Race?* (London: Marshall, Morgan and Scott, 1980), pp. 68, 69.

82. As cited by Simon, *op. cit.*, p. 341.

83. *Ibid.*, pp. 342, 343.

84. George J. Annas, "What Should We Do With Surplus Humans?" *Washington Post* (March 31, 1985), p. K1.

CHAPTER TWELVE: FRIENDLY FASCISM

1. Jacques Ellul, *The Political Illusion* (New York: Vintage Books, 1972), p. 9.

2. *Ibid.*
3. *See generally* Paul Johnson, *Modern Times: The World from the Twenties to the Eighties* (New York: Harper and Row, 1983).
4. Bertram Gross, *Friendly Fascism: The New Face of Power in America* (New York: M. Evans, 1980), p. 124.
5. Ellul, *op. cit.*, p. 10 (emphasis supplied).
6. Gross, *op. cit.*, p. 3.
7. *Ibid.*
8. Kenneth Dolbeare, "Alternatives to the New Fascism," paper delivered at The American Political Science Association (September 1976), as quoted in Gross, *op. cit.*, p. 2.
9. Francis A. Schaeffer, *How Should We Then Live?* (Old Tappan, N.J.: Revell, 1976), p. 228 (emphasis in original).
10. *Ibid.*, pp. 244, 245.
11. Kevin P. Phillips, *Post-Conservative America: People, Politics, and Ideology in a Time of Crisis* (N.Y.: Random House, 1981), p. 164.
12. William L. Shirer, *The Rise and Fall of the Third Reich: A History of Nazi Germany* (New York: Simon and Schuster, 1960).
13. As noted in Gross, *op. cit.*, p. 6.
14. Roland Huntford, *The New Totalitarians* (New York: Stein and Day, 1972), p. 11.
15. Neil Postman, *Amusing Ourselves to Death: Public Discourse in the Age of Show Business* (New York: Viking Books, 1985), p. 8.
16. *Ibid.*
17. *Ibid.*, p. 141.
18. *See generally* Samuel Blumenfeld, *Is Public Education Necessary?* (Greenwich, Conn.: Devon-Adair, 1981).
19. Postman, *op. cit.*, p. 8.
20. *Ibid.*, pp. 155, 156.
21. *Ibid.*, p. 163.
22. Schaeffer, *op. cit.*, p. 245.
23. William Irwin Thompson, "'What's Past Is Prologue,' The Past—What's That?," *New York Times* (June 10, 1976), p. 37.
24. *Ibid.*

CHAPTER THIRTEEN: THE NEW DESPOTISM

1. Bertram Gross, *Friendly Fascism: The New Face of Power in America* (New York: M. Evans, 1980), p. 2.
2. As quoted in David Burnham, *The Rise of the Computer State* (New York: Random House, 1983), p. 47.
3. As quoted in Leonard Peikoff, *The Ominous Parallels: The End of Freedom in America* (New York: Stein and Day, 1982), p. 7.
4. *See* John W. Whitehead, *The Stealing of America* (Westchester, Ill.: Crossway Books, 1983), pp. 115, 116.
5. As quoted by Ted Gest and Patricia M. Scherschel, "Who Is Watching You?" *U.S. News & World Report* (July 12, 1982), p. 34.
6. *Ibid.*
7. *Ibid.*, p. 35.

8. *Ibid.*
9. *Ibid.*, p. 36.
10. *Ibid.*
11. *Ibid.*
12. As quoted in Burnham, *op. cit.*, pp. 47, 48.
13. Jacques Ellul, *The Technological Society* (New York: Vintage, 1964), p. 274.
14. *Ibid.*, p. 275.
15. *See generally* John Kenneth Galbraith and M. S. Randhawa, *The New Industrial State* (Boston: Houghton Mifflin, 1967).
16. As quoted in Francis A. Schaeffer, *How Should We Then Live?* (Old Tappan, N.J.: Revell, 1976), p. 225.
17. *Ibid.*
18. *Ibid.*
19. *Ibid.*
20. Zbigniew Brzezinski, *Between Two Ages: America's Role in the Technetronic Era* (New York: Penquin, 1976), p. 260 (emphasis supplied).
21. *See* John W. Whitehead, *The Second American Revolution* (Elgin, Ill.: David C.Cook, 1982), pp. 89-92.
22. Ellul, *op. cit.*, p. 258.
23. Anthony Burgess, *A Clockwork Orange* (New York: W. W. Norton, 1963).
24. *See generally* Whitehead, *The Second American Revolution, op. cit.*
25. Ellul, *op. cit.*, p. 275.
26. As quoted in Burnham, *op. cit.*, p. 104.
27. *Ibid.*, p. 105.
28. *Ibid.*, pp. 105, 106.
29. As quoted in James Martin, *The Telematic Society: A Challenge For Tomorrow* (Englewood Cliffs, N.J.: Prentice Hall, 1981), p. 203.
30. Burnham, *op. cit.*, p. 107.
31. *Ibid.*, p. 109.
32. *Ibid.*, p. 110.
33. *Ibid.*
34. *Ibid.*, p. 111.
35. *Ibid.*, p. 112.
36. *Ibid.*, p. 122. For a detailed study of The National Security Agency *see* James Banford, *The Puzzle Palace: A Report on NSA, America's Most Secret Agency* (Boston: Houghton Mifflin, 1982).
37. *Ibid.*, p. 123.
38. *Ibid.*, p. 124.
39. *Ibid.*, pp. 126, 127.
40. *Ibid.*, p. 127.
41. *Ibid.*, p. 128.
42. *Ibid.*, p. 130.
43. *Ibid.*, p. 254.
44. Os Guinness, *The Dust of Death* (Downers Grove, Ill.: InterVarsity Press, 1973), p. 134.
45. Ellul, *op. cit.*, p. 97.

46. Guinness, *op. cit.*, p. 134.
47. Ellul, *op. cit.*, p. 100.
48. *Ibid.*, p. 102.
49. Burnham, *op. cit.*, pp. 152, 153.
50. Ellul, *op. cit.*, p. 102.
51. Aldous Huxley, *Brave New World* (New York: Bantam, 1968), p. xii.
52. Christopher Evans, *The Micro Millennium* (New York: Washington Square Press, 1969), p. 156.
53. *See* Burnham, *op. cit.*, pp.235-241.
54. Seymour Hersch, "Laird Approved False Reporting of Secret Raids," *New York Times* (August 10, 1973), p. 1.
55. *Ibid.*
56. *Ibid.*
57. Joseph Weizenbaum, *Computer Power and Human Reason: From Judgment to Calculation* (San Francisco: W. H. Freeman, 1976), p. 239.
58. *Ibid.*, p. 241 (emphasis in original).
59. Burnham, *op. cit.*, p. 253.
60. *See* George Gallup, Jr., *Forecast 2000: George Gallup, Jr., Predicts the Future of America* (New York: William Morrow, 1984), pp. 30-38.
61. *Ibid.*, pp. 33, 34.
62. *Ibid.*, p. 27.
63. *Ibid.*, p. 28.
64. *See, for example*, Edward T. Hall, *The Hidden Dimension* (Garden City, N.Y.: Anchor Books, 1969), pp. 3, 4
65. Evans, *op. cit.*, p. 280.

CHAPTER FOURTEEN: FREEDOM AND HUMANITY

1. Jean-François Revel, *How Democracies Perish* (Garden City, N.Y.: Doubleday, 1983), p. 3.
2. *Ibid.*
3. *Ibid.*, pp. 3, 4 (footnote omitted).
4. Fyodor Dostoyevski, *The Brothers Karamazov* (New York: Bantam Books, 1970).
5. *Ibid.*, pp. 297-319.
6. *Ibid.*, p. 304.
7. Matthew 4:3.
8. Matthew 4:4.
9. Dostoyevski, *op. cit.*, p. 305.
10. Aldous Huxley, *Brave New World and Brave New World Revisited* (New York: Harper and Row), Foreword.
11. Alexis de Tocqueville, *Democracy in America* (Garden City, N.Y.: Anchor Books, 1960), p. 61.
12. *See* Robin Lloyd, *For Money or Love: Boy Prostitution in America* (New York: Vanguard Press, 1976).
13. As quoted in B. F. Skinner, *Beyond Freedom and Dignity* (New York: Knopf, 1971), p. 34.
14. *Ibid.*
15. *Ibid.*, p. 40.

16. Dostoyevski, *op. cit.*, p. 307.
17. *See* Jacques Ellul, *The Political Illusion* (New York: Vintage Books, 1972), p. 6.
18. Aleksandr Solzhenitsyn, "Gulag Survivor Indicts Western 'Freedom,'" *Los Angeles Times* (June 13, 1976), Part IV, p. 1.
19. *Ibid.*
20. Matthew 4:8; Luke 4:5.
21. Matthew 4:9.
22. Matthew 6:24.
23. Daniel P. Mannix, *Those About to Die* (New York: Ballantine Books, 1958), p. 27.
24. Luke 1:28.
25. Pierre Grimal, *The Civilization of Rome* (New York: Simon and Schuster, 1963), pp. 332, 456.
26. Ethelbert Stauffer, *Christ and the Caesars* (Philadelphia: Westminster Press, 1965), p. 86.
27. Acts 4:12.
28. Matthew 4:10.
29. Dostoyevski, *op. cit.*, p. 307.
30. Matthew 4:6.
31. Matthew 4:7.
32. Dostoyevski, *op. cit.*, p. 308.
33. Ellul, *op. cit.*, p. 61.
34. Matthew 27:42.
35. Dostoyevski, *op. cit.*, p. 308.
36. Francis A. Schaeffer, *The Complete Works of Francis A. Schaeffer*, Vol. 4 (Westchester, Ill.: Crossway Books, 1982), p. 184.

SELECT
BIBLIOGRAPHY

As the heading suggests, this bibliography makes no pretense to be exhaustive. I have listed only the works I have actually used and cited in the text and/or referred to in the process of writing this book. Even so, for a subject as complex and multidimensional as set forth in the text, it is impossible to remember, let alone do full justice to, all the writings which have helped to form my opinions.

Abbey, Edward. *Desert Solitaire.* New York: Ballantine Books, 1971.

Agar, Herbert. *The Price of Union.* Boston: Houghton Mifflin, 1950.

Andrew, Brother. *The Ethics of Smuggling.* Wheaton, Ill.: Tyndale House, 1979.

Annas, George J. "What Should We Do With Surplus Potential Humans?" *Washington Post,* 31 March 1985.

Aristotle. *Politics.* Cambridge: Harvard University Press, 1932.

Ascherson, Neal, ed. *The French Revolution: Extracts from the Times 1789-1794.* London: Times Books, 1975.

Bailyn, Bernard, David Brian Davis, David Herbert Donald, John L. Thomas, Robert H. Wiebe, and Gordon S. Wood. *The Great Republic: A History of the American People.* Boston: Little, Brown, 1977.

Banbury, Richard F. "A Humanistic View of Abortion." 31 *Yale Law Report* (Fall 1984).

Banford, James. *The Puzzle Palace: A Report on NSA, America's Most Secret Agency.* Boston: Houghton Mifflin, 1982.

Barber, Noel. *Seven Days of Freedom: The Hungarian Uprising 1956.* New York: Stein & Day, 1974.

Barbour, Ian G. *Science Ponders Religion*. New York: Appleton-Century-Crofts, 1960.

Barzun, Jacques. *Darwin, Marx and Wagner*. Boston: Peter Smith, 1946.

Bass, Archer B. *Protestantism in the United States*. New York: Thomas Y. Crowell, 1929.

Bauer, P. T. *Equality, the Third World and Economic Delusion*. Cambridge: Harvard University Press, 1981.

Baumer, Franklin L. *Modern European Thought*. New York: Macmillan, 1977.

Becker, Carl. *The Declaration of Independence*. New York: Knopf, 1942.

_____. *The Eve of the Revolution*. New Haven: Yale University Press, 1918.

Begley, Sharon. "How the Brain Works," *Newsweek*, 7 February 1983.

Bergler, Edmund. *The Psychology of Gambling*. New York: Hill & Wang, 1957.

Birth Control Review. October 1926.

Blamires, Harry. *The Christian Mind*. Ann Arbor, Mich.: Servant Books, 1978.

Blanshard, Paul. "Three Cheers for Our Secular State." *The Humanist*, March/April 1976.

Blumenfeld, Samuel L. *Is Public Education Necessary?* Greenwich, Conn.: Devon-Adair, 1931.

Bonafield, Michael. "Soviet World-Record Abortion Rate Undermines Drive for More Births." *Washington Times*, 19 August 1985.

Boorstin, Daniel. *Image; or, What Happened to the American Dream*. New York: Atheneum, 1962.

Borisov, Vadim. "Personality and National Awareness," *From Under the Rubble*. Boston: Little, Brown, 1975.

Bosworth, Allan R. *America's Concentration Camps*. New York: Bantam Books, 1968.

Bourdeaux, Michael, and Michael Rowe. *May One Believe—in Russia?* London: Darton, Longman & Todd, 1980.

Brackman, Arnold C. *A Delicate Arrangement: The Strange Case of Charles Darwin and Alfred Russel Wallace*. New York: Times Books, 1980.

Bradbury, Ray. *Fahrenheit 451*. New York: Ballantine Books, 1979.

Bradley, Harold Whitman. *The United States 1492-1877*. New York: Charles Scribner's Sons, 1972.

Bridenbaugh, Carl. *Mitre and Sceptre: Transatlantic Faiths, Ideas, Personalities & Politics 1689-1775*. New York: Oxford University Press, 1962.

Broom, Leonard, and Philip Selznick. *Sociology: A Text with Adapted Readings*, 4th ed. New York: Harper & Row, 1968.

Brown, Harold O. J. *The Reconstruction of the Republic*. New Rochelle, New York: Arlington House, 1977.

_____. *Heresies*. Garden City, N.Y.: Doubleday, 1984.

Brown, Martin, ed. *The Social Responsibility of the Scientist*. New York: Free Press, 1971.

Brezezinski, Zbigniew. *Between Two Ages: America's Role in the Technetronic Era*. New York: Penguin, 1970.

Bullock, Alan. *Hitler: A Study in Tyranny*, rev. ed. New York: Harper & Row, 1962.

Burgess, Anthony. *A Clockwork Orange*. New York: W. W. Norton, 1963.

Burlingame, L. *Heredity and Social Problems*. New York: McGraw-Hill, 1940.

Burnham, David. *The Rise of the Computer State*. New York: Random House, 1983.

Burton, Alan C. "The Human Side of the Physiologist, Prejudice and Poetry," *Physiologist*, Vol. 1, No. 1, 1957.

Callahan, Daniel, ed. *The American Population Debate*. New York: Anchor Books, 1971.

Campbell, Joseph. *The Masks of God*. New York: Viking, 1969.

Camus, Albert. *The Rebel*, trans. Anthony Bower. New York: Knopf, 1969.

Canby, Vincent. "'A Clockwork Orange': Dazzles the Senses and Mind." *New York Times*, 20 December 1971.

Carlson, A. J. "Science and the Supernatural," *Science*, Vol. 78, 1931.

Carroll, Peter N. *Puritanism and the Wilderness*. New York: Columbia University Press, 1969.

Centre Calling, Vol. 10, 1975.

Clapperton, Jane Hume. *Scientific Meliorism*. London: K. Paul, Trench & Co., 1885.

Clark, Kenneth. *Civilisation: A Personal View*. New York: Harper and Row, 1969.

Clarke, Robert E. D. *Darwin: Before and After*. London: Paternoster Press, 1948.

Cohen, Carl. *Civil Disobedience: Conscience, Tactics and the Law*. New York: Columbia University Press, 1971.

Colby, K. M., J. B. Watt, and J. P. Gilbert. "A Computer Method of Psychotherapy: Preliminary Communication," *The Journal of Nervous and Mental Disease*, Vol. 142, No. 2 (1966).

Collingwood, R. G. *The Idea of Nature*. Oxford: Clarendon Press, 1945.

Commager, Henry Steele. *The Empire Of Reason*. Garden City, N. Y.: Anchor Press-Doubleday, 1977.

Conklin, Edwin G. *Man Real and Ideal: Observations and Reflections on Man's Nature, Development and Destiny*. New York: Charles Scribner's Sons, 1943.

Cotham, Perry C. *Politics, Americanism and Christianity*. Grand Rapids, Mich.: Baker Book House, 1976.

Cousins, Norman. *In God We Trust*. New York: Harper & Brothers, 1958.

Cowen, Robert. "Biological Origins: Theories Evolve," *Christian Science Monitor*, 4 January 1962.

Cox, Harvey. *The Secular City*. New York: Macmillan, 1965.

Craig, Gordon A. *Germany: 1866-1945*. New York: Oxford University Press, 1978.

Craven, Erma Clardy. "Abortion, Poverty and Black Genocide: Gifts to the Poor," *Abortion and Social Justice*. New York: Sheed and Ward, 1972.

Crick, Francis. *Of Molecules and Men*. Seattle: University of Washington Press, 1967.

Cura, Roberto, and Catherine Pierce. *Experiments in Family Planning: Lessons from the Developing World*. Baltimore: Johns Hopkins Press, 1977.

Custance, Arthur C. *The Mysterious Matter of Mind*. Grand Rapids, Mich.: Zondervan, 1980.

Darwin, Charles. *Autobiography*. New York: Dover Publications, 1958.

————. *The Descent of Man*. London: John Murray, 1871.

————. *The Illustrated Origin of Species*. New York: Hill & Wang, 1979.

_____. *The Origin of Species by Means of Natural Selection or the Preservation of Favoured Races in the Struggle for Life.* New York: D. Appleton, 1872.

_____. *The Origin of Species by Means of Natural Selection or the Preservation of Favoured Races in the Struggle for Life.* L. Valorium, ed. Philadelphia: University of Pennsylvania Press, 1959.

Davidheiser, Bolton. *Evolution and Christian Faith.* Philadelphia: Presbyterian & Reformed, 1969.

Davis, Kingsley. "The Climax of Population Growth: Past and Future Perspective," *California Medicine,* Vol. 113, 1970.

Dewar, Douglas, and H. S. Shelton. *Is Evolution Proved?* London: Hollis & Carter, 1947.

Dewey, John. *A Common Faith.* New Haven: Yale University Press, 1934.

Dillard, Annie. *Pilgrim at Tinker Creek.* New York: Harper and Row, 1974.

Dobzhansky, Theodosius. "A Biologist's World View," *Science,* Vol. 175, 1972.

_____. "On Methods of Evolutionary Biology and Anthropology," *American Scientist,* Vol. 45, 1957.

Doerflinger, William. *The Magic Catalog.* New York: Dutton, 1977.

Donahue, Phil. *The Human Animal.* New York: Simon and Schuster, 1985.

Dostoyevski, Fyodor. *The Brothers Karamazov.* New York: Bantam Books, 1970.

Drew, Donald. *Images of Man.* Downers Grove, Ill.: Inter-Varsity Press, 1974.

Drucker, Peter F. *The Unseen Revolution.* New York: Harper & Row, 1976.

Durant, Will. *The Story of Philosophy.* New York: Simon & Schuster, 1961.

Durant, Will and Ariel. *The Age of Faith.* New York: Simon & Schuster, 1950.

_____. *The Age of Napoleon: A History of European Civilization from 1789 to 1815.* New York: Simon & Schuster, 1975.

_____. *The Age of Reason Begins.* New York: Simon & Schuster, 1961.

_____. *The Lessons of History.* New York: Simon & Schuster, 1968.

_____. *The Life of Greece*. New York: Simon & Schuster, 1939.

_____. *The Story of Civilization*. 11 vols. New York: Simon & Schuster, 1954-1975.

Einstein, Albert. *Ideas and Opinions*. New York: Bonanza Books, 1954.

_____. *Out of My Later Years*. London: Thames and Hudson, 1950.

Elliott, Robin, Lynn C. Landman, Richard Lincoln, and Theodore Tsuruoka. "U.S. Population and Family Planning: A Review of the Literature," *Family Planning Perspectives*, Vol. 2, as reprinted in Daniel Callahan, ed., *The American Population Debate*. New York: Anchor books, 1971.

Ellul, Jacques. *The Meaning of the City*. Grand Rapids, Mich.: Eerdmans, 1970.

_____. *The Political Illusion*. New York: Vintage Books, 1972.

_____. *The Technological Society*. New York: Vintage Books, 1964.

_____. *The Theological Foundation of Law*. New York: Seabury Press, 1969.

Ely, John H. "The Wages of Crying Wolf: a Comment on *Roe v. Wade.*" *Yale Law Journal* 82 (1973): 920.

Ericson, Jr., Edward E. *Solzhenitsyn: The Moral Vision*. Grand Rapids, Mich.: Eerdmans, 1980.

Erikson, Erik. *Childhood and Society*. New York: W. W. Norton, 1963.

Erlich, Paul. *The Population Bomb*. New York: Ballantine Books, 1968.

Evans, Christopher. *The Micro Millennium*. New York: Washington Square Press, 1979.

Fernbach, David. *Karl Marx: Surveys from Exile*. New York: Vintage Books, 1974.

Ferrero, Guglielmo, and Corrado Barbagallo. *A Short History of Rome*. 2 vols. New York: Knickerbocker Press, 1919.

Feuer, Kathryn, ed. *Solzhenitsyn: A Collection of Critical Essays*. Englewood Cliffs, N.J.: Prentice-Hall, 1976.

Fiske, Edward B. "Computers Alter Life of Pupils and Teachers," *New York Times*, 4 April 1982.

Flake, Carol. *Redemptorama: Culture, Politics, and the New Evangelicalism.* New York: Anchor Press, 1984.

Foerster, Norman. *Image in America.* Notre Dame, Ind.: University of Notre Dame Press, 1962.

Foster, George Burman. *Friedrich Nietzsche.* New York: Macmillan, 1931.

Fraser, J. T. *Of Time, Passion and Knowledge: Reflections on the Strategy of Existence.* New York: George Braziller, 1975.

Freed, Stanley A. and Ruth S. Freed. "One Son Is No Sons," *Natural History,* January 1985, p. 10.

Freeman, David Hugh. *A Philosophical Study of Religion.* Nutley, N.J.: Craig Press, 1964.

Freud, Sigmund. *Civilization and Its Discontents.* New York: Doubleday, 1958.

_____. *The Future of an Illusion.* Garden City, N.Y.: Anchor Books, 1964.

_____. *Moses and Monotheism.* New York: Knopf, 1949.

Gabriel, Ralph Henry. *The Course of American Democratic Thought,* 2nd ed. New York: John Wiley & Sons, 1956.

Galbraith, John Kenneth. *The Affluent Society.* Boston: Houghton Mifflin, 1958.

_____. *The Age of Uncertainty.* Boston: Houghton Mifflin, 1977.

Galbraith, John Kenneth, and M. S. Randhawa. *The New Industrial State.* Boston: Houghton Mifflin, 1967.

Gallup, Jr., George. *Forecast 2000: George Gallup Jr. Predicts the Future of America.* New York: William Morrow, 1984.

Galton, Francis. "Eugenics: Its Definition Scope and Aims," *Sociological Papers.* London: Macmillan, 1905.

_____. *Memories of My Life.* London; Methven & Co., 1908.

Gaucher, Roland. *Opposition in the U.S.S.R. 1917-1967.* New York: Funk & Wagnalls, 1969.

Gay, Peter, ed. *The Enlightenment.* New York: Simon & Schuster, 1973.

Gest, Ted, and Patricia M. Scherschel. "Who Is Watching You?" *U.S. News & World Report,* 12 July 1983.

Gibbon, Edward. *The Decline and Fall of the Roman Empire.* 6 vols. 1776-1788. Reprint. New York: Dutton, 1910.

Gilder, George. *Naked Nomads.* New York: Quadrangle-New York Times, 1974.

_____. *Sexual Suicide*. New York: Quadrangle-New York Times, 1973.

_____. *Wealth and Poverty*. New York: Basic Books, 1981.

Gish, Duane T. *The Fossils Say No!* San Diego: Creation-Life Publishers, 1978.

Gish, Duane T., and Clifford Wilson. *Manipulating Life: Where Does It Stop?* San Diego: Master Books, 1981.

Glick, T.F., ed. *The Comparative Reception of Darwinism*. Austin: University of Texas Press, 1974.

Goddard, Donald. *The Last Days of Dietrich Bonhoeffer*. New York: Harper & Row, 1976.

Goldman, Lucien. *Le Dieu Caché*. Paris: Gallimard, 1955.

Gorman, Michael J. *Abortion and the Early Church*. Downers Grove, Ill.: InterVarsity Press, 1982.

Gould, Stephen Jay. *The Mismeasure of Man*. New York: W. W. Norton, 1981.

Grant, Michael. *History of Rome*. New York: Charles Scribner's Sons, 1978.

Grassé, Pierre. *Evolution of Living Organisms: Evidence for a New Theory of Transformation*. New York: Academic Press, 1977.

Greer, Germaine. *Sex and Destiny*. New York: Harper & Row, 1984.

Gregory, R. L. "The Brain as an Engineering Problem," *Current Problems in Animal Behavior*. Cambridge: Cambridge University Press, 1961.

Grene, Marjorie. *The Understanding of Nature*. Dordrecht: D. Reidel, 1974.

Grimal, Pierre. *The Civilization of Rome*. New York: Simon & Schuster, 1963.

Gross, Bertram. *Friendly Fascism: The New Face of Power in America*. New York: M. Evans, 1980.

Guinness, Os. *The Dust of Death*. Downers Grove, Ill.: InterVarsity Press, 1973.

_____. *Violence: A Study of Contemporary Attitudes*. Downers Grove, Ill.: InterVarsity Press, 1974.

Haile, H. G. *Luther: An Experiment in Biography*. New York: Doubleday, 1980.

Haldeman, H. R. *The Ends of Power*. New York: Times Books, 1978.

"Half U.S. Population Is Over 31 Years Old," *Washington Post*, 11 April 1985.

Hall, Edward T. *The Hidden Dimension*. Garden City, New York: Anchor Books, 1969.

Hall, Thomas Cuming. *The Religious Background of American Culture*. Boston: Little, Brown, 1930.

Harden, Blaine. "Birth Control Raises Scare in Kenya," *Washington Post*, 8 April 1986.

Hardin, Garrett. *Nature and Man's Fate*. New York: Mentor Books, 1961.

Harrington, Michael. *The Politics of God's Funeral: The Spiritual Crisis of Western Civilization*. New York: Holt, Rinehart & Winston, 1983.

Harrington, Walt. "The Heretic Becomes Respectable," *Washington Post Magazine*, 18 August 1985.

Harris, Marvin. *Cultural Materialism: The Struggle for a Science of Culture*. New York: Random House, 1979.

Hatfield, Charles, ed. *The Scientist and Ethical Decision*. Downers Grove, Ill.: InterVarsity Press, 1973.

Hegel, George W. F. *The Logic of Hegel*. New York: Oxford University Press, 1892.

_____. *Philosophy of Right*. New York: Oxford University Press, 1962.

Heidegger, Martin. *Being and Time*. New York: Harper & Row, 1962.

_____. *The Question of Being*. Boston: Twayne, 1958.

Heilbroner, Robert L. *The Worldly Philosophers*. New York: Simon & Schuster, 1953.

Heimert, Alan, and Perry Miller, eds. *The Great Awakening*. Indianapolis: Bobbs-Merrill, 1967.

Heine, Heinrich. *Selected Works*. New York: Vintage, 1973.

Heirich, Max. *The Beginning: Berkeley 1964*. New York: Columbia University Press, 1977.

Henig, Robin Marantz. "The Sterilization Option," *Washington Post Health*, 19 March 1986.

Henry, Carl F. *Christian Mindset in a Secular Society*. Portland, Ore.: Multnomah Press, 1984.

Herdman, Marie L. *The Story of the United States*. New York: Grossett & Dunlap, 1916.

Hersch, Seymour, "Laird Approved False Reporting of Secret Raids," *New York Times*, 10 August 1973.

Hertz, Richard. *Chance and Symbol.* Chicago: University of Chicago Press, 1948.

Hill, Christopher. *The Century of Revolution 1703-1714.* New York: Nelson, 1961.

Hillel, Marc, and Clarissa Henry. *Of Pure Blood.* New York: McGraw-Hill, 1976.

Hillerbrand, Hans J. *The Protestant Reformation.* New York: Walker, 1968.

Hilsman, Roger. *The Crouching Future: International Politics and U.S. Foreign Policy—A Forecast.* Garden City, N.Y.: Doubleday, 1975.

Hitchcock, James. *What Is Secular Humanism?* Ann Arbor, Mich.: Servant Books, 1982.

Hodge, Charles. *What Is Darwinism?* New York: Scribner, Armstrong & Company, 1874.

Holler, Jr., John S. *Outcasts from Evolution: Scientific Attitudes of Racial Inferiority.* New York: McGraw-Hill, 1971.

Holyoake, George. *The History of the Last Trial by Jury for Atheism in England,* Madalyn Murray O'Hair, ed. New York: Arno Press, 1973.

_____. *Life of Holyoake—Sixty Years of an Agitator's Life.* London: T. F. Unwin, 1906.

_____. *Secularism: The Practical Philosophy of the People.* London: Holyoake & Co., 1845.

Howgate, George W. *George Santayana.* New York: A. S. Barnes, 1938.

Hudson, Winthrop S. *Religion in America.* New York: Charles Scribner's Sons, 1973.

Hull, Charles Henry. *The Economic Writings of Sir William Petty,* Vol. I. Cambridge: Cambridge University Press, 1889.

Huntford, Roland. *The New Totalitarians.* New York: Stein & Day, 1972.

Huxley, Aldous. *Brave New World.* New York: Harper and Row, 1946.

_____. *The Doors of Perception.* New York: Harper & Row, 1954.

_____. *Heaven and Hell.* New York: Harper & Row, 1956.

_____. *Science, Liberty, and Peace.* New York: Harper & Row, 1946.

Huxley, Julian. "At Random—A Television Preview," *Evolution After Darwin*, Vol. I. Chicago: University of Chicago Press, 1960.

_____. "Evolution and Genetics," *What Is Science?*, J. R. Newman, ed. New York: Simon & Schuster, 1955.

_____., ed. *The Humanist Frame*. New York: Harper & Row, 1962.

Hyde, Douglas. *Dedication and Leadership*. Notre Dame, Ind.: University of Notre Dame Press, 1966.

International Life Times, 7 November 1980.

Jackson, Jeremy. *No Other Foundation*. Westchester, Ill.: Cornerstone Books, 1980.

Jacobsen, Thorkild. "Enuma Elish—'The Babylonian Genesis,'" *Theories of the Universe*. M. K. Munitz, ed. New York: Free Press of Glencoe, 1957.

Jaspers, Karl. *Man in the Modern Age*. New York: Doubleday, 1957.

_____. *The Enchanted Loom: Mind in the Universe*. New York: Simon & Schuster, 1981.

_____. *God and the Astronomers*. New York: W. W. Norton, 1978.

_____. *Until the Sun Dies*. New York: W. W. Norton, 1977.

Johnson, Paul. *Modern Times: The World from the Twenties to the Eighties*. New York: Harper & Row, 1983.

Jones, Gareth. *Brave New People*. Downers Grove, Ill.: InterVarsity Press, 1984; Grand Rapids, Mich.: Eerdmans, 1985.

Jordan, Mary. "Suicides Plague College Campuses," *Washington Post*, 12 November 1984.

Jung, C. G. *Collected Works*, Vol. 11. Princeton, N.J.: Princeton University Press, 1969.

Kahn, M. E., and C. V. S. Prasad. *Fertility Control in India*. New Delhi: Manohar, 1980.

Kant, Immanuel. *Critique of Pure Reason*. 1781. Reprint. New York: Wiley, 1943.

_____. *Gesammelte Schliften*. Berlin: George Reiner, 1911.

Kauffmann, Walter, trans. *The Portable Nietzsche*. New York: Viking Press, 1968.

Keith, Arthur. *Evolution and Ethics*. New York: G. P. Putnam's Sons, 1949.

_____. "Galton's Place Among Anthropologists," *Eugenics Review*, Vol. 12, 1920-21.

Kenealy, Arabella. "A Study of Degeneracy," *Eugenics Review*, Vol. 3, 1911.

Keppel, Francis. *The Necessary Revolution in American Education.* New York: Harper & Row, 1966.

Kerkut, G.A. *Implications of Evolution.* New York: Pergamon Press, 1960.

Kevles, Daniel J. *In the Name of Eugenics: Genetics and the Uses of Human Heredity.* New York: Knopf, 1985.

Key, Wilson Bryan. *Media Sexploitation.* Englewood Cliffs, N.J.: Prentice-Hall, 1976.

_____. *Subliminal Seduction.* New York: Signet Books, 1973.

Kiesel, Diane. "Subliminal Seduction: Old Ideas, New Worries," *American Bar Association Journal* 70 (July 1984): 25.

Kirk, Russel. *The Roots of American Order.* LaSalle, Ill.: Open Court, 1974.

Koch, G. Adolf. *Religion of the American Enlightenment.* New York: Thomas Y. Crowell, 1968.

Koch, H. W. *Hitler Youth: The Duped Generation.* New York: Ballantine Books, 1972.

Koestler, Arthur. *Darkness at Noon.* New York: Bantam Books, 1968.

_____. *The Ghost in the Machine.* New York: Macmillan, 1968.

Kolenda, Konstantin. *Religion Without God.* Buffalo, N.Y.: Prometheus Books, 1976.

Koop, C. Everett. *The Right to Live, The Right to Die.* Wheaton, Ill.: Tyndale House, 1976.

Kuehnelt-Leddihn, Erik von. *Leftism: From de Sade and Marx to Hitler and Marcuse.* New Rochelle, N.Y.: Arlington House, 1974.

Kyemba, Henry. *A State of Blood: The Inside Story of Idi Amin.* New York: Grossett & Dunlap, 1977.

Lamont, Corliss. *The Philosophy of Humanism.* New York: Frederick Ungar, 1972.

Laqueur, Walter. *Terrorism.* Boston: Little, Brown, 1977.

_____, ed. *Fascism—A Reader's Guide: Analyses, Interpretations, Bibliography.* Berkeley: University of California Press, 1976.

Lasch, Christopher. *The Culture of Narcissism.* New York: W. W. Norton, 1979.

Laughlin, H. H. "Immigration Control," *A Report of the Special Committee on Immigration and the Alien Insane Submitting a Study on Immigration Control.* Chamber of Commerce of the State of New York, 1934.

Leder, Lawrence H., ed. *The Meaning of the American Revolution.* Chicago: Quadrangle Books, 1969.

Lenski, Gerhard. *The Religious Factor: A Sociological Study of Religion's Impact on Politics, Economics and Family Life.* Garden City, N.Y.: Doubleday, 1961.

Lewis, C. S. *The Abolition of Man.* New York: Macmillan, 1947.

──────. *The Discarded Image.* New York: Cambridge University Press, 1964.

Littlewood, Thomas B. *The Politics of Population Control.* Notre Dame, Ind.: University of Notre Dame Press, 1977.

Lloyd, Robin. *For Money or Love; Boy Prostitution in America.* New York: Vanguard Press, 1976.

Locke, John. *Essay Concerning Human Understanding.* 1690. Reprint. Gloucester, Mass.: Peter Smith, 1973.

──────. *On the Reasonableness of Christianity.* 1695. Reprint. Chicago: Henry Regnery, 1965.

Lovelace, Richard F. *Dynamics of Spiritual Life: An Evangelical Theology of Renewal.* Downers Grove, Ill.: InterVarsity Press, 1979.

Lygre, David G. *Life Manipulation: From Test-tube Babies to Aging.* New York: Walker, 1979.

Machen, J. Gresham. *The Christian Faith in the Modern World.* Grand Rapids, Mich.: Eerdmans, 1965.

Machiavelli, Niccolo. *The Prince.* 1513. Reprint. New York: Penguin Books, 1961.

Malbin, Michael J. *Religion and Politics: The Intentions of the Authors of the First Amendment.* Washington, D.C.: American Enterprise Institute for Public Policy Research, 1978.

Mallove, Eugene T. "Einstein's Intoxication with the God of the Cosmos," *Washington Post,* 22 December 1985.

Mander, Jerry. *Four Arguments for the Elimination of Television.* New York: William Morrow, 1978.

Mannix, Daniel P. *Those About to Die.* New York: Ballantine Books, 1958.

Marcuse, Herbert. *One Dimensional Man*. Boston: Beacon Press, 1964.

Martin, James. *The Telematic Society: A Challenge for Tomorrow*. Englewood Cliffs, N.J.: Prentice-Hall, 1981.

Marx, Karl, and Friedrich Engels. *The Manifesto of the Communist Party*. 1848. Reprint. San Francisco: China Books, 1965.

May, Henry F. *The Enlightenment in America*. New York: Oxford University Press, 1976.

McAuliffe, Sharon and Kathleen. *Life for Sale*. New York: Coward, McCann & Georg Hegan, 1981.

McCorduck, Pamela. *Machines Who Think*. San Francisco: W. H. Freeman, 1979.

McDonald, Forrest. *E. Pluribus Unum: The Formation of the American Republic 1776-1790*. Boston: Houghton Mifflin, 1965.

McGory, Mary. "Relentless Pro-Lifers," *Washington Post*, 27 January 1985, p. Cl.

McLuhan, Marshall. "Cybernation and Culture," *The Social Impact of Cybernetics*. New York: Simon & Schuster, 1966.

_____. *The Gutenberg Galaxy*. Toronto: University of Toronto Press, 1962.

_____. *Understanding Media: The Extension of Man*. New York: McGraw-Hill, 1964.

McManners, John. *The French Revolution and the Church*. New York: Harper & Row, 1969.

Meehan, Mary. "Foundation Power," *Human Life Review*, Vol. X, 1984.

Methvin, Eugene H. *The Rise of Radicalism*. New Rochelle, N.Y.: Arlington House, 1973.

Mickleson, Sig. *The Electric Mirror: Politics in an Age of Television*. New York: Dodd, Mead, 1972.

Middelmann, Udo. *Pro-Existence*. Downers Grove, Ill.: InterVarsity Press, 1974.

Miller, Perry. *The Life of the Mind in America*. London: Victor Gallancz, 1966.

Minkler, Meredith. "Consultants or Colleagues: The Role of the U.S. Population Advisers in India," *Population and Development Review*, December 1977.

Mises, Ludwig von. *Omnipotent Government: The Rise of the State and Total State*. New Rochelle, N.Y.: Arlington House, 1969.

Moberly, Sir Walter. *The Crisis in the University*. New York: Macmillan, 1949.

Monaghan, Patrick, "'Substantively Due Processing' the Black Population," 4 *Lincoln Review* 45 (1983).

Monod, Victor. *Dieu dans l'Univers. Essai sur l'action exercée sur lon pensée chrétienne par les grands systemes cosmologiques depuis Aristote jusqu'à nos jours*. Paris: Librarie Fischbacher, 1933.

Monsma, Stephen V. *The Unraveling of America*. Downers Grove, Ill.: InterVarsity Press, 1974.

Moore, Jr., Barrington. *Social Origins of Dictatorship and Democracy*. Boston: Beacon Press, 1966.

Morris, Henry M. and John Whitcomb. *The Genesis Flood*. Philadelphia: Presbyterian & Reformed, 1961.

_____. *The Twilight of Evolution*. Grand Rapids, Mich.: Baker Book House, 1963.

Morris, Richard B. *Seven Who Shaped Our Destiny*. New York: Harper & Row, 1973.

_____, ed. *Encyclopedia of American History* (1953). New York: Harper & Row, 1976.

Morris, Richard. *Dismantling the Universe: The Nature of Scientific Discovery*. New York: Simon and Schuster, 1983.

Mosher, Steven W. *Broken Earth: The Rural Chinese*. New York: Free Press, 1983.

Muggeridge, Malcolm. *Christ and the Media*. Grand Rapids, Mich.: Eerdmans, 1977.

Mumford, Lewis. *Technics and Civilization*. New York: Harcourt, Brace & Jovanovich, 1963.

Myrdal, Alva. *Nation and Family*. New York: Harper & Brothers, 1941.

Myrdal, Gunnar. *Beyond the Welfare State*. New York: Bantam Books, 1967.

Naisbitt, John. *Megatrends*. New York: Warner Books, 1982.

Nathanson, Bernard N. *Aborting America*. Garden City, N.Y.: Doubleday, 1979.

Newton, Isaac. *The Mathematical Principles of Natural Philosophy*. 2 vols. 1729 ed. Atlantic Highlands, N.J.: Humanities, 1968.

Nietzsche, Friedrich Wilhelm. "Thus Spake Zarathustra," Vol. 1, *Philosophy of Nietzsche*. New York: Modern Library, 1937.

Noonan, Jr., John T. *A Private Choice: Abortion in America in the Seventies*. New York: Free Press, 1979.

North, Gary. *The Dominion Covenant: Genesis*. Tyler, Tex.: Institute for Christian Economics, 1982.

Novak, Michael. *The Experience of Nothingness*. New York: Harper and Row, 1970.

_____. *Marx's Religion of Revolution: The Doctrine of Creative Destruction*. Nutley, N.J.: Craig Press, 1968.

Ogilvy, David. *Ogilvy on Advertising*. New York: Crown, 1983.

Olson, Everett Claire. "The Evolution of Life," *Evolution After Darwin*. Sol Tax, ed., Vol. 1. Chicago: University of Chicago Press, 1960.

"On the Edge of the Pit: Abortion as a Racist Tool," *The Daily Californian*, 14 October 1982.

Oparin, Aleksandr. *Life: Its Nature, Origin and Development*. London: J. M. Dent & Sons, 1971.

Orwell, George. *Animal Farm*. New York: Harcourt, Brace & World, 1946.

Overend, William. "Two Looks into the Future and Past," *Los Angeles Times*, 9 November 1977.

Padover, Saul K., ed. *The World of the Founding Fathers*. New York: Thomas Yoseloff, 1960.

"Planned Parenthood's Plans," *Wall Street Journal*, 19 December 1984.

Pascal, Blaise. *Pensées*. New York: Dutton, 1931.

Parrington, Vernon Louis. *Main Currents in American Thought*. New York: Harcourt, Brace, 1927.

Patterson, Colin. Speech delivered at the American Museum of Natural History. New York, N.Y., 5 July 1981.

Peikoff, Leonard. *The Ominous Parallels: The End of Freedom in America*. New York: Stein & Day, 1982.

Perry, Ralph Barton. *Puritanism and Democracy*. New York: Vanguard Press, 1944.

Perry, Roland. *Hidden Power: The Programming of the President*. New York: Beaufort Books, 1984.

Peters, Charles. *How Washington Really Works*. Reading, Mass.: Addison-Wesley, 1980.

Phillips, Kevin P. *Post-Conservative America: People, Politics, and Ideology in a Time of Crisis.* New York: Random House, 1982.

Pirsig, Robert. *Zen and the Art of Motorcycle Maintenance.* New York: Morrow, 1974.

Pit, Jan. *Persecution: It Will Never Happen Here?* Orange, Calif.: Open Doors, 1981.

"Planned Parenthood Plans," *Wall Street Journal,* 19 December 1984.

Plato. *Laws.* Penguin Books, 1970.

_____. *Republic.* New York: Basic Books, 1968.

Polanyi, Michael. *Personal Knowledge: Towards a Post-Critical Philosophy.* Chicago: University of Chicago Press, 1958.

_____. *The Tacit Dimension.* New York: Doubleday, 1967.

Pontecorvo, G. *Trends in Genetic Analysis.* New York: Columbia University Press, 1958.

"Post-Abortion Fetal Study Stirs Storm," *Medical World News,* 8 June 1973.

Postman, Neil. *Amusing Ourselves to Death: Public Discourse in the Age of Show Business.* New York: Viking Books, 1985.

Ranford, Victor. "Sociology." *Encyclopedia Britannica,* Vol. 20. 1949.

Reich, Charles. *The Greening of America.* New York: Bantam Books, 1971.

Reincourt, Amaury de. *The Coming Caesars.* New York: Coward-McCam, 1957.

Remsberger, Boyce. "Scientists Hail Gene Transfers as Promising," *Washington Post,* 20 November 1984.

Restak, Richard M. *Pre-Meditated Man: Bioethics and the Control of Future Human Life.* New York: Viking Press, 1975.

Revel, Jean-Francois. *How Democracies Perish.* Garden City, N.Y.: Doubleday, 1983.

_____. *The Totalitarian Temptation.* Garden City, N.Y.: Doubleday, 1977.

Rich, John Martin. *Humanistic Foundations of Education.* Worthington, Ohio: Charles A. Jones, 1971.

Rifkin, Jeremy. *Algeny.* New York: Viking, 1983.

Roe v. Wade, 410 U.S. 113, 1973.

Rogers, Michael. *Biohazard.* New York: Knopf, 1977.

Rookmaaker, H. R. *Modern Art and the Death of a Culture.* Downers Grove, Ill.: InterVarsity Press, 1970.

Rose, Arnold M. "The Slow Painful Death of the Race Myth," *Society Today and Tomorrow*. New York: Macmillan, 1961.

Rose, Fran K. *Into the Heart of the Mind: An American Quest for Artificial Intelligence*. New York: Harper & Row, 1984.

Rosenblueth, A., N. Wiener and J. Biegelow. "Behavior, Purpose and Teleology," *Philosophy of Science*, Vol. 101, 1943.

Rosenfeld, Albert. *The Second Genesis: The Coming Control of Life*. New York: Vintage Books, 1975.

Rosenstock-Huessy, Eugen. *Out of Revolution*. New York: William Morrow, 1938.

Rosten, Leo, ed. *Religions of America*. New York: Simon & Schuster, 1975.

Roszak, Theodore. *Person/Planet: The Creative Disintegration of Industrial Society*. New York: Anchor Books, 1978.

Rousseau, Jean-Jacques. *The Social Contract*. 1762. Reprint. New York: Oxford University Press, 1972.

Rushdoony, Rousas John. *Freud*. Philadelphia: Presbyterian & Reformed, 1975.

_____. *Intellectual Schizophrenia*. Philadelphia: Presbyterian & Reformed, 1961.

_____. *The Messianic Character of American Education*. Nutley, N.J.: Craig Press, 1972.

_____. *The Politics of Pornography*. New Rochelle, N.Y.: Arlington House, 1974.

Russell, Cristine. "Activist Challenges Gene-Transfer Research," *Washington Post*, 20 November 1984.

_____. "Gene Panel Rejects Ban: Interspecies Transfer Seen Useful by NIH," *Washington Post*, 30 October 1984.

_____. "Private Report Shows High Price of Living Longer," *Washington Post*, 5 September 1984.

_____. "U.S.D.A. Using Human Gene in Effort to Grow Super Livestock," *Washington Post*, 1 October 1984.

Sagan, Carl. *Cosmos*. New York: Random House, 1980.

_____. "In Praise of Robots." *Natural History*, Vol. 84, No. 1, January 1975.

_____. *The Dragons of Eden*. New York: Random House, 1977.

Salomon, Michael. *Future Life*. G. Daniels, trans. New York: Macmillan, 1983.

Sanger, Margaret. *An Autobiography*. New York: Dover Publishers, 1971.

Savage, M. J. *The Religion of Evolution*. Boston: Lockwood, Brooks, 1876.

Savan, Leslie. "Abortion Chic: The Attraction of Wanted— Unwanted Pregnancies," *Village Voice*, 4 February 1981.

Schaeffer, Francis A. *A Christian Manifesto*. Westchester, Ill.: Crossway Books, 1981.

————. *Back to Freedom and Dignity*. Downers Grove, Ill., InterVarsity Press, 1972.

————. *The Complete Works of Francis A. Schaeffer*, Vol. 4. Westchester, Ill.: Crossway Books, 1982.

————. *Escape from Reason*. Downers Grove, Ill.: InterVarsity Press, 1968.

————. *Genesis in Space and Time*. Downers Grove, Ill.: InterVarsity Press, 1972.

————. *The God Who Is There*. Downers Grove, Ill.: InterVarsity Press, 1968.

————. *The Great Evangelical Disaster*. Westchester, Ill.: Crossway Books, 1984.

————. *How Should We Then Live?* Old Tappan, N.J.: Revell, 1976.

————. *The Mark of the Christian*. Downers Grove, Ill.: InterVarsity Press, 1970.

————. *Pollution and the Death of Man: The Christian View of Ecology*. Wheaton, Ill.: Tyndale House, 1970.

Schaeffer, Francis, and C. Everett Koop. *Whatever Happened to the Human Race?* London: Marshall, Morgan & Scott, 1980.

Schaeffer, Franky. *A Time for Anger: The Myth of Neutrality*. Westchester, Ill.: Crossway Books, 1982.

————. *Addicted to Mediocrity*. Westchester, Ill.: Crossway Books, 1981.

————. *Bad News for Modern Man*. Westchester, Ill.: Crossway Books, 1984.

Schaeffer, Franky, and Harold Fickett. *A Modest Proposal for Peace, Prosperity and Happiness*. Nashville, Tenn.: Thomas Nelson, 1985.

Schlossberg, Herbert. *Idols for Destruction: Christian Faith and Its Confrontation with American Society*. Nashville: Thomas Nelson, 1983.

Schmeck, Jr., Harold M. "Animals Given a Human Gene: Growth Hormone Gene Yields Dramatic Results," *New York Times*, 6 December 1983.

Scott, Otto J. *Robespierre: The Voice of Virtue.* New York: Mason & Lipscomb, 1974.

_____. *The Secret Six: John Brown and the Abolitionist Movement.* New York: Times Books, 1979.

Sealey, Raphael. *A History of the Greek City States 700-338 B.C.* Berkeley: University of California Press, 1976.

Selby, W. Gardner. "Teen Suicides Portrayed as 'Epidemic,'" *Washington Post*, 16 December 1984.

Sennett, Richard. *The Fall of Public Man.* New York: Knopf, 1977.

Shearer, Lloyd. "No Babies for Many U.S. Women," *Parade*, 23 June 1985.

Shirer, William L. *The Rise and Fall of the Third Reich: A History of Nazi Germany.* New York: Simon & Schuster, 1960.

Simon, Herbert A. "What Computers Mean for Man and Society," *Science*, 18 March 1977.

_____. *The Sciences of the Artificial.* Cambridge, Mass.: M.I.T. Press, 1964.

Simon, Herbert A., and Allen Newell. "Heuristic Problem Solving: The Next Advance in Operation Research," *Operations Research*, Vol. 6, Jan.-Feb. 1985.

Simon, Julian L. *The Ultimate Resource.* Princeton, N.J.: Princeton University Press, 1981.

Simon, Julian L., and Herman Kahn, eds. *The Resourceful Earth: A Response to Global 2000.* New York: Basil Blackwell, 1984.

Simon, William E. *A Time for Truth.* New York: McGraw-Hill, 1978.

Simpson, George Gaylord. *The Meaning of Evolution.* New Haven, Conn.: Yale University Press, 1950.

Singer, C. Gregg. *A Theological Interpretation of American History.* Nutley, N.J.: Craig Press, 1969.

_____. *From Rationalism to Irrationality: The Decline of the Western Mind from the Renaissance to the Present.* Phillipsburg, N.J.: Presbyterian & Reformed, 1979.

Singer, Ethan. "Recombinant DNA: It's Not What We Need." Written remarks presented at the NAS Forum, 7, 8, 9 March 1977.

Sire, James W. *The Universe Next Door.* Downers Grove, Ill.: InterVarsity Press, 1976.

Sisson, Daniel. *The American Revolution of 1800.* New York: Knopf, 1974.

Skinner, B. F. *Beyond Freedom and Dignity.* New York: Knopf, 1971.

Smith, A. E. Wilder. *The Creation of Life.* San Diego, Calif: Creation-Life, 1981.

Smith, Anthony. *The Human Pedigree.* Philadelphia: J. B. Lippincott, 1975.

Smith, Page. *The Nation Comes of Age: A People's History of the Ante-Bellum Years,* Vol. 4. New York: McGraw-Hill, 1981.

Smulders, Peter, *The Design of Teilhard de Chardin.* A. Gibson, trans. Westminster, Md;: Newman Press, 1967.

Sobel, Robert. *The Manipulators.* Garden City, N.J.: Anchor Press-Doubleday, 1976.

Solzhenitsyn, Aleksandr I. "Gulag Survivor Indicts Western 'Freedom,'" *Los Angeles Times,* 13 June 1976.

————. *August 1914.* New York: Farrar, Straus & Giroux, 1972.

————. *The Gulag Archipelago 1918-1956.* New York: Harper & Row, 1973.

————. *The Gulag Archipelago 1918-1956 (Two).* New York: Harper & Row, 1975.

————. *The Gulag Archipelago 1918-1956 (Three).* New York: Harper & Row, 1978.

————. *Lenin in Zurich.* New York: Farrar, Straus & Giroux, 1976.

————. *Letter to the Soviet Leaders.* New York: Harper & Row, 1974.

————. *The Oak and the Calf.* New York: Harper & Row, 1980.

Speer, Albert. *Infiltration.* New York: Macmillan, 1981.

————. *Inside the Third Reich.* New York: Macmillan, 1970.

————. *Spandau: The Secret Diaries.* New York: Macmillan, 1976.

Spencer, Herbert. *Principles of Sociology.* 1880-1897. 3 vols. Westport, Conn.: Greenwood Press, 1974.

Spengler, Oswald. *The Decline of the West.* 2 vols. New York: Knopf, 1926, 1928.

Stauffer, Ethelbert. *Christ and the Caesars.* Philadelphia: Westminster Press, 1965.

"Sterilization Leads Birth-Control List: Popularity Exceeds Pill's," *Washington Post,* 6 December 1984.

Sterling, Theodor D., and Seymour V. Pollack. *Computers and the Life Sciences.* New York: Columbia University Press, 1965.

Stott, John R. W. *Christ the Controversialist.* Downers Grove, Ill.: InterVarsity Press, 1970.

Stycos, J. Mayone. "Demographic Chic at the Union," as reprinted in Thomas Robert Malthus. *An Essay on the Principle of Population.* New York: W. W. Norton, 1976.

Sussman, Gerald J. *The Computer Model of Skill Acquisition.* New York: American Elsevier, 1975.

Tatarkiewiez, Wladyslaw. *Nineteenth Century Philosophy.* Belmont, Calif.: Wadsworth, 1973.

Teich, Albert H., ed. *Technology and Man's Future.* 2nd ed. New York: St. Martin's Press, 1977.

Teilhard de Chardin, Pierre. *The Phenomenon of Man.* B. Wall, trans. New York: Harper & Row, 1959.

_____. *The Vision of the Past.* J. Cohen, trans. New York: Harper & Row, 1966.

Thielicke, Helmut. *The Evangelical Faith,* Geoffrey W. Bromiley, trans. Grand Rapids, Mich.: Eerdmans, 1974.

"Theological Survey Finds Tolerance for Pre-Marital Sex," *Washington Post,* 29 December 1984.

Thomas, Lewis. *Late Night Thoughts on Listening to Mahler's Ninth Symphony.* New York: Viking, 1983.

_____. *The Lives of A Cell.* New York: Viking, 1986.

_____. *The Youngest Science.* New York: Viking, 1983.

Thompson, William Irwin. "'What's Past Is Prologue' The Past—What's That?" *New York Times,* 10 June 1976.

Thompson, W. R. *Introduction to Charles Darwin, The Origin of the Species.* New York: E. P. Dutton, 1956.

Thoreau, Henry David. *Walden.* Princeton, N.J.: Princeton University Press, 1971.

Thorpe, William H. "The Frontiers of Biology," *Mind in Nature.* Washington, D.C.: University Press of America, 1977.

Thorpe, William H., and Oliver L. Zangwill. *Current Problems in Animal Behavior*. Cambridge: Cambridge University Press, 1980.

Tillich, Paul. *Dynamics of Faith*. New York: Harper & Row, 1957.

_____. *Systematic Theology*. 3 vols. Chicago: University of Chicago Press, 1967.

Tocqueville, Alexis de. *Democracy in America*. Garden City, N.Y.: Anchor Books, 1960.

Toffler, Alvin. *The Eco-Spasm Report*. New York: Bantam Books, 1975.

_____. *Previews and Premises*. New York: Morrow, 1983.

_____. *The Third Wave*. New York: Morrow, 1980.

Tomlin, E. W. F. *The Great Philosophers*. New York: A. A. Wyn, 1952.

Toynbee, Arnold. *A Study of History*. 12 vols. New York: McGraw-Hill, 1972.

Tucker, Robert C., ed. *The Marx-Engels Reader*. W. W. Norton, 1978.

Turkle, Sherry. *The Second Self: Computer and the Human Spirit*. New York: Simon & Schuster, 1984.

Tuveson, Ernest Lee. *Redeemer Nation: The Idea of America's Millennial Role*. Chicago: University of Chicago Press, 1968.

Twain, Mark. *Autobiography of Mark Twain*, Charles Neider, ed. New York: Harper and Row, 1959.

Velikovsky, Immanuel. *Mankind in Amnesia*. Garden City, N.Y.: Doubleday, 1982.

VerSteeg, Clarence L., and Richard Hofstadter, eds. *Great Issues in American History: From Settlement to Revolution 1584-1776*. New York: Vintage Books, 1969.

"Vietnam Sets Penalties to Stem Births," *Washington Post*, 26 December 1984.

Viorst, Milton. *Fire in the Streets: America in the 1960s*. New York: Simon & Schuster, 1979.

Vitz, Paul C. *Psychology as Religion: The Cult of Self-worship*. Grand Rapids, Mich.: Eerdmans, 1977.

Wade, Nicholas. *The Ultimate Experiment: Man-Made Evolution*. New York: Walker, 1977.

Waldholz, Michael. "The Diagnostic Power of Genetics Is Posing Hard Medical Choices," *Wall Street Journal*, 18 February 1986.

Wallace, Alfred Russel. *The Action of Natural Selection on Man.* New York: AMS Press, 1983.

Wallis, E. A., trans. *The Book of the Dead.* New York: University Books, 1960.

Walter, J. A. *The Human Home: The Myth of the Sacred Environment.* Icknield Way, Tring, Herts, England: Lion Publishing Co., 1982.

Walzer, Michael. *Exodus and Revolution.* New York: Basic Books, 1985.

Warwick, Donald. *Bitter Pills.* New York: Cambridge University Press, 1982.

Weiner, Philip P. *Dictionary of the History of Ideas*, Vol. II. New York: Charles Scribner's Sons, 1973.

Weisskopf, Michael. "Abortion Policy Tears at Fabric of China's Society," *Washington Post*, 7 January 1985.

_____. "Shanghai's Curse: Too Many Fight for Too Little: Tough Birth Control Policy Shakes Chinese Society," *Washington Post*, 6 January 1985.

Weizenbaum, Joseph. *Computer Power and Human Reason: From Judgment to Calculation.* San Francisco: Walt Freeman, 1976.

Wells, H. G. *The Outline of History.* Garden City, N.Y.: Doubleday, 1971.

_____. *The Shape of Things to Come.* New York: Macmillan, 1945.

Wertenbaker, Thomas J. *The First Americans 1607-1690.* Chicago: Quadrangle Books, 1971.

West, Geoffrey. *Charles Darwin: A Portrait.* New Haven, Conn.: Yale University Press, 1938.

White, Lynn. "The Historical Roots of Our Ecologic Crisis," *Science*, Vol. 155, 10 March 1967.

Whitehead, Alfred North. *Nature and Life.* New York: Greenwood Press, 1968.

_____. *The Principles of Natural Knowledge.* Cambridge, England: Cambridge University Press, 1925.

_____. *Science and the Modern World.* New York: Macmillan, 1925.

Whitehead, John W. *The Second American Revolution.* Elgin, Ill.: David C. Cook, 1982.

_____. *The Stealing of America.* Westchester, Ill.: Crossway Books, 1983.

_____ and Wendell R. Bird. *Home Education And Constitutional Liberties: The Historical and Constitutional Arguments in Support of Home Instruction.* Westchester, Ill.: Crossway Books, 1984.

Whitney, Leon F. *The Case for Sterilization.* New York: Frederick A. Stokes, 1934.

Wiedmann, Franz, trans. *Hegel.* New York: Western, 1968.

Wiener, Norbert. *God and Golem, Inc.* Cambridge, Mass.: M.I.T. Press, 1964.

Wilder-Smith, A. E. *He Who Thinks Has to Believe.* Minneapolis, Minn.: Bethany House, 1981.

Willis, Garry. *Inventing America.* Garden City, N.Y.: Doubleday, 1978.

Wish, Harvey. *Society and Thought in Early America,* Vol. 1. New York: Longmans, Green, 1950.

Wolstenholme, Gordon, ed. *Man and His Future: A CIBA Foundation Volume.* Boston: Little, Brown, 1963.

Wood, Garth. *The Myth of Neurosis: Overcoming the Illness Excuse.* New York: Harper and Row, 1986.

Woodside, Moya. *Sterilization in North Carolina: A Sociological and Psychological Study.* Chapel Hill, N.C.: University of North Carolina Press, 1950.

Wysong, R. L. *The Creation-Evolution Controversy.* Midland, Mich.: Inquiry Press, 1976.

Zohn, Gordon. "Abortion and the Corruption of the Mind," *New Perspectives on Human Abortion.* Frederick, Md.: University Publications of America, 1981.

INDEX

Abbey, Edward, 72
Abortion, xi, 18, 32, 43, 45, 48,
  68, 74, 83, 85, 145, 161, 173,
  177, 182, 183, 184, 185, 186,
  194, 195, 196, 197, 199, 200,
  240, 243
Absolutes, 18, 19, 23, 24, 26, 37,
  41, 43, 45, 46, 49, 57, 59, 60,
  96, 97, 150, 184, 243
Accommodation, 29
Accountability, 18, 19, 79
Action of Natural Selection on Man,
  The (Alfred Russel Wallace), 165
Acton, Lord, 85
Activism, 21
Adam, 76, 79
Adam, Dr. Peter A. J., 145
Adams, John, 19, 207
Adventures of Huckleberry Finn
  (Mark Twain), 19
Advertising industry, the, 15
Age of Faith, The (Will Durant), 88
Agnosticism, 92
Albertus Magnus, 88
Algeny (Jeremy Rifkin), 81
Anaxagoras, 69
Antihumanism, 39, 101, 206
Antithesis, 26, 27
Aristotle, 51, 88, 152
Armstrong, Scott, 183
Art, 23, 32, 36, 37, 60, 131
Artificial intelligence, 41, 129, 147
  (Chapter 9 passim), 235
Atheism, 31, 40, 52, 54, 68,
  75, 245
Audit Information Management
  System (AIMS), 222
Authoritarianism, xi, 47, 48, 49,

63, 187, 199, 204, 205, 206,
  207, 208, 212, 213, 235, 240
Automated Wants and Warrants
  System, 229

Bacon, Roger, 88, 90, 99
Baig, Tara Ali, 193
Barzun, Jacques, 56
Beal v. Doe, 183
Behaviorism, 42, 112
Bell, Alexander Graham, 169
Bell, Daniel, 215, 216
Bentley, Richard, 52
Bergson, Henri, 136
Bernard, St., 88
Between Two Ages (Zbigniew
  Brzezinski), 117, 216
Beyond Freedom and Dignity
  (B. F. Skinner), 241
Bible, the, 17, 20, 21, 27, 30, 32,
  37, 75, 89, 239
Biotechnology, 135, 139, 143, 147
Blackmun, Justice Harry, 183, 184
Blamires, Harry, 31
Boice, James, 71
Borisov, Vadim, 45
Brave New People (Gareth Jones), 184
Brave New World (Aldous
  Huxley), 39, 63, 207, 208,
  230, 240
Brethren, The (Bob Woodward and
  Scott Armstrong), 183
Brothers Karamazov, The (Fyodor
  Dostoyevski), 239
Brown, Ford Madox, 55
Brown, Harold O. J., 17, 20, 95
Brzezinski, Zbigniew, 117, 216
Buck, Carrie, 169, 170

Buck v. Bell, 170
Buddhism, 35
Burgess, Anthony, 217
Burnham, David, 219, 221, 222, 224, 228
Burroughs, John, 72
Burton, Allen G., 66
Byron, Lord, 115

Calvin, John, 37
Cambodia, 232
Campbell, Joseph, 70
Camus, Albert, 18
Canby, Vincent, 93
Capitalism, 33, 53, 116, 204
Carnegie, Andrew, 53
Carter Administration, 216
Catholicism, 30, 55
Chargaff, Erwin, 82, 85, 96
China, 48, 85, 161, 164, 187, 193, 194, 195, 196, 197
Christ, 18, 20, 25, 27, 28, 39, 60, 71, 88, 89, 95, 108, 135, 239, 240, 243, 244, 245, 246
Christ the Controversialist, 28
Christianity, 16, 20, 21, 22, 25, 26, 27, 28, 29, 30, 31, 32, 34, 40, 57, 58, 70, 71, 79, 80, 88, 89, 100, 107, 110, 137, 184, 247
Christian Mindset in a Secular Society, The (Carl F. H. Henry), 184
Christian nation, 20
Civilization of Rome, The (Pierre Grimal), 244
Clapperton, Jane Hume, 165
Claus, Carl, 51
Clock, the, 113, 114, 115, 121
Clockwork Orange, A, 93, 217
Cloning, 43, 145
Cobbett, William, 115
Colby, K. M., 123, 124
Collingwood, R. G., 136
Coming of Post-Industrial Society, The (Daniel Bell), 215
Commentariolus (Copernicus), 51
Communism, 35, 48, 68, 107, 193, 197, 203, 208, 226, 237, 238
Communist Manifesto, The (Karl Marx), 116
Computers, 41, 55, 61, 79, 84, 96, 109, 115, 119, 121, 122, 124, 125, 126, 127, 128, 129, 130, 131, 132, 139, 140, 142, 143, 147, 148, 149, 150, 151, 153, 154, 155, 156, 206, 212, 213, 216, 219, 220, 221, 222, 223, 224, 225, 226, 228, 229, 230, 231, 232, 233, 234, 245
Conditioners, the, 39, 42, 82, 84, 85, 86, 161, (Chapter 10 *passim*), 197, 215, 216
Confrontation, 28
Conklin, Edwin G., 64
Copernicus, 51, 92
Cox, Harvey, 41
Crick, Francis, 44, 45, 75, 82, 187
Critique of Pure Reason (Immanuel Kant), 91
Cults, the, 16
Curie, Marie, 43
Current Problems in Animal Behavior (William H. Thorpe and Oliver L. Zangwill), 141
Custance, Arthur C., 155
Cybernetics, 140, 141, 142, 143, 147, 155

Darwin, Charles, Darwinianism, 22, 25, 45, 51 (Chapter 3 *passim*), 69, 71, 72, 80, 81, 96, 113, 131, 132, 133, 134, 135, 138, 141, 142, 165, 166, 167, 171
Darwin, Erasmus, 54
Darwinism (Alfred Russel Wallace), 53
Darwin, Marx and Wagner (Jacques Barzun), 56
Das Kapital (Karl Marx), 68
Da Vinci, Leonardo, 95, 96
Davis, Kingsley, 187
Dean, John, 219
Death of God movement, 35, 38, 41, 93
De Chardin, Teilhard, 46, 62
Declaration of Independence, 18, 19, 238
Deism, 38, 39, 70
De Lamarck, Marquis Jean Baptiste, 54
Democracy, 77, 206, 219, 237, 238, 240, 242
De Reincourt, Amury, 55
Descartes, Rene, 90, 91, 154
Descent of Man (Charles Darwin), 52
Determinism, xi, 33, 52, 69, 94, 95

De Tocqueville, Alexis, 240
Dewey, John, 59
Dickens, Charles, 163
Diderot, 94
Dillard, Annie, 70
Discoverie of Witchcraft, The
(Reginald Scot), 99
"Dismal theorem," 162
*Dismantling the Universe: The
Nature of Scientific Discovery*
(Richard Morris), 66
Doerflinger, William, 99, 100
Dolbeare, Kenneth, 205
Dominion, 77, 78, 79, 82, 119
Donahue, Phil, 42, 172
Dostoyevski, Fyodor, 239, 242,
245, 246
Drescher, Gary, 153
Dreyfus, Herbert, 148
Durant, Will, 74, 75, 88
Durant, Will and Ariel, 163

Eastern religion, 16
Ecology, 71, 72
Eden, 78, 79
Education, public and private,
19, 22, 25, 37, 42, 58, 59, 60,
63, 83, 84, 119, 129, 132, 133,
164, 173, 179, 190, 206, 207,
208, 216
Egypt, 97
Einstein, Albert, 23, 24, 43, 128
Eisenhower, President Dwight, 211
Elijah, 89
Eliot, T. S., xiii, 16, 105, 243
ELIZA, 121, 122, 123, 124, 125
Ellul, Jacques, 97, 119, 203, 204,
215, 216, 217, 219, 227, 228,
233, 242, 246
Emerson, Ralph Waldo, 70, 87
Empiricism, 35, 42, 102
*Enchanted Loom: Mind in the
Universe, The* (Robert
Jastrow), 154
Encyclopedia (Diderot), 94
"End times" thinking, xii
Enlightenment, the, 20, 22, 23, 25,
27, 41, 55, 91, 93, 162, 164
Enuma Elish, 61
Epistemology, 22, 26, 93, 137, 208
Erikson, Erik, 78
Erlich, Paul, 173, 187
*Essay on the Principle of Population
As It Affects the Future
Improvement of Society*

(Thomas Malthus), 162, 163
Ethics, 19, 28, 30, 31, 38, 46, 57,
100, 144, 145, 184, 187, 208
Euclid, Euclidean geometry, 23
Euclides, 98
Eugenics, 82, 83, 84, 85, 165, 166,
167, 168, 169, 170, 171, 172,
180, 181, 182, 184, 197
Eugenics (Education) Society, 166
Euhemerus, 74, 75
Europe, 22, 23, 54, 58, 88, 90,
115, 164
Euthanasia, xi, 45, 88, 199, 200,
240, 243
Evangelicalism, 27, 29, 30, 184
Evangelism, 25, 27, 58
Evans, Christopher, 127, 231, 234
Evolution, 22, 38, 41, 42, 43, 46,
51 (Chapter 3 *passim*), 54, 75,
95, 113, 131, 132, 133, 134,
135, 138, 139, 142, 143, 154,
156, 165, 234
Existentialism, 47, 58
Experience of Nothingness, The
(Michael Novak), 42
Experimentation, xi, 43, 68,
144, 145

Faith, 19, 25, 29, 35, 36, 40, 41,
46, 61, 64, 65, 67, 89, 96, 133,
134, 209, 245
Fall, the, 18, 27, 32, 76, 77, 78,
108, 112
Family Planning Association of
India (FPAI), 188
Fascism, 67, 204, 205, 206, 209
Fickett, Harold, 187
Floyd, Jay, 183
Foerster, Norman, 17
Forecast 2000 (George
Gallup, Jr.), 29, 234
Founding fathers, 19, 45
France, 91, 179, 195, 204,
205, 234
Franklin, Benjamin, 19
Fraser, J. T., 138
Fredkin, Edward, 154
Freedom, 17, 23, 32, 34, 42, 48,
67, 87, 88, 89, 125, 206, 214,
224, 227, 237, 238, 239, 240,
241, 242, 243, 246, 247
French Revolution, 47, 115,
208, 238
Freud, Freudianism, 25, 46,
51, 128

Friedrich, John P., 42

Gabriel, Ralph Henry, 55
Galbraith, John Kenneth, 215
Galileo, 23, 25, 90
Gallup, George Jr., 29, 234
Galton, Sir Francis, 83, 166, 167
Gandhi, Indira, 192
Genetics, 43, 83, 84, 134, 143,
   144, 145, 166, 186, 187
Germany, 49, 68, 84, 179, 180,
   181, 184, 204, 205, 212
Gest, Ted, 213
Gibbon, Edward, 88
Gilbert, J. P., 123
Global village, 117, 119
God, 17, 19, 24, 30, 32, 38, 39, 40,
   44, 55, 70, 71, 74, 77, 78, 79,
   87, 89, 92, 94, 95, 96, 101, 108,
   131, 135, 136, 155, 243, 245; as
   Creator, 17, 18, 19, 32, 35, 38,
   45, 46, 51, 54, 55, 56, 62, 69,
   70, 71, 75, 76, 77, 87, 88, 89,
   90, 91, 93, 95, 96, 100, 107,
   108, 125, 147, 156, 245, 246
Golem, 153
Goncourt brothers, 240, 241
Gould, Stephen Ray, 68
Government, xi, 20, 25, 47, 58,
   175, 203, 204, 205, 206, 208,
   212, 213, 214, 215, 216, 218,
   222, 223, 225, 230, 232, 237, 239
Grassé, Pierre P., 65, 142
Great Britain, 19, 21, 91, 115,
   163, 167, 204, 205, 242
Great Evangelical Disaster, The
   (Francis A. Schaeffer), 27
Greece, Greeks, 23, 24, 69, 75, 79,
   98, 107, 109, 119, 135
Greenwalt, Kent, 212
Greer, Germaine, 74, 172, 174,
   180, 189, 191, 199
Gregory, R. L., 141
Grimal, Pierre, 243
Gross, Bertram, 204, 211
Grosseteste, Bishop, 88
Guiness, Os, 41, 43, 227
Gutenberg Galaxy (Marshall
   McLuhan), 112

Hardin, Garrett, 132
Harrington, Michael, 30, 31, 33,
   35, 90
Hegel, Georg Wilhelm Friedrich, 58

Heine, Heinrich, 36
Henning, Doug, 100
Henry, Carl F. H., 184, 186
Hinduism, 28
Hitchcock, James, 39, 47, 48
Hitler, Adolf, 25, 48, 49, 68, 77,
   84, 85, 184, 204, 206
Hobbes, Thomas, 91, 94
Hodge, Charles, 56
Hollow Men, The (T. S. Eliot),
   xiii, 105
Holmes, Justice Oliver Wendell
   Jr., 170
Holocaust, the, 18
Holyoake, George, 40, 41, 43
How Democracies Perish
   (Jean-Francois Revel), 237
Human Animal, The
   (Phil Donahue), 15, 43
Humanism, 22, 35 (Chapter 2
   passim), 41, 42, 44, 45, 46, 48,
   49, 107, 187, 245
Human Numbers, Human Needs,
   193
Hume, David, 91, 162
Huntford, Roland, 206
Huxley, Aldous, 39, 63, 100, 207,
   208, 230, 240, 241
Huxley, Julian, 59, 63, 132
Huxley, Thomas Henry, 56

Idealism, 25, 58
Ideas, consequences of, 16, 24,
   25, 35, 53, 204
Idols for Destruction (Herbert
   Schlossberg), 35
Illustrations and Proofs of the
   Principle of Population
   (Francis Place), 164
Image of God, imago Dei, 17, 36,
   54, 55, 75, 76, 108, 131, 144,
   156, 184, 246, 247
Impersonalism, 15, 16, 27, 31, 38,
   44, 45, 61, 67, 87
Implications of Evolution
   (G. A. Kerkut), 134
India, 85, 161, 164, 178, 187, 188,
   189, 190, 191, 192, 193
Industrial Revolution, 22, 23,
   54, 55, 81, 95, 113, 114, 115,
   163, 164
Infant Doe, 84
Infanticide, xi, 43, 162, 177, 186,
   194, 195, 196, 200, 240, 243
Ingersoll, John, 224

Intelligence Gathering Retrieval
System, 220
Internal Revenue Service (IRS),
214, 217, 218, 219, 220, 221,
222, 226
Italy, 204, 205
It Can't Happen Here (Sinclair
Lewis), 204

Jackson, Jeremy, 88, 89
Japan, 204, 205
Jastrow, Robert, 64, 154
Jefferson, Thomas, 18, 19, 39,
207, 238
Johnson, Paul, 23, 24, 203
Johnson Administration, 226
Jones, Gareth, 184, 185
Jonestown, 18
Judaism, 29, 71
Judeo-Christian values, 25, 125

Kant, Immanuel, 58, 90, 91, 92,
93, 94, 126
Kashiwagi, Hiroshi, 159
Keith, Arthur, 166
Kekomaki, Dr. Martii, 145
Kennedy Administration, 219
Kerkut, G. A., 65, 133
Kierkegaard, Soren, 58
Koestler, Arthur, 46
Koop, C. Everett, 199
Kubrick, Stanley, 93, 217

Laughlin, H. H., 168, 169
Law, xi, 25, 30, 32, 58
Laws (Plato), 37
Leary, Timothy, 61
Lenin, V. I., 48
Lenski, Gerhard, 35
Lewis, C. S., 83, 85, 96, 99, 145
Lewis, John, 189, 190
Lewis, Sinclair, 204
Ley, Robert, 212
Life of Greece, The (Will Durant), 74
Life of the Mind in America, The
(Perry Miller), 21
Liverpool, Lord, 115
Locke, John, 91
Loew, Rabbi, 153
Los Angeles Center for Law in the
Public Interest, 229
Ludd, Ned, 115
Lyell, Charles, 54

McGuffey Readers, 60

Machen, J. Gresham, 33, 34
McLuhan, Marshall, 108, 109,
112, 116, 117, 118, 119
Mackworth head-camera,
118, 119
Madison, James, 207
Magic, 96, 97, 98, 99, 100,
150, 151
Magic Catalogue, The (William
Doerflinger), 99
Malthus, Daniel, 162
Malthus, Thomas, 161, 162,
163, 164, 165, 167, 171, 172,
178, 197
Man, nature of, 15, 18, 32, 34, 37,
38, 39, 43, 44, 52, 67, 87, 93,
100, 101, 112, 127, 131, 132,
137, 157, 241, 247; extensions
of, 107, 108, 109, 111, 112,
114, 116, 117, 118, 119, 121,
128, 129, 131, 137, 208
Manipulation, 15, 42, 43, 69, 77,
78, 81, 83, 95, 96, 98, 107, 139,
143, 147, 200, 205, 206, 208,
216, 237, 240, 241
Marshall, Justice Thurgood, 183
Marxism, Marx, Karl, 20, 25, 45,
68, 116, 205
Mary, 243
Masks of God, The (Joseph
Campbell), 70
Materialism, 15, 32, 35, 38, 44,
45, 67, 98, 155, 175, 188
Media, the, 15, 16, 29, 48, 58,
116, 117, 206, 208, 209, 211,
227, 241, 245
Medicine, medical research, xi,
32, 43, 128, 172
Meehan, Mary, 173
Meeting at Tule Lake, A
(Hiroshi Kashiwagi), 159
Megatrends (John Naisbitt), 140
Mein Kampf (Adolf Hitler), 68
Micro Millennium, The
(Christopher Evans), 127
Miller, Perry, 21
Milton, John, 37
Minsky, Marvin, 156
Modern Times (Paul Johnson), 203
Monaghan, Patrick, 182
Moores, Admiral Thomas, 232
Morality, 17, 20, 24, 25, 26, 30,
31, 39, 40, 42, 46, 48, 57, 67,
85, 94, 99, 100, 101, 165,
231, 242

Morris, Henry M., 62
Morris, Richard, 66
Moses, 30
Mumford, Lewis, 113, 114
Mussolini, Benito, 68, 204
Myrdal, Alva, 198
Mysticism, 16, 53, 57

Naisbitt, John, 140, 143
Napoleon, 38
Narcissus, narcissism, 108, 109,
    126, 129
National Security Agency (NSA),
    223, 224, 225
Nationalism, 22, 39, 53, 165
Natural selection, 53, 56, 67, 135,
    141, 165
Nazis, the, 84, 85, 184, 204, 213,
    229, 243
Nehru, Jawaharlal, 188
Neo-Malthusians, 164, 165, 184
Neoplatonism, 25, 58
Neuroscience, 127
"New despotism, the," 211
Newell, Alan, 129, 149
Newspeak, 206
Newton, Isaac, Newtonian
    cosmology, 23, 24, 25, 38, 52,
    90, 92, 134, 135
New Totalitarians, The
    (Roland Huntford), 206
Nietzsche, Friedrich, 45, 68
Nineteen Eighty-four
    (George Orwell), 201
Nixon, Richard, 219
Noah, 186
No Other Foundation
    (Jeremy Jackson), 88
Novak, Michael, 42
Nuclear war, 233, 234

Occult, the, 16
Of Time, Passion, and Knowledge
    (J. T. Fraser), 138
Ogilvy, David, 15
Oparin, Aleksandr, 134
Oppenheimer, J. Robert, 90
Origen, 30
Origin of Species (Charles
    Darwin), 52, 56, 62, 68
Orthodoxy, 20
Orwell, George, 201, 206
Overton, Judge William, 60

Paley, William, 54

Papert, Seymour, 129
Pascal, Blaise, 38, 87, 90, 92
Patterson, Colin, 63, 133
Paul, 77, 79, 108
Pearson, Karl, 167
Pennfield, Dr. Wilder, 155
Perfectibility, 22, 27
Peter, 244, 247
Petty, William, 179
Phillips, Kevin, 206
Pietism, 20, 21, 22, 30, 58
Pilgrim at Tinker Creek
    (Annie Dillard), 70
Pitt, William, 163
Place, Francis, 164, 165
Planned Parenthood, 74, 83, 147,
    171, 173, 174, 188, 193
Platonism, 21, 37, 152
Plesser, Ronald, 213
Polanyi, Michael, 87, 124
Political Illusion, The
    (Jacques Ellul), 242
Pollution, 73
Pope, Alexander, 36
Population Bomb, The
    (Paul Erlich), 173
Population planners, xi, 42, 43,
    83, 84, 147, 165, 171, 172, 175,
    177, 178, 180, 187, 196
Pornography, 213, 240, 241
Postman, Neil, 25, 31, 118,
    207, 208
Presuppositions, 16, 26, 27,
    96, 154
Principles of Geology
    (Charles Lyell), 54
Privacy, 212, 213, 224
Process philosophy, 137, 152
Protestantism, 17, 20, 30, 33, 37,
    55, 60, 118
Ptolemy, 51
Puritans, the, 17
Pygmalion (My Fair Lady), 122

Quakers, the, 21
Quarry, The (Jean Jacques
    Rousseau), 55

Racism, 25, 67, 68, 167, 172, 180,
    181, 182, 186, 204
Radio, 29, 118
Rationalism, 41, 45, 94, 103
Reason, 22, 27, 37, 41, 58, 87, 90,
    91, 93, 94, 162, 232

Reasonableness of Christianity (John Locke), 91
Redeemer Nation (Ernest Tuveson), 21
Redemption, 21, 43, 55, 58, 77, 246
Reformation, the, 89
Relativity, relativism, 23, 24, 25, 32, 33, 57, 67
Religion, 20, 25, 28, 29, 30, 31, 32, 33, 35, 37, 38, 42, 45, 46, 48, 51, 57, 60, 63, 64, 67, 71, 90, 93, 96, 107, 108, 118, 125, 130, 151, 153, 178, 205, 207
Renaissance, the, 89, 107, 135
Renewal, 20
Revel, Jean-Francois, 237
Revelation, 22
Revival, 21
Rich Christians in an Age of Hunger (Ronald Sider), 186
Rifkin, Jeremy, 81, 135
Rights, 18, 19, 49, 153, 183, 187, 199, 200, 231, 243
Rise and Fall of the Third Reich, The (William L. Shirer), 206
Rise of the Computer State, The (David Burnham), 219, 228
Robespierre, 93
Rockefeller, J. D., 53, 169, 172
Roe v. Wade, 145
Rogerian psychotherapy, 122
Rookmaaker, H. R., 89, 91, 95
Rousseau, Jean Jacques, 55, 91, 162, 241
Russell, Bertrand, 128
Russian Revolution, 208

Sagan, Carl, 64, 97, 123
Salvation, "salvation experience," 21, 27, 43, 239, 244
Sanger, Margaret, 83, 171, 172
Sartre, Jean-Paul, 74, 80
Schaeffer, Francis A., 26, 27, 28, 29, 37, 45, 46, 67, 74, 76, 108, 199, 205, 208, 246
Schaeffer, Franky, 186
Schank, Roger, 152
Scherschel, Patricia, 213
Schlossberg, Herbert, 35
Schmeck, Harold M. Jr., 144
Science, 15, 22, 24, 25, 32, 34, 38, 39, 42, 43, 45, 46, 49, 52, 57, 58, 60, 61, 64, 66, 67, 68, 76, 78, 79, 80, 82, 83, 87, 88, 89,
90, 91, 92, 93, 95, 96, 97, 98, 99, 100, 101, 102, 103, 107, 114, 119, 124, 125, 126, 128, 132, 134, 137, 140, 141, 144, 145, 147, 150, 151, 154, 161, 211, 230
Scientific Meliorism (Jane Hume Clapperton), 165
Scientific method, the, 22, 66, 96, 134
Scot, Reginald, 99
Second American Revolution, The (John Whitehead), xi
Second Self, The (Sherry Turkle), 148
Secular City, The (Harvey Cox), 46
Secularism, secularization, xi, 15, 16, 22, 27, 29, 31, 32, 33, 34, 35, 36, 37, 38, 39, 40, 41, 42, 43, 44, 45, 47, 48, 60, 61, 68, 75, 84, 87, 91, 101, 107, 144, 175, 199, 208
Seneca, 37
Sex and Destiny (Germaine Greer), 74, 172
Sharp, Dr. Harry, 167
Shaw, George Bernard, 53
Shelley, Mary, 157
Sherrington, Sir William Charles, 155
Shirer, William L., 206
Sider, Ronald, 186, 187
Simon, Herbert A., 100, 101, 127, 147, 148, 149
Simon, Julian, 74, 164, 171, 178, 179, 180, 181, 198, 200
Singer, C. Gregg, 19, 22, 55, 56, 58
Singer, C. J., 137
Singer, Ethan, 84
Skepticism, 22, 66, 152
Skinner, B. F., 42, 44, 101, 241, 242
Slavery, 21
Smith, Adam, 53
Smith, Leonard, 228, 229
"Social contract," 94
"Social Darwinsim," 41, 58, 69
Socialism, 59, 68, 107, 172, 191, 197, 205, 208
Solzhenitsyn, Aleksandr, 214, 238, 242, 243
Soviet Union, 48, 171, 179, 199, 204, 224, 234, 238, 242, 244
Stalin, Josef, 29, 48, 77

State, the, 15, 34, 42, 47, 48, 60, 84, 116, 131, 166, 183, 196, 197, 203, 204, 205, 207, 208, 212, 215, 216, 240, 241, 243, 244, 245, 246, 247
Stealing of America, The (John Whitehead), xi
Sterilization in North Carolina: A Sociological and Psychological Study (Moya Woodside), 181
Stott, John R. W., 28, 29
Surveillance, 212, 213, 214, 224, 225, 227, 228, 231
"Survival of the fittest," 25, 53
Sussman, Gerald, 151, 152
Sweden, 206

Taxpayer Compliance Measurement Program (TCMP), 221
Technics and Civilization (Lewis Mumford), 113
Technology, xi, 32, 33, 42, 46, 49, 54, 61, 78, 79, 82, 95, 103, 107, 109, 110, 111, 112, 113, 115, 116, 118, 121, 125, 128, 131, 135, 139, 141, 142, 143, 144, 147, 151, 180, 190, 206, 207, 208, 209, 211, 212, 216, 218, 222, 226, 227, 228, 229, 230, 231, 232, 233
Television, 29, 117, 118, 119, 206, 207, 208, 209
Theism, 16, 17, 18, 19, 20, 27, 29, 39, 40, 43, 45, 48, 52
Theobald, Robert, 215
Theological Interpretation of American History, A (C. Gregg Singer), 19
Thielecke, Helmut, 35
Thomas, Lewis, 43, 71, 121, 148
Thompson, William Irwin, 209
Thoreau, Henry David, 70
Thorpe, William H., 141, 142
Tibetan Book of the Dead, 61
Tillich, Paul, 30
Time, 23, 24, 39, 44, 45, 54, 92, 114, 116, 121, 135, 137, 139, 140, 143
Toffler, Alvin, 110, 111
Totalitarianism, 33, 46, 47, 48, 57, 67, 203, 204, 205, 208, 227, 237, 240
Trubow, George, 214
Tse-tung, Mao, 48

Turkle, Sherry, 126, 127, 148, 152, 155, 156
Tuveson, Ernest, 21
Twain, Mark, 19, 21
Tyranny, 19, 47, 67, 77, 88, 217, 240

Ultimate Resource, The (Julian Simon), 74, 178, 180
Understanding Media (Marshall McLuhan), 108, 116
Urey, Harold, 64
Utopianism, 47, 78, 116, 128, 147, 162, 163, 164, 175

Values, 17, 77, 94, 100, 101, 117, 246
Vietnam, 197, 232
Vietnam War, 81, 225, 231

Wald, George, 65
Wallace, Alfred Russel, 53, 54, 165
Walter, J. A., 71, 72, 73
Warwick, Donald, 187
Wasteland, The, 16
Watson, James D., 44, 75, 82
Watt, J. B., 123
Weber, Max, 35
Weiner, Norbert, 140, 141, 155
Weisskopf, Michael, 194, 195, 196
Weizenbaum, Joseph, 101, 102, 121, 122, 123, 124, 125, 129, 149, 150, 151, 232
Whatever Happened to the Human Race? (Francis A. Schaeffer and C. Everett Koop), 199
White, Lynn Jr., 71
Whitehead, Alfred North, 24, 90, 136, 137, 138
Whitney, Leon F., 180
Wilberforce, Rev. Samuel, 56
Wilberforce, William, 21
Wilder-Smith, A. E., 61, 75
William of Auvergne, 88
Woodside, Moya, 181
Woodward, Bob, 183
Work (Ford Madox Brown), 55

Xinzhong, Qian, 194

Zahn, Gordon, 182
Zangwill, Oliver L., 141
Zen and the Art of Motorcycle Maintenance (Robert Pirsig), 26